COMPARATIVE POLITICS

COMPARATIVE POLITICS

Dr. Archna Chaturvedi

Commonwealth

Comparative Politics

Edition : 2024

ISBN 81-7169-969-3

Published by :

COMMONWEALTH PUBLISHERS
4831/24, Prahlad Street,
Ansari Road, Darya Ganj,
New Delhi - 110002
Ph. : 23275511, 23257835
e-mail : commonwealthbooks@gmail.com

Typesetting by :

Rishu Computers
Delhi - 110051

Printed at :
Roshan Offset Printers
Delhi

PREFACE

Aim of the book on comparative politics is to make a comparative study of political institution and its limitations. It examines classification of governments, organisation of governments, division of powers and the separation of powers.

Meaning, evolution and problems of comparative methods have been discussed. Material on political systems and political culture have been included. To facilitate research bibliographical details for further studies have been provided with each chapter.

We gratefully acknowledge the authorities on the subject.

We have received all possible co-operation and help from the librarians and their staff members. We are thankful to them all.

Hardwork and co-operation from my publisher have facilitated completion of this work in record time. They deserve the love and patronage of my readers.

Dr. Archna Chaturvedi

Contents

1

Forms of Government

COMPARATIVE STUDY OF POLITICAL INSTITUTIONS AND ITS LIMITATIONS

1. Comparative Approach in Political Theory and Governmental Machinery

Contents of Political Theory and Governmental Machinery

On Political Theory we discussed the meaning and nature of Political Science, its methodology, its relation to cognate subjects, the evolution of political theory, state and its nature, sovereignty, state authority and power, obligations and rights of the individual, liberty and equality, the end and functions of the state and theories of state activity.

On Governmental Machinery, we shall discuss political institutions, which carry political principles or give expression to them. Forms of government, comparative study of political institutions, constitutionalism, the branches of government, executive, legislature and judiciary, civil service, political parties, local government, international organizations and other topics constitute the subject matter.

Comparative Study in Political Theory

In studying political theory, the political scientist takes into consideration the evolution of political ideas in the various states in the past and in the present. Since the days of Aristotle, many political thinkers did make in their own way a comparative study of political principles evolved in different states. The study of the evolution of the state, of the development of the concept of sovereignty, of the formation of legal codes, of the concepts of obligations and rights, of the emergence of the principles of liberty and equality, of the study of Idealism, Individualism, Capitalism, Democratic Socialism, Communism, Collectivism, Fabianism, Syndicalism, Anarchism, Fascism, Nazism and other topics necessitates a comparative study of political principles all over the world.

Comparative Study of Political Institutions

The study of political institutions statewise is not conducted. We do not undertake to study the political institutions of a single state at a stretch separately. Had this been the case, we would have studied all the political institutions of a country like England, and only after completing this study we would have proceeded to study the political institutions of each of the other states separately; but this procedure is not followed. What we seek to do is to make a *comparative study of political institutions* located in various states or political systems. For example, when we discuss forms of governments and constitutions, we make a comparative study. The study of unitary government takes us to Britain and France as the study of federalism draws us to states like the United States of America, Canada, Switzerland, Australia, Soviet Russia and India. Similarly, the study of the cabinet system brings within its fold the most important states having such a system. Here we cannot resist the temptation of striking comparison and contrast between the British and Indian parliamentary systems. The study of democratic institutions would take in its sweep Britain, the U.S.A., India and other states. The study of legislature, including bicameralism and unicameralism embraces the legislatures of several important states at a stretch. The same is the procedure or technique of study followed in discussing judiciary, civil service, public opinion, political parties, local government and other topics. The straight study of all topics connected with the political institutions of one state alone is not conducted by the student of political science. The method followed is comparative.

2. Meaning of Comparative Method

Need of Competence

The comparative method is one of the ways of acquiring political knowledge. For political and other reasons or both, the study of comparative government has assumed a great importance in the study of the discipline. Such a study has to be conducted by those who are competent, if it is to be purposeful and fruitful. The researcher should be fully conversant with all the necessary methods and techniques to make the study truly comparative. He should have a deep knowledge and thorough grasp of sociological, anthropological, socio-psychological and general systems theory. He should not be found wanting while dealing with culture, socialization processes, attitudes and motivations.

Use of Comparative Method along with Historical Method

The comparative method is the one which studies the states of the past and the present for collecting definite data from which the political scientist culls matter for comparative study in the fields of political theory and governmental machinery. Comparative methodology is based on inductive logic. By a scientific study of various states, the researcher is able to draw a definite set of principles and generalizations. He studies the geographical features, historical basis, social strata, economic conditions and political institutions of a particular state and tries to strike a comparison or contrast between them and similar conditions in another state. In the study of the executive, a researcher may try to strike a contrast between Britain and the United States of America. The former has a parliamentary system in a unitary set-up. A thorough study of the historical background, political institutions, social life and economic systems of both the states will enable the researcher to account for the contrast. It is apt to mention here that political institutions of Britain are several centuries older than those of the U.S.A., whose political system was developed in the course of the last two centuries only. It may also be pointed out that the authors of the American federal system were those who had rebelled against Britain and had taken part in the successful American Revolution (1776-83). Similarly, a critical study of the conditions in Britain and India will explain why the parliamentary system was found to be congenial in Britain, while a similar system did not meet with the expected success in India. A comparative study of the conditions in Russia and China will show why a one party totalitarian government has struck deep roots in both the states. In the instances, cited above, we note that the scholar uses that comparative method side by side with the historical method.

Different Ways of Comparative Study

John Stuart Mill speaks of the different ways in which the comparative method is used. He refers to the methods of (1) single factor difference, (2) indirect difference, and (3) agreement. Besides the methods advocated by Mill, the method of residues and the method of concomitant variations can be employed.

Framework for Treatment of Governments

In his article on *A Comparative Method for the Study of Politics* (November 1958) David E. Apter spelt out the purpose of the comparative method: "Its purpose is to create a framework for the treatment of governments in diverse social settings in order to make possible some generalization about how the presence, absence or clustering of certain combinations of variables affect politics."

Explaining Types of Government

The comparative method helps the researcher to understand what particular types of government emerge under a given set of circumstances. It is true that certain constitutions are the result of deliberations and discussions; but a comparative study explains why these discussions favoured a particular type of constitution. The researcher is able to understand the principle of interplay of variables as the cause of the establishment of certain types of constitutions.

Common Factors Facilitating Comparative Study

Certain common factors among states or political systems will facilitate comparative study. One common factor is contemporaneity. States of a given period can be easily brought under comparative research. Another common factor is historical basis. Two or more states, sharing a common or similar historical background will meaningfully lend themselves to comparative study. Thirdly, states having common or similar political, social, cultural and economic institutions can be brought together for comparative study.

3. Evolution of Comparative Study

Aristotle

The comparative method of studying political science was evolved in course of a long time. In fact the method is as hoary as Aristotle himself. Aristotle (384-322 B.C.) who lived in the 4th century B.C. had a penchant for comparative study in a scientific manner. It is recorded that he conducted political research in the course of surveying institutions in as many as 158 states. The *Politics* of Aristotle, which has been praised as a pillar of light for all those who came after him, was written with the help of the vast data collected by him by the study of actual governments of his time including those of Crete, Carthage, Sparta and Athens and by the scholarly works of his predecessors, like Phaleas, Hippodamus and Plato. The study enabled Aristotle to draw his own generalisations, and he conceived of the evolution of a particular political pattern in a given set of circumstances. When he classified governments in his own scientific manner, he blended two criteria (1) empirical, and (2) normative. Aristotle not only described political institutions, but compared and contrasted them. He drew definite inferences of forms of government with reference to the number of persons exercising supreme power and the purpose (good or evil) of wielding it. Peter Merkl says in *Political Continuity and Change* (1967): "In addition to these philosophical insights into the ends of politics, Aristotle laid the groundwork for the scientific analysis of politics by his discovery of the comparative method. As a tool of political analysis the comparative method can be compared to the role of experimentation in natural sciences." Harry Eckstein explains why the name of Aristotle has to be mentioned while studying comparative politics. "The field of comparative politics has a long and honourable past. That its pedigree reaches back as far as Aristotle is not unusual, since just about every discipline can in one way or another, trace its origin to Aristotle. Comparative, politics, however, has a particular right to claim Aristotle as an ancestor because of the primacy that he assigned to politics among the sciences and because the problems he raised and the methods he used are similar to those still current in political studies." (Eckstein and Apter, 1963).

Polybius

The political thought of the historian Polybius (204-122 B.C.), a Greek hostage who wrote his celebrated *History of Rome* is of much significance. He discussed the different types of government and the natural cycle of political changes after making a comparative study, which enable him to draw the inference that the mixed form of government organized by the Romans was the best.

Machiavelli

In the history of political, thought, the Florentine writer Machiavelli (1469-1527) occupies an important place. He was an eminent diplomat and powerful writer extolling the qualities of a ruler, who built up and maintained his power by questionable and crooked methods. The significant use of the historical and comparative methods is clearly brought out in his celebrated works, *The Prince* (1513) and *Discourses* (1519). Machiavelli's knowledge is not merely bookish. Besides his wide range of studies, he had opportunities to have a close look at the actual functioning of governments in the various Italian city states, and in France and Germany. Political scientists say that the earliest source of comparative politics in modern times is Renaissance political thought, most clearly that of Machiavelli. In the words of Macridis and Brown, "the technique of government was that of securing, maintaining and extending power. How could this be done? Only by understanding human nature and by drawing as many examples as possible from the past. History can give us guidance to successful rulership."

Bodin

Jean Bodin (1530-1596) who marks the beginning of modern political thought employed the historical and comparative methods. He studied the past and present conditions of various states, borrowed much from Greek and Roman political thought, and analysed and drew his own political inferences.

Montesquieu

Montesquieu (1689-1755) whose greatest legacy in his celebrated classic *Spirit of the Laws* (1748) commands our special attention in the study of the comparative method. His book had a profound impact on the constitution makers in America, France and other European governments. His wide and deep studies made him competent to employ the comparative method and draw generalisations. He believed that historical events and processes were governed by definite principles, which would be understood by a thorough study and dispassionate and objective analysis. The history of Rome was the starting point for the construction of his pet political principles, one of which was the famous Theory of Separation of Powers. His methodology was like that of Aristotle and not of Plato, like that of Bodin and not Hobbes, Locke or Rousseau. In making a comparative study of political institutions, Montesquieu gave importance to climatic factors, soil, economic conditions, trade and commerce, religion, forms of government and other influences.

Tocqueville

Alexis de Tocqueville (1805-1859), another great gifted political thinker follower the comparative methodology of Aristotle, Polybius, Machiavelli, Bodin and Montesquieu. He had ample opportunities of observing political institutions at a close range in countries like France, England and Germany. Tocqueville said: "I have had occasion to study the political institutions of medieval France, England and Germany, and the more deeply I went into the subject, the more I was struck by the remarkable similarity between the laws and institutions in all the three countries; indeed it seems extraordinary that nations so unlike and having so little intercourse with each other should have built up systems of law so closely akin."

Mill

John Stuart Mill (1806-1873), the great political scientist, essayist, economist, philosopher and social reformer, gave much prominence to the comparative method which according to him assumes several forms. Mill was a voracious reader interested in the works of many great Greek scholars and philosophers including Plato, Aristotle, Herodotus, Isocrates, Diogenes and Xenophon. He also read the works of Adam Smith and Ricardo. Mill wielded a prolific pen and wrote several books on various branches of knowledge including political science.

Freeman

Edward A. Freeman (1823-92) was another eminent scholar, who was also among the first to develop the comparative method. Freeman wrote: "The establishment of the comparative method of study has been the greatest intellectual achievement of our time. It has carried light and order into whole branches of human knowledge which before were shrouded in darkness and confusion."

Bryce

Among the political scientists, who widely used the comparative method was the British historian and diplomat Viscount James Bryce (1838-1922). Commenting on the comparative method, Byrce said: "That which entitles it to be called scientific is that it reaches general conclusions by tracing similar results to similar causes, eliminating those disturbing influences which present in one country and absent in another, make he results in examined cases different in some points while similar in others." (J.W. Garner, *Political Science and Government*—1951, p. 21). He read widely and wrote scholarly works including *Modern democracies* (1921) and *International Relations* (1922), which bore testimony to his pursuit of the comparative method. As an eminent historian and diplomat, who occupied high offices, he had opportunities to have a close look at the events and hence could profitably use the comparative method. In 1886 he was Under-Secretary of Foreign Affairs and later found a place in Gladstone's Cabinet. During 1907-12 he was British Ambassador to the USA. While Bryce conducted research on the actual working of democratic institutions in several countries, he effectively used the comparative method. His *Modern Democracies* was the result of a comparative study of many democratic countries including ancient Athens, the republics of Latin America, France, Switzerland, Canada, the United States of America and New Zealand. In his studies, Bryce tried to establish first principles of empirical grounds.

Friedrich

Friedrich's great work in comparative study *Constitutional Government and Democracy* is filled with discussions of abstract political theories and comparative material on political parties, interest groups and media of political communication. He lays great emphasis on the interplay between political forms and social conditions. He organizes his empirical materials in terms of many structural and functional categories, and succeeds in giving a truly modern and full-fledged comparative synthesis. In his studies, he amasses facts, thinks upon them and draws his generalisations.

Ostrogorski

Ostrogorski went "beyond describing events or institutions in a single country" and made generalisation in the field of comparative government. In his studies he drew a contrast between the British and American party systems. (See D.E. Butler, *the Study of Political Behaviour*—1958, p. 49).

Wheare

K.C. Wheare is another political scientist, who took the full advantage of the comparative approach. His monumental work, *Federal Government*, is an example of "the process of juxtaposing descriptions of similar situations in different countries."

Duverger

Maurice Duverger also meaningfully employed the comparative method in bringing out his significant pioneering book *Political Parties* (1951).

Dissatisfaction on the Traditional Comparative Approach

During the recent years, several political scientists have expressed dissatisfaction on the traditional approach and emphasis on the comparative study. R.C. Macridis, while making a survey of the field of comparative government, points out that comparative study has so far been comparative just in name only. Really speaking, it is nothing but a descriptive, historical or legalistic study of foreign governments with emphasis on written documents and "the legal prescription for the allocation of political power." The so-called comparative study covers only Western democracies or the political systems of Western Europe, Great Britain and the Dominions. It does not go deep into true comparison and is superficial. Criticising the books on the comparative study in the traditional manner, Macridis says that they "are limited summarily to political morphology or what might also be called political anatomy. They describe various political institutions generally without attempting to compare them. What comparison is made is limited exclusively to the identification of differences between types or systems, such as federal versus unitary system or parliamentary versus presidential system or the more elusive differences between democratic and totalitarian systems." (Jean Blondel, 1969). G.A. Almond and G.B.

Powell in their *Comparative Politics—A Developmental Approach* (1972) also express dissatisfaction on the comparative study of political science along traditional lines.

4. Political Systems and Political Culture

Political Systems

In the comparative study conducted critically by political scientists like David Easton in recent years, the term *Political Systems* and not *Sates* has found favour. They say that the principle of political system is applicable to the entire scope of political activities in a society. Almond and Powell say in *Comparative Politics—A Developmental Approach* (1972): "The Political system includes not only governmental such as legislatures, courts and administrative agencies but *all structures in their political aspects.* Among these are traditional structures such as kinship ties and caste groupings; and anomic phenomena such as assassinations riots and demonstrations; as well as formal organizations like parties, interest groups, and media of communications." In a political system, the various component parts are interdependent. Any change in one part has its repercussions on others. In an organism or a machinery, if one part is affected, the entire organism or machine is consequently affected. The emergence of political parties, for instance, brings about a great change in the other components of the political system. The term structure is applied to all those activities, which can be observed in a political system. These activities have a set pattern or have a certain regularity in them.

Political Culture

In a political system, the underlying propensities or inclinations and the actual performance or activities are known as *political culture.* It is difficult to define precisely political culture, and political scientists differ among themselves about the definition and meaning of two words. Hence, a definition may be given only in broad and general terms. Whatever its definition, the concept of political culture has entered into the stream of political vocabulary of the recent political researchers. It seems the first use of the term Political Culture was made by Gabriel Almond in his article "Comparative Political Systems" in the *Journal of Politics,* Vol. 18, 1956. Its early use was also made in

Patterns of Government (Random House, New York, 1958) edited by Samuel Beer and Adem Ulham. A study of political culture, which is a natural evolution in the development of the behavioral approach, enables us to understand the political ideals and standards of behaviour people have set for themselves in a polity. Political culture constitutes an important link between the behaviour of individuals and political events. Wars, election campaigns, laws, acts of government officials etc. affect the behaviour of individuals and groups. Scholars have evolved the concept of political culture to take seriously into account the great influence of social customs, attitudes, beliefs, emotions, values and ideals on the nature and functioning of the governmental system. Political culture "consists of attitudes, beliefs, values and skills which are current in an entire population, as well as those special propensities and patterns which may be found within separate parts of that population. Thus regional groups or ethnic groups or social classes which make up the population of a political system may have special propensities and tendencies." (See Almond and Powell, *Comparative Politics—A Developmental Approach*—1972, p. 23).

Lucian Rye says in *Political Culture and Political Development* (edited by Pye and Verba, Princeton University, New Jersey—1969): "Indeed, political culture is a recent term, which seeks to make more explicit and systematic much of the understanding associated with such long-standing concepts as political ideology, national ethos and spirit, national political psychology, and the fundamental values of a people. Political culture, by embracing the political orientations of both leaders and citizens, is more inclusive than such terms as political style or operational code which focus on elite behaviour. On the other hand, the term is more explicit and hence more restrictive than such concepts as public opinion and national character." It should be noted here that only those attitudes, beliefs, emotions and values of society related to the political system and political issues are included in political culture. At times the beliefs and attitudes may be held only unconsciously. In societies, which are quite stable, political culture is likely to be homogeneous. But if there is a vast difference between one group and another, and a consensus is not possible, there prevails a political sub-culture. Alan R. Ball says in *Modern Politics and Government* (1971): "The blacks in the United States constitute a political sub-culture. Sub-cultures may not necessarily be divisive; the separate communities of the English, Welsh and Scots in Great Britain do not place a great strain on the political system, although Northern Ireland, because of religious cleavages, does produce-different political attitudes and emotions from those of the United Kingdom."

Political Culture a Part of Larger Culture

Political culture is only the part of a whole, that is, larger or general culture. Political culture includes only the set of political beliefs held by an individual, and obviously these beliefs are only a part of the totality of beliefs. Dennis Kavanagh says that political culture may be regarded as a sub-culture influenced by the general culture. He gives the example of France in which widespread popular distrust of government is connected with the low levels of interpersonal trust in French social relations. As regards Britain, he says that as the people are accommodative in personal relationships, they are broadly speaking loyal to the government. (See *Political Culture*, Macmillan, 1972, p. 10). A study of political culture inevitably makes us study the process of political socialization (formation and development of attitudes to and beliefs about the political system) and how political culture is transmitted from one generation to another.

Political Socialization

The method by which political cultures are preserved and transformed is known as political socialization. Research into political socialization enables us to understand political stability and growth. Political socialization by which individuals are drawn into political culture and led to develop particular attitudes towards political objects is a continuous process. The family, the church, the school, the office or institution of employment and mass media are important agents of political socialization. Through various agents political socialization works in many formal and informal ways. Among the agents the most conspicuous is the government itself. G.A. Almond says: "Political socialization is the process of induction into the political culture. Its end product is a set of attitudes—cognitious, value standards, and feelings—towards the political system, its various roles, and role incumbents. It also includes knowledge of, values affecting, and feelings toward the inputs of demands and claims into the system, and its authoritative outputs." (See *The Politics of the Developing Areas*, edited by G.A. Almond and J.S. Coleman, Princeton University, New Jersy, 1970, p. 27). Political socialization is a continuous process, commencing from childhood and ending only with the individual's death. The agents that undertake the function of political socialization in a political system are: (1) the family, (2) the educational institutions, (3) the voluntary groups, (4) the mass media, (5) the political parties, and (6) the government.

5. Comparative Study Since World War I

Much Progress by Researchers

Between the First World War (1914-18) and the Second (1939-45) political scientists began to take a keen interest in large-scale comparisons. In fact the study of political science as an entire discipline evoked unprecedented interest and enthusiasm among political researchers, and comparatively speaking, the discipline began to take long strides on its path of progress.

Round Table Conference

In April 1954 the International Political Science Association organised a round table conference in Florence to discuss the study of comparative government. Not less than fifty participants at the round table reached an agreement on the great significance of a comparative study of political science. In his report Professor Gunnar Heckscher stated: "If we regard our field of study as mainly descriptive, comparisons are required to help us refine our tools of description. If we have hopes of establishing a general theory on an inductive basis, we do so only through comparison. If we attempt to test specific hypothesis, this is possible only if we bring a sufficient number of examples, to be investigated by the comparative method."

New Trends in Comparative Politics

After the Second World War, new trends were clearly visible in the study of comparative politics, and these may be briefly summarised as follows:

Empirical Field Enlarged

The field of comparative study was enlarged in a two-fold manner. Firstly, intensive research of non-Western political systems was undertaken. Secondly, aspects of political science hitherto neglected by political scientists were brought under study. The emergence of new states since the First World War, the interest provoked by the political developments in the Afro-Asian countries, the emergence of Japan as a great power to challenge Western democracies, the upheavals in India, China and Turkey and the availability of lavish funds, which were limited till the First World War were some of the factors prompting researchers to turn their attention to the political fields of Asia and Africa. The failure of democracy in the inter-war period, the striking emergence of totalitarian dictatorship in Italy, Germany and Russia and other causes drew the attention of political scientists to areas, which they formerly ignored totally or partially.

Study More Scientific

The study of comparative politics was made more scientific. The development of new and unconventional concepts, thoroughly systematic analysis, and introduction of sophisticated testing procedures marked the scientific study of comparative politics. The development of the behavioural approach, the growing influence of the methods adopted by other social sciences on political science, the new interest cultivated in the study of Afro-Asian countries, the scientific research work of sociologists and anthropologists in the new countries and the realisation by political scientists of the inadequacy of techniques of Bryce and Friedrich compelled critically-minded political practitioners to follow thoroughly rigorous scientific methods in comparative study.

Emphasis on Social Groups

The political researcher began to realise the tremendous significance of the role of social groups in the political field, and paid greater attention to their study than in the past. He became aware that social institutions played a special part in moulding political values, loyalties and identifications. The importance of the social setting of politics and agencies working between the social and the political institutions was being increasingly realised.

It was becoming clear to political scientists that a political system is embedded in social relations. The keen desire to study politics led to the emulation of the methods of the sociologist and the cultural anthropologist. Advanced comparative technique brought to light the fact that social phenomena are all inter-related.

Structural Functional Analysis

Critical analysis of political systems has been started. Questions have been raised about the political systems "in terms of conceptual schemes largely imported from other social sciences, above all in terms of structural functional analysis." M.J. Levy has explained the meaning of the term. What is called structural functional analysis includes a wide range of analytical questions and procedures. It applies to the definitions of political science or political system or governments or states or social structures engaged in political activities. The use of the term structural functional analysis is becoming common in the study of comparative politics. Harry Eckstein observes; "We tend no longer to think of political systems solely as sovereign states and their formal subdivisions but as any "collective decision-making structure" or as any set of structures for "authoritatively allocating social values," or as structures that perform the function of "maintaining the integration of society" or as structures that perform the functions of the "integration and adaptation of societies by means of the employment, or threat of employment of more or less physical compulsion" and in many other ways in similar vein." [See Eckstein and Apter (Ed.), *Comparative Politics: A Reader*—1963, p. 26].

The study of structural functionalism of G.A. Almond may be taken into consideration here. Almond built up his views on the ground work provided by the theoretical sociological analysis of Talcott Persons and on the decision making analysis of Lasswell. Almond's starting point was David Easton's analysis which speaks of "inputs and outputs": I. On the input side are demands which are (1) formulated (or articulated), and (2) combined (or aggregated), II. On the output side are rules, which are (3) formulated (rule-making), (4) applied (rule-application), and (5) adjudicated in individual cases (rule-adjudication). III. The different activities in the political system (about which Easton speaks) are (6) communicated within the system and outside.

Almond says that inputs are converted into outputs and the political system maintains and adapts itself through a process of political socialization. (See Jean Blondel, *Comparative Politics: A Reader*—1969, p. XXVII.) Almond while explaining David Easton's political system, refers to two types of inputs (See Almond and Powell, *Comparative Politics—A Developmental Approach*—1922, pp. 25-26): (1) Demand and (2) Supports. There is a wide range and variety of demands: (1) demands for allocation of goods and services like demands for labour legislation, educational opportunities, recreational facilities; (2) demands for laws for providing for public safety, for controlling markets, for health and sanitation, and so on; (3) demands for franchise, for holding office, for expressing grievances and for forming political associations; (4) demands for communication and information. As regards supports, the classification is fourfold: (1) national supports like tax payment and rendering military service; (3) obedience to laws and rules; (2) political activities like voting and political discussion; (4) attention to government information and respect for authority. Inputs are created by the executive, legislature and judiciary.

Then again, referring to Easton's outputs, Almond speaks of four types of transactions (*Ibid*, p. 27): (1) imposing taxes and demanding tribute, personal service etc.; (2) regulating human behaviour; (3) allocating and distributing goods and services; (4) issuing policy statements, upholding values and displaying political symbols.

Almond's general model is known as structural functionalism. The detailed variables, which are called structural, include executives, legislatures, groups, parties and other institutions in the political system. He does not apply particular norms and values in the comparative study, but takes into consideration behavioural patterns. Gabriel A. Almond, Taylor Cole and Roy C. Macridis while writing on "a Suggested Research Strategy in Western European Government and Politics" say that after the First World War in the USA the scope of political science underwent a change to some extent unless the stimulus of great European political innovators like Ostrogorski, Bryce, Weber, Pareto and Michels. Political scientists "began to probe into the non-legal levels and processes of politics and substantial literature developed including in addition to realistic and functional analysis of the presidency, the courts, the Congress, and the bureaucracy—studies of non-legal or semi-legal institutions and processes such as political parties, pressure groups, public opinion and political behaviour." [See Eckstein and Apter (Ed.), *Comparative Politics: A Reader*—1973, p. 53].

Structural-Functional Similitude. Structural-functional similitude can be struck in several ways. A few of these may be briefly reviewed:

(1) The political institutions of similar states or political systems may be compared. For example, the political institutions of Britain may be compared to those of the Commonwealth countries. A similitude may be projected between the totalitarian systems of Soviet Russia and People's Republic of China. Similarly, political institutions of the USA and those of the Latin American republics may be compared.

(2) Political institutions of different political systems may be compared. The legislatures of the USA (having the presidential system) and Britain (having the parliamentary system) may be brought under comparative research. The Prime Minister of the Soviet Union (which has a single party totalitarian system) and the Prime Minister of Britain (which has two-party democratic system) may be amenable to comparison and contrast.

(3) Political institutions of one and the same system may be studied together for comparison. The Supreme Court and the High Courts in India, the Prime Minister and the Chief Minister in India, Parliament and State Legislatures in India may be compared.

6. Drawbacks and Problems of the Comparative Method

While it is true a large number of distinguished political scientists have produced works of a high standard and surpassing scholarship in the field of comparative study, the fact remains that the method is beset with several drawbacks and problems. We may briefly examine these limitations. Jean Blondel observes in *Comparative Government—A Reader* (page xxv) (1969): "The study of comparative government is thus fraught with special difficulties. There are difficulties arising from the nature of the data and the desire of secrecy which governments often display. There are difficulties arising from the nature of variables which have to be used in the study of government: the pull of comparative government is towards the use of 'general' or 'cross-national' variables but unique character of each policy has in some form to be measured, if comparisons are realistically to account for the presence of a particular type of government."

The following are the drawbacks of the comparative method:

Many Basic Questions Unanswered

The practitioners of the comparative method have not yet succeeded in answering many basic questions. Why particular types of government exist in certain parts of the world only and not in others, why certain governments are stable, while others suffer from the chronic infirmity of instability, why liberal democracies and dictatorships assume different manifestations, forms and sub-forms—such and many other questions have not been cogently answered by comparative methodologies. Political scientists using the comparative method are unable to understand fully and analyse satisfactorily the complex political institutions and processes, special features of political life, countless variables and relationship between law and practice, norms and realities.

Difficulty of Gathering Vital Information

The political scientist engaged in studying political institutions through the comparative method finds the task of gathering information and data vital to his study pretty formidable. In several states, invaluable data, which can revolutionize the study, are kept beyond the reach of the scholar for political and other reasons. Only when the scholar finds all important source material within his easy reach, he can think in terms of making a genuine comparative study. In several Western democracies, the required information is readily available, and hence, there has been a profit growth of comparative political literature. But the story as regards totalitarian regimes is totally different. In certain democracies researchers are able to gather information directly from the principal actors of the political drama; but in totalitarian dictatorships such actors keep their lips sealed and their doors permanently shut to information seekers. Even in Western democracies, many facts go undisclosed strictly in "public interest". Researchers may not be able to know what precisely happened at the highest decision-making levels in the chambers of Presidents and Prime Ministers. In authoritarian regimes in which the radio, television, newspapers and other media of mass communication are disciplined and controlled by government, what is found in cold print or what is heard over the air may be apocryphal News items may be misleading and in wrong perspective, and statistical data highly inflated and imaginary.

Difficulty of Measuring Political Decisions

Another great obstacle on the path of the practitioners of the comparative method is the real difficulty of measuring precisely what we call political decisions. This hurdle comes in the way of bringing vital information under comparative treatment. A researcher will not be able to know the true relationship between the executive and the legislature of a state (as against what is given in the press) as he is not able to assess correctly the power and influence of each of the two branches of government. Similarly, the researchers may not be able to subject certain important developments or events to comparative study, as he may not be able to know their true nature and intensity. He may wrongly regard certain episodes or decisions as unique and may be tempted to put them in a special category altogether without bringing them within his purview of comparative study.

Bewildering Variety of Variables

The political scientist encounters a bewildering variety of variables in the course of his rigorous investigation. Even in a single state the activities of members of political parties, big leaders, local leaders, members of the legislature, voters, demonstrators, trade unionists and other people of different types make a confused picture of a large number of variables. A researcher is likely to ignore some of them or pay only scant attention to others. Historical background, cultural peculiarities, climatic conditions, soil, economic problems and other factors go far in contributing to the emergence of these variables. Comparative study cannot be precise unless all the significant variables are paid due attention by the political scientist. Jean

Blondel refers pointedly to the tendency of researchers to reduce the number of variables in *Comparative Government—A Reader* (1969): "Admittedly, some students of governments have at times been tempted to reduce these variables to a much smaller number. Marxist or neo-Marxist explanations of society have emphasised economic factors and among these, ownership of capital as the major variable. Theories based on climate or geography (sea-faring countries *v.* land based politics) have sometimes been put forward for accounting for the major differences between types of governments. But none of these theories has satisfactorily *explained* more than a fraction of differences which exist among political systems."

One of the most difficult problems is of multi-variate analysis. While it is difficult to measure certain variables with comparative ease, it is well-high impossible to do the same with others. Researchers were able to establish an unmistaken connecting link between the birth of political parties in Western Europe and the emergence of urban working classes, between liberal democracy and a high standard of living, between military rule and backward countries. But researchers were unable to note a clear line of difference between unique historical events like the French Revolution and socio-economic features of a country.

Much Disagreement

Want of agreement among political scientists is another drawback. In the field of comparative politics, there is no unanimity of opinion about the exact procedure to be followed. In fact there is acute disagreement among those who have been working in the comparative field. For instance, since the middle of the 19th century, there has been a medley of classificatory schemes, Max Weber, Robert A. Dahl, David Apter, James S. Coleman, Harold D. Lasswell, David Easton, Gabriel A. Almond and others have used different schemes. Among the numerous classificatory schemes, we may mention only a few: Weber's traditional, national-legal and charismatic types, Marxists' feudal, bourgeois and proletarian systems, Coleman's competitive, semi-competitive and authoritarian systems, Dahl's democracy, hierarchy and bargaining systems, Apter's dictatorial, oligarchical, indirectly representational and directly representational. Almond's

Anglo-American, Continental European, totalitarian and pre-industrial, and Edward Shils's five-fold classification of *new* states: (1) political democracies, (2) tutelatory democracies, (3) modernising oligarchies, (4) totalitarian oligarchies, and (5) traditional oligarchies.

Political scientists have not been able to find a precise measuring rod for use against each governmental system. In the absence of this, comparative studies have not always been exact, but vague or even erroneous.

Problem of Norms, Institutions and Behaviour

Another problem challenging the study of the political scientist dealing with comparative study is concerning norms, institutions and behaviour. Jean Blondel observes: "But the relationship between these three elements is not simple: norms and institutions are not associated in a direct and uniform fashion. Some structures may be produced by certain types of norms, but be used in a different normative context. Dictatorships use legislatures and parties to their own ends; hierarchies exist outside authoritarian rule; and the practices of legislature have often been modified by custom." (See *Comparative Government : A Reader*—1969, p. XXIII). A researcher is likely to commit serious mistakes, if he is unable to observe and understand the vast difference between the constitutional norms laid down for individuals and institutions and their actual functioning. If he had a look at the written word only without turning his searching gaze at the political behaviour of individuals and bodies, he would be working under an illusion, and no comparative study worth the name will be possible. The researcher, making a comparative study, has to be extremely cautious in his approach. He should be a scholar of vast erudition, competent to strike comparison and contrast, to distinguish between the true and the false, to discriminate between real difference, and superficial difference to differentiate between the norms and actual behaviour and have the tremendous patience of gathering vital information and data germane for comparative study. At every stage he should beware of the possible hurdles and pitfalls. Then alone he will be in a position to make his job purposeful and draw correct conclusions.

REFERENCES

Almond, G.A. and Powell, G.B., *Comparative Politics, A Developmental Approach*, 1972, Amerind Publishing Co. Pvt. Ltd., New Delhi.

Ball, Alan R., *Modern Politics and Government*, 1971, Macmillan.

Blondel Jean, *Comparative Government*, 1969, Amerind Publishing Co. Pvt. Ltd., New Delhi.

Butler, D.E., *The study of Political Behaviour*, 1958, Hutchinson of London.

Dahl, Robert, A., *Modern Political Analysis*, 1963, Prentice Hall, New Jersey.

Dyke, Vernon, Van, *Political Science, A Political Analysis*, 1960, Standard University Press, California.

Eckstein and Apter (Ed.), *Comparative Politics*, 1963, The Free Press, Glencoe, London.

Field, G.L, *Comparative Political Development*, 1967.

Freeman, E.A., *Comparative Politics*, 1873.

Fried, R.C., *Comparative Political Institutions*, 1966.

Garner, J.W., *Political Science and Government*, 1955, The World Press, Calcutta.

Heckscher, Gunnar, *The Study of Comparative Government and Politics.*

Johari, J.C., *Comparative Politics*, 1972.

Kavanagh, Dennis, *Political Culture*, 1972, Macmillan.

Lasswell, Harold D., *The Policy Orientation of Political Science*, 1971, Lakshmi Narain Agarwal, Agra 3.

Macridis, R.C. and Brown, E., *Comparative Politics : Notes and Readings*, 1968.

Pinney, B.L. *Comparative Politics and Politics*, 1966.

Pye, Lucian, *Politics, Personality and Nation Building*, 1962, New Haven.

Pye and Verba (Ed.), *Political Culture and Political Development*, 1969, Princeton University, New Jersy.

UNESCO, *Contemporary Political Science, 1950.*

Waldo, Dwight, *Political Science in the United States of America*, UNESCO.

2

The Organisation of Government

THEORY OF THE SEPARATION OF POWERS

The Traditional classification of the organs of government has been into the legislative, the executive, and the judicial; but this classification is considered to be too simple to suit modern conditions.

Aristotle, the father of Western political thought, distinguishes between the deliberative, the magisterial, and the judicial powers. Although in theory Aristotle found it easy to separate these three powers, in practice they were all exercised by the same persons in ancient Greece.

The Roman thinkers who came after Aristotle—particularly Polybius (a Greek taken to Italy as a hostage) and Cicero—stress the importance of a 'balanced equilibrium of powers'. They find the monarchic, aristocratic, and democratic elements embodied respectively in the Consuls, the Senate and the popular assembly, each part of government acting as a check upon the others. Both these writers consider a 'mixed' form of government embodying a system of checks and balances as being essential for stability.

During the Middle Ages no contribution was made to the doctrine of the separation of powers.

Bodin, one of the earliest thinkers of the modern period, sees the importance of separating executive and judicial powers. He insists that the Prince should not administer justice himself, but should delegate this power to an independent tribunal, his argument being that not to separate the two powers would mean the indiscriminate mixture of justice and mercy, of strict adherence of law and arbitrary departure from it.

In his *Civil Government*, Locke makes a casual reference to the theory of the 'Separation of Powers'. According to him civil society was constituted for the protection of life, liberty, and property, and the means for the attainment of these ends are as definite as the ends themselves. These means express themselves in a three or four-fold division of governmental activity, namely legislation, which provided for a 'standard interpretation' of the law of nature which fixes these rights; the judicial side of governmental activity, namely the provision for an authority just and impartial, for applying the interpretation of the Laws of Nature as between the individuals in a community; and the executive side of it, the provision for employing the force of the community in enforcing by penalties the prescriptions in the laws. The function of maintaining the interest of the community and of its individuals in relation to other communities Locke calls the 'Federative' duty.

His doctrine of the separation of powers breaks new ground. The functions of legislation and execution must needs be separated; and certainly it is unwise to invest the makers of laws with the duty of enforcing them, for either they may exempt themselves from the operations of such laws of may suit the laws to serve their own ends.

As to Locke's treatment of the theory, the principle is merely suggested as a determinant of the relations between the Legislature and the Executive. The 'tripartite' division of functions, familiar to-day, and the complementary doctrine of mutual checks and balances which it entails, do not find a place in the speculation of Locke, but owe their development to Montesquieu, the French Philosopher, who expanded the English Philosopher's suggestions.

It was Montesquieu (1698-1755), the celebrated French writer, who made the doctrine his own in his *Esprit des Lois* (1/48). Curiously enough, after studying the working of the English constitution on the spot for two years, Montesquieu gave it as his considered judgment that the stability of the English constitution was due to its adherence to the separation of powers. It is agreed by all to-day that Montesquieu was mistaken in his interpretation of the English constitution. Even though the cabinet system of government which is a direct violation of the separation of power was not fully developed in the eighteenth century when Montesquieu wrote his work, there was no clear separation of powers even in England of his day. It is instructive to note that even the English jurist, Blackstone who wrote twenty years later, repeated the error committed by Montesquieu in holding that the fundamental principle of the English system of government was its clear-cut distinction between the legislative, executive and judicial powers. The fact of the matter is that both Montesquieu and Blackstone concerned themselves with the principle of the English constitution and not with its actual practice thus laying themselves open to the charge of being superficial.

By temperament and upbringing Montesquieu was an aristocrat. Nevertheless he had a profound respect for liberty, which he considered to be the greatest of all human goods. It was for the securing of this good that Montesquieu advocated the separation of powers. He realised that it was in the nature of authority to abuse itself and that unless, therefore, clear limitations were laid down, arbitrary rule would be inevitable. Moderation in exercise of governmental authority, he considered, was the *sine qua non* of good government. In the interest of such moderation, he enunciated his well-known theory of the separation of powers, according to which each power should be exercised by a different organ of government and between the various organs of government there should be a system of checks and balances so that no one organ might become all-powerful. The doctrine as stated by Montesquieu himself is:

> 'When the legislative and executive powers are united in the same person or body, there can be no liberty. . . . If the power of judging were joined to the legislative power, the life and liberty of the subject would be exposed to arbitrary control. . . . if it were jointed to the executive, the judge might behave as an oppressor'.

Montesquieu particularly emphasised the separation of the executive and legislative powers. Within the legislature itself there were to be two chambers, one acting as a check upon the other.

The doctrine has a profound influence on the framers of the American constitution as well as upon revolutionary France. While in France the theory broke down, leaving only administrative courts as a tribute to the doctrine of the separation of powers and the cabinet system was adopted by the 1875 constitution, in the United States of America it has come down to modern times.

Even to-day the legislature, the executive, and the judiciary are organised independently of each other. Thus, the President of the U.S.A. who is the chief executive and his cabinet are not members of the legislature, and the close contact between the legislature and the executive found in countries which have adopted the British system as government is unknown in America. The two houses of the legislature are separately constituted with different periods of tenure and with different powers. The judges of the Supreme Court are appointed by the executive with the consent of the Senate, but the terms of appointment are such as to make the judiciary practically an independent branch.

Not only are the organs of government separate from each other, but each organ exercises certain checks upon the rest. Thus, the consent of the Senate is require to all the appointments of chief officials made by the President. War and peace are to be declared by the Congress, and treaties entered into by the executive require ratification by the Senate. The President is empowered to sent messages to the Congress outlining his legislative programme, but a convention of the constitution prevents him or any of the members of his cabinet from appearing on the floor of the Congress to elucidate or defend the government policy. The President has the power of veto on the acts of the legislature, but it is a suspensive, and not an absolute veto.

Criticism

While the principle of the separation of powers is generally admitted as valid, embodying as it does the scientific principle of differentiation, the practical difficulties experienced in working it makes it of little value to us to-day. Even the U.S.A. does not possess a rigid separation of powers. In modern governments every legislature performs some executive duties; and the executive has certain judicial functions. The chief value of the theory is in emphasising the independence of the judiciary; but this end is attained more easily by other means such as security tenure to the judges, liberal salaries which are independent of annual budgetary provision, and freedom of the judges from party alignments or control

principle that government must act according to well-established rules or laws. Arbitrary rule is a negation of good government.

The theory admonishes the executive and administrative officials not to interfere with the processes of law and justice. In the words of Finer, it imposes upon each power the need to explain itself.

In justification of the doctrine, some have argued that while functions may be combined, powers should always remain supreme. This seems to us to a distinction without a difference. How functions can be performed without the necessary power to perform them it is difficult to see.

The doctrine of the separation of powers was of great value against the despotism of the King at one time and, at a later date, against the despotism of Parliament. But there is no danger of either of these despotisms today. In democratic countries we may require protection against the domination of parties and the 'despotism' of civil servants, while, in countries with a dictatorial form of government we need protection against the dictatorship of the party and the Leader. Against none of these types of domination, the separation of powers is of any avail. It is too mechanical in nature. The best safeguard of individual liberty in a democratic country is a well-informed and vigilant electorate.

The smooth working of government under modern conditions calls not so much for separation of powers as for the 'con-ordination' or 'articulation' of powers. Each organ should regard itself as a servant of the public and do everything in its power to advance its end. Apropos of this H.J. Laski writes:

> 'Legislatures could not fulfil their task unless they were able both to interfere in the execution of law, and also on occasion, to overrule by statute the decisions of the judges the results of which are widely felt to be unsatisfactory. As executive is bound, in applying the law to clothe the general principle in the garment of detail; and in the modern State, this function covers so wide ambit that it is often difficult to distinguish it from the work of the legislature. The judiciary, finally, which settles either the competence of the executive (in which case it determines the substance of legislative will) or dispute between two citizens (in which case it extends the legal imperatives of a state to cover new ground, or denies that the ground involved comes within the ambit of those imperatives) is in fact performing a function which is legislative in character'.[1]

As against what Laski writes, the doctrine of the separation of powers, while making for a certain degree of efficiency, places a premium on jealousy, suspicion, and inner friction. The nature of power is such that anybody entrusted with it wants to press it to the utmost limits possible and prevent others from exercising their power. The serious limitations of the doctrine of the separation of powers were clearly brought out during the second term, as president, of Woodrow Wilson, when the State refused to ratify the treaty which the President had concluded. In the picturesque language of Finer, the theory of the separation of powers throws 'government into alternating conditions of coma and convulsion'. In modern democracies the legislature, representing the people as it does, occupies a more important place than that occupied by the executive or the judiciary.

There is no doubt that the British system of government which knows of little or no separation of powers as understood by Montesquieu, and in which there is an intimate and continuous relation between the executive and legislature, works more efficiently than the American system. It provides for 'a single focus of government'. Writing on the contrast between the two systems, Ramsay Muir says: 'If the Separation of Powers is the essential principle of the American constitution, concentration of Responsibility is the essential principle of the British constitution'. Another writer has said: 'Separation of powers means confusion of powers'.

Willoughby, who adopts a slightly different point of view, argues that in the English government there is a separation of powers organically but a union of powers personally, while in America there is a union of powers organically, but a separation of powers personally. The principle strictly adhered to in England is that of vesting the exercise of each power in a distinct organ, but this distinction is ignored in the United States. What prevails in this latter country is a personal separation of powers, but not an organic separation.

In the British ministry or cabinet we find a good illustration of union of person[2] but a separation of organs. The ministry acts as an executive organ, a legislative organ, and an administrative board. When it acts in one capacity it keeps in abeyance it powers in other capacities. To paraphrase Willoughby on this question:

when the ministry acts as executive organ, it acts independently of Parliament and as representative of the Crown. When it acts as a legislative organ, it keeps within the legislative field and does not seek to take to itself strictly either executive or administrative functions. When it acts as an administrative board, it does not seek to exercise either executive or legislative powers, but confines itself strictly to the problems of administration.

Thus in the British constitution the several branches of government are kept separate. But they are made to realise that they are part and parcel of a common mechanism by placing the same persons in charge of several organs.

As regards the American constitution, Willoughby writes that many people imagine that the public liberties of the American people are safeguarded by a strict separation of powers. But the fact of the matter is there is considerable union of powers. The difficulty of working the American constitution is not due to the separation of powers, but is due to a joint exercise of powers by two or more authorities.

In the American constitution, says Willoughby, neither the union of powers not the separation of powers is consistently carried out; and the consequence has been a chronic struggle between the executive and the legislature. This struggle has been intensified by the failure of the American constitution to realise the importance of administration as a separate branch of government.

Seeing the futility of a rigid application of the theory of the separation of powers to modern conditions, H. Finer divides the powers of government into *resolving* powers and *executive* powers, the former including the electorate, political parties, parliament, cabinet, and the chief of state; and the latter including the cabinet, chief of state, the civil service and the courts of justice. To a discussion of some of these we shall now turn our attention.

ORGANS OF GOVERNMENT

In modern democratic States, there no three, but seven organs of government, closely related to each other and capable of being grouped under 'policy-making' organs of government and 'policy-enforcing' organs of government.

The Electorate

This is the body of people in any country who have the power of vote. By the exercise of this power they make and unmake governments in the last analysis. It is only seldom that whole country acts as a single constituency, as in Fascist Italy. The usual practice is to divide the country into easily manageable constituencies with nearly equal population. Where a constituency is entitled to one and only one representative, it is called a single-member constituency. Constituencies sending up more than one representative are called multi-member constituencies. England and India have single-member constituencies for the most part. 576 out of the 615 seats in the British House of Commons are filled up by single-member constituencies.

In India we find separate constituencies for minorities and for special interests such as commerce and the landed aristocracy, as well as University constituencies. All this is undemocratic and stands in the way of India evolving a genuinely national and democratic State. Communalism is a survival of tribalism, and representation of special interests is a vestige of feudalism.

Representation by estates was common in several of the European countries till comparatively recent times. Political reformers in England agitated for a long time for the principle of 'one member, one vote'. In the words of J. Bentham, the prince among reformers, 'Each (was) to count for one; and nobody for more than one'. This reform has come to pass in all democratic countries, in spite of a few anomalies here and there. Even to-day plural voting exists in England according to which a person may vote as a member of the constituency in which he lives as well as an occupier of business premises worth £ 10 a year. University graduates, too, may exercise a second vote in voting for the member for whom the constituency is entitled.

Women were denied the franchise till very recent times, especially for national elections. Partly as a result of continuous and even militant agitation and partly as a result of the notable part played by them during the Great War, women above 30 secured the vote in England in 1918. In 1928 this age discrimination was abolished and both men and women were placed on the same footings. The U.S.A. extended the franchise to women by the 19th Amendment to the Constitution in 1919, and Germany provided for women franchise in the Weimar constitution. France and Italy to this day refuse the right of vote to women for fear that it might unduly strengthen the influence of the clergy on politics, while Spain, another Catholic country, has removed the restriction. Soviet Russia treats both men and women alike as regards the franchise. Even foreign residents are allowed to vote. In India women enjoy the franchise for all elections on the same terms as men.

The extension of the franchise to women was heralded by many as inaugurating an era of purity and social justice and humanitarianism in politics. But it has done none of these things. Women as a whole have not exercised the vote any more discriminately than men. After fighting for the vote, several have failed to use it. Still, as a result of the presence of women representatives in the legislature and of the increasing interest of individual women and women's associations in the civic life of the country, greater attention is being paid to social questions and, in a country like India, to the removal of the legal and social disabilities of women and to the satisfaction of the needs of children.

The age at which a person is entitled to vote varies in different countries, the prevailing age being 21, as in Great Britain and India. Turkey and Soviet Russia enfranchise their young people at 18, when a great many are still immature. The German constitution of 1919 threw open the franchise to men and women above 20. In some countries the right to vote is not given till a person is 25. Some have argued that it is a mistake to enfranchise youth who are often irresponsible and radical in their outlook. But the prevailing opinion is that by the time youth reaches 21 he has enough knowledge of the world around him to exercise his vote intelligently. Even his alleged radicalism is not to be frowned upon in view of the preponderance of conservatism in positions of authority. Besides, youth is bound to learn by experience.

The age at which a person may contest a seat to the national legislature is usually fixed at a higher level than the age at which he can vote. Thus in the U.S.A., Germany, and France a candidate has to be at least 26; in Japan he has to be 30. In Great Britain and Russia the same age is fixed for both candidature and voting.

In India the qualifying age for the candidate is 25 for the provincial Assemblies and 30 for the Provincial Councils. No maximum age limit seems to be fixed anywhere. In England a candidate is not required to be a resident of the constituency from which he proposes to stand, but not so in the United States.

Modern theory and practice are in favour of universal, equal, and adult suffrage. But certain classes of people are excluded—such as the insane, certified mental defectives, certain classes of criminals, paupers, and bankrupts. Aliens are excluded from the franchise in all countries, except in Russia. Most countries lay down rules for the naturalisation of aliens. The usual qualification is residence in the country for a period of years. In the U.S.A. each state has its own rules for the naturalisation of aliens. The usual qualification is residence in the country for a period of years. In the U.S.A. each state has its own rules regarding electoral qualifications. Some state require a citizenship and literacy test in English in addition to residence. The 15th Amendment to the Constitution provides that no person may be excluded for the vote merely on the ground of race or colour. But the southern states which are colour-ridden have devised several subterfuges by which to keep the Negroes out. In the South African Union the black people who form 9/10ths of the population have no vote. Germany denies all political rights to the Jews. In several of the European countries national minorities are excluded from the vote. Certain classes of government servants such as election officers and soldiers are excluded from the vote in some countries.

Property and educational qualifications are usually insisted upon and conditions for voting. But with the advance of democracy these qualifications are fixed at as low a level as possible. The earlier theory was that only those who had 'a stake in the country', that is, propertied classes, should vote. But this resulted in the creation of many vested interests and the perpetuation of much injustice. The Reform Bills of 1832 and 1867 in England fought against restrictions based on high property qualifications. Till 1919 the three class system based upon the direct amount of taxation paid prevailed in Prussia, according to which a voter in the first class roughly possessed four times the political power of a man belonging to the second class and sixteen times that of a member of the third class. Even to-day higher property and educational qualifications are required in India for election to the upper chambers.

As regards educational qualifications, simple literacy in the language of the area is considered adequate. While literacy is no doubt a great advantage, mere illiteracy ought not to be considered a serious disqualification. As the Lothian Committee observes in relation to the Indian situation: 'Illiteracy by no means implies that the individual is not capable of casting an intelligent vote on matters within the range of his own knowledge and experience'. This does not mean that a premium is to be placed on illiteracy. Mr. S. Srinivasa Iyengar says: 'Ability to follow the debates in the newspapers and to read books and papers containing an exposition of facts and arguments bearing on rival policies and measures, is indispensable to a sound scheme of democracy'. Political parties can do a great deal in educating the electorate.

We no longer subscribe to the old theory that the right to vote implies the duty to back up one's vote by physical strength, if necessary. No one claims to-day that women should be excluded from the vote because they do not bear the brunt of the battlefield as much as men. Therefore, military qualification for voting is irrelevant to-day. Everybody has a right to good life and as such every normal person who is not an enemy of the State should have the vote.

In the view of many thinkers the right to vote is not a right which automatically belongs to every citizen. It is a privilege which can be conferred only upon those who are capable of exercising it for public good. This being so, some argue that the duty to vote is not only a moral duty but also a legal obligation. Thus we find that some of the Cantons of Switzerland, Australia, Belgium, and the Argentine Republic make voting compulsory. In Mexico a person who has failed to exercise his vote once without sufficient excuse is debarred from voting at the next election. Compulsion in this matter, as in many other matters, is undesirable and defeats its own end. The proper remedy for non-voting is not compulsion, but the stimulation of interest and the avoidance of too many and too frequent elections.

The old theory of representation was 'Community' representation. People were grouped according to classes or estates, and each class voted separately. The system which has been in vogue in modern times is territorial representation. Recently this system has come in for much criticism. It has been argued by guild socialism, syndicalism, etc. that the mere fact that people live together in a given locality does not mean that their interests are common or tend to become common. A coal miner, for instance, is certain to have more in common with another coal miner living fifty miles away from him than with a commercial traveller or a school master who may be his next-door neighbour. On the basis of this argument, it is said that a truer form of representation is the vocational. The system is in practice in the corporative State of Italy and the communist State of Russia. It is too early to say whether the system will work more efficiently than territorial representation. One of the chief criticisms of vocational representation is that it is not always easy to say what occupations should be recognised as entitled to representation and what amount of representation should be given to each of them. Besides, this system is likely to multiply rival interests and groups and militate against the creation and maintenance of a spirit of true citizenship. 'Neighbourhood' is just as important a factor in man's social life as 'profession'. The primary function of a legislature is not to protect the interests of rival economic groups, but to secure and advance the interests of the nation as a whole.

Proportional Representation

Single member constituencies often lead to anomalous results when there are more than two candidates contesting for a seat. Votes are so divided that the successful candidate frequently represents the minority, and not the majority, of the electorate. In the General Election of November, 1935 in Great Britain the pro-Baldwin group secured 430 seats in the House of Commons, although their total voting strength in the country was only 11,764,660; while the parties opposed to the Baldwin ministry, though securing 10,071,993 votes, obtained only 185 seats. To remedy such an anomalous state of affairs, several devices have been put forward such as the Second Ballot, the Alternative Vote, the Comulative Vote, the Limited Vote, and Pro-portional representation by single transferable vote.

Of these the last mentioned, known also as the Hare plan, seems best fitted for producing the most equitable electoral results.

But as yet there is no great enthusiasm for it although it has been tried in India, the Dominions and certain constituencies of Great Britain such as University Constituencies.

According to this scheme, the quota required for the election of any candidate is fixed before hand in accordance with the formula

$$\text{Quota} = \frac{\text{Valid votes}}{\text{Number of candidates} + 1} + 1$$

In the voting paper the elector indicates his preference with numbers 1, 2, 3, 4, 5, and so on. After the polling is over, the first preferences are all counted and candidates securing more than the quota are declared elected. As the effect of no vote is to be lost, the superfluous first votes (that is votes above the quota) of any candidate or candidates are passed down the list in accordance with the order of preference indicated in the ballot paper. Votes are transferred according to the order of preference indicated not only from those candidates who have enough and to spare but also from those who have no chance of being elected at all on account of the few first votes cast in their favour. Their ballot papers are scrutinised to find out their second, third, fourth preference, etc., and the votes are transferred accordingly. This two-fold transference of votes is kept up among the 'continuing' candidates till a point is reached when the number securing the quota is equal to the number of candidates to be returned from the constituency in question. At this point the process of transfer stops and the results are announced. The transference of votes from the bottom is resorted to at a later state in the process than transference from above since it means the exclusion of certain candidates.

There is no doubt that, more than any other system, the system of Proportional Representation will more accurately represent the relative strength of the parties in the country. But it has certain defects. Instead of reducing in number of parties in a country to two of there main parties, it has a tendency to multiply them and stereotype the existing ones. Every small group is encouraged to maintain its own peculiarity without seeking to find points of contact with other groups and eventually be merged in them. The system is likely to increase the importance of the party machine.

The successful candidate is not likely to take the same personal interest in the welfare of his constituency, as his election depends upon the working of a mathematical formula and not upon his having successfully wooed a definite body of known voters. With a heterogeneous group of representatives in Parliament, a strong, united, and homogeneous cabinet becomes well nigh impossible. Besides, there will be no periodical bye-elections which provide a rough indication of the degree of confidence in which the government of the day is held by the electorate. Furthermore, the process is too complicated for the average voter.

All these arguments have been countered by the advocates of proportional representation. In smaller bodies such as municipal councils in Canada and the United States, the system has proved useful. While the Liberal party in England is a staunch supporter of the proportional representation system, the two major parties have not taken to it kindly.

Political Parties

Political parties are considered to be indispensable for the successful working of modern democracy. By a political party we mean an organised body of people who stand for certain principles and policies in the political life of the country by whose operation they seek to promote the interests of the country as a whole. Burke defines a party as 'a body of men united for promoting by their joint endeavours the national interest upon some particular principle in which they are all agreed'. A political party, it must be born in mind does not mean a faction and sharp differences of opinion between party leaders are not to be interpreted in terms of a personal quarrel. A political party without definite political principles and a clear programme is not worthy of the name.

It is a well-known fact that even in the same family members differ from each other in temperament and outlook. Some are by nature timid, cautions and afraid to launch out on bold schemes. Others, on the contrary, are bold, adventurous, and radical in their thinking. Such differences are found on a wider scale when we are dealing with a large group of free people keenly interested in advancing the welfare of the country.

Parties with differing policies and programmes have no place under despotism. They are simply not tolerated. Modern dictatorships are all governments by one party, being a euphemism for the arbitrary rule of a few people. Parliamentary government, on the other hand, is essentially a party government. It allows full freedom of thought and discussion within, of course, the limits of constitutional propriety and ordinary decency. As a consequence, people divide themselves into such groups as Conservatives, Liberals, and Labourites or Republicans and Democrats. Owing to periodical changes in the general life and thought of the country, party labels do not always clearly indicate the programmes for which the parties stand. Thus at one time in the history of England the Liberals stood for a policy of non-intervention in the industrial life of the country and the Conservatives stood for considerable regulation of industry and for programmes of social reconstruction. Later on, however, the two parties changed places almost completely. Even on such fundamental issues as free trade and protection the attitudes of parties have not been consistent. Whatever difference in principle there may have been between the Republicans and Democrats of the United States of America in the past, they have largely disappeared to-day.

The party system is especially valuable in countries which have adopted parliamentary democracy, for it helps to bring about a harmonious relation between the executive and the legislature which is the bedrock of successful party government. The party in power in the legislature is the party from which the executive is drawn. When, owing to a national crisis, a coalition government is formed the parties are represented in the Cabinet or ministry roughly in proportion to their strength in the popular house.

This advantage of a harmonious relation between the executive and the legislature is found lacking in the constitution of the U.S.A. where it is possible to have those two organs of government controlled by the two rival parties in the country. Even in such a country parties play a very important role in creating public opinion on the momentous questions of the day.

There can be no doubt that under the complex conditions which prevail in modern states, parties render a valuable service in clarifying issues and policies. The party system helps a person to see his way through a maze of conflicting politics and intricate details. The issues before any modern government are so complex and difficult of comprehension that without the systematic guidance offered by political parties, the average voter will find himself entirely at sea. Parties perform in politics a function similar to that performed by lawyers in arguing the different sides of a case. Just as a it is possible for a clever lawyer to make right appear wrong and wrong appear right, a party by means of false propaganda, catchwords, and shibboleths may mislead the public altogether. But such tactics do not always succeed, especially if the electorate is educated, well-read and discriminating. Generally speaking, the party discussion enables the voter to discover the truth for himself. Lowell rightly says that the party serves as 'the broker of ideas'. Parties present alternative programmes and rival candidates and the voter is asked to choose between them. Parties further help in the evolution of a general will which is the core of democracy.

To sum up the discussion so far in countries which have adopted the parliamentary system of government parties help to make the government strong and stable; and in both parliamentary and non-parliamentary forms of democratic government they help to make the opinions of the electors articulate.

Recent thinkers, however, have seriously questioned the validity of the party system. Mr. S. Srinivasa Iyenger of Madras, a former president of the Indian National Congress, has severely criticised the party system in his 'Problems of Democracy in India'. He writes: The beneficent possibilities of the party system in the West appear to be exhausted.

Against the continuance of the party system, it is said that party mentality is very often a partisan mentality and that parties lean to bribery and corruption and exercise a tyranny of the most thorough-going kind both over their representatives in the legislature and over the general public. All these charges no doubt contain enough truth to make them appear plausible, but it must be remembered that it is easy to exaggerate them.

The primary aim of a party is to succeed. And in its craze for success a party frequently adopts dubious vote-catching devices. The party platform is made as broad and as nebulous as possible so as to catch the largest number of votes. Promises are made which are never meant to be fulfilled. Political opponents and rival political programmes are misrepresented, if not ridiculed. The choice before the voter if so limited that at times he is forced to choose between a knave and a fool. Party spirit and party loyalty are so worked up that passion and prejudice gain precedence over calm thinking and cool action. When it comes to appointments made by the government of the day, loyal supporters of the party are chosen in preference to well-qualified men who belong to the opposite party or to no party whatever. Party corrupts even the administration in a country like the U.S.A. where the 'Spoils System' has reigned supreme for generations. Voters are bribed, flattered and cajoled. In the words of Lord Bryce, the party system has 'demoralised politics and made them sorbid'. Such rigid discipline is exercised over the members of a party that very little room is left for individual judgement or independent voting. Party members in the legislature often play the role of 'dumb driven cattle'. They obey meekly the behests of the party whip. Decisions are made outside the legislature in party conclaves and the legislature is used only to register them. Individuality is crushed and members are encouraged to be insincere and hollow in thought and action. The party machine is controlled by a few selfish individuals and 'bosses' who declare a secret or open war upon ability and integrity of character.

The fair-minded student of public affairs is bound to admit the weight of many, if not all, of these criticisms. Yet he may not be prepared to throw the baby along with the bath water. Mr. S.S. Iyengar is much concerned about the loss of freedom of the average member of the legislature. But it must be remembered that not all out legislators are power-houses of ideas. Many of them are probably happier to have a party programme and policy which they can blindly follow than take the trouble of examining every detail for themselves for which they may not have the requisite qualification. Besides, it is always possible for an active member to influence policies and decisions in party meetings. Party discipline is undoubtedly a check upon the egotism of individual members. It curbs their ambitions and eccentricities and enables them to take their proper place alongside of others who think and act with them. In a country like India, as elsewhere, to destroy parties altogether would mean undue development of individualism each person playing the game for himself. If undue regimentation is bad, so is undue individualism. To the charge that the party system leads to dictatorship, our answer is that dictatorship is not the result of a well-organised party system working within the constitutional framework. It is the result of the disintegration of the party system, as is the case in Fascist Italy and Nazi Germany. Without a well-organised party system with adequate resources behind, able but poor candidates will have little chance of being elected.

Even if we abolish party funds and party organisation by means of legislation as Mr. Iyengar suggests, there is no doubt that parties will come back to life under some other form, less desirable than before. Being driven underground, parties are bound to transform themselves into secret cliques struggling to advance their own selfish ends. It is instructive to note at this point that even in Switzerland where the party spirit has been least developed the trend is in the direction of strengthening the party system.

Conditions for the successful working of party

The party system has worked exceedingly well in countries which have a strong two-party system. A strong government and an almost equally strong opposition presenting alternative programmes of public interest seem to be necessary if parties are not to degenerate into cliques. The opposition in England plays a very vital part in the conduct of public affairs. By its responsible criticism of the measures proposed by the government, it not only keeps the government alert and watchful, but also renders a great public service. It is no wonder, therefore, that it is described as 'His Majesty's Opposition'. Canada pays a salary to the Leader of the Opposition in recognition of the fact that his work in the House is just as important as that of any member of the Government in power.

France has demonstrated in no uncertain terms the weakness of the multiple party system. Government is formed by continuous bargaining and trafficking between members of different groups who have no scruples in changing their allegiance on the slightest pretext possible. It is no wonder that French governments have been exceedingly unstable, altogether at the mercy of the legislature. When the history of the present war comes to be written, it is more than likely that the historian will find in the multiple party system making for instability and weakness a potent case for the defeat of France at the hands of Nazi Germany.

If public opinion is not able to prevent the formation of frivolous or avowedly selfish parties we may have to resort to legislation. Any new party should be put on probation for some years and be obliged to establish its *bona fides* before it is allowed to become permanent. Parties which have no clear programmes or policies substantially different from those of existing parties have no right to exist. Our constant endeavour should be to integrate groups which are similar to each other in order that there may not be more than two strong parties in the country. No tolerance should be shown to a party whose avowed object is to break up all other parties and establish a dictatorship of its own.

Parties founded merely on differences of class, caste or community have no abiding place in politics. They are a fruitful cause of national weakness. By perpetuating fissiparous tendencies they place themselves entirely at the mercy of the interested outsider. Even broad national questions which should be judged purely on their own merit are approached from the caste or communal angle. The caste and communal spectacles distort the vision with regard to economic, social, and political policies and programmes. At times of national crisis parties should be prepared to lay aside their differences and work together as a single unit.

In no circumstance a party should be allowed to have a private military force, knowing as we do that the Nazis in Germany and the Fascists in Italy rode to power on the backs of their private armies. The only legitimate weapons which a party may use in winning adherents are persuasion and conviction. The long tongue and recourse to physical force are signs of barbarism. Democracy can function only if political minorities defeated at elections accept their defeat manfully. Their only constitutional right is to convert themselves into a majority by argument and persuasion.

If party government should succeed, it is necessary to keep the administration outside the reach of parties and politicians. Government officers from top to bottom should be elected on the basis of merit by a body which commands the respect of everybody by its stern impartiality. Government officials who are found guilty of favouring men of their own caste or community should be dealt with mercilessly. Recruitment, transfer, and promotion of public servants should follow the recognised canons of public service.

Everything possible should be done to break up the control of party 'bosses' and time-servers. Those who seek to control the party machine for their own selfish ends should be hounded out of the party. For accomplishing this end sound public opinion is necessary. Leaders of outstanding a ability and unimpeachable character are the life breath of a party.

The failure of the party system is partly a reflection on the people themselves. If the electorate is not intelligent, critical and discriminating, party dictatorship is inevitable. It is absurd to say that a person should vote in a particular way because his father and grandfathers before him voted that way; or because the members of his class or profession want him to vote in that manner. The intelligent voter should be prepared to defy customs and conventions when necessary and vote according to the dictates of his conscience and judgment.

The party system is bound to fail if there is a lack of character among politicians and the people at large. A high degree of public honesty and honour is the first requisite of successful party government. Without truthfulness, honesty, and a single-minded devotion to public weal, parties become mere cliques, corrupting the people and eating into the vitals of the country. The voter on his part should cultivate independence and judgment, a horror or bribery and corruption, and a keen sense of public duty. Parties should become a synonym for cooperative methods of realizing the common good. Without character of a very high order widely prevalent among the people any type of government, particularly the democratic, will come to grief. An honest and well-informed press and platform can do much in making the party follow the narrow and strict path of public morality.

The Legislature

Among the organs of government, especially in democratic countries, the pride of place is given to the legislature. But such has not been the case always. In olden days, as Jenks points out, laws were not made but discovered. They were folk laws based upon the customs of the people, and it was the business of what governmental and religious authorities there were to discover these laws. As time advanced folk laws became less important, and laws took the form of ordinances or decrees issued by the executive for the maintenance of peace. These were not as permanent as folk laws and did not cover such a wide range. At a still later state came laws by established estates which were more or less representative assemblies. Finally there came into being Parliaments and Parliamentary sovereignty.

When Parliaments were first summoned, the object was not to secure their help in law-making, but to vote supplies for the carrying out of the king's policy. A place in Parliament at this time was not a position of honour and influence to be covered, but an onerous responsibility to be avoided. Soon, however, representatives in Parliament realised that before supplies could be voted they could insist upon the redress of grievances, which a harassed king, involved in foreign wars and domestic difficulties, felt obliged to do. From this time on began the continuous history of law-making by the legislature. It is instructive to note that even to-day in England while laws are made by 'the Kings Most Excellent Majesty by and with the advice and consent of the Lords Spiritual and Temporal in the Parliament assembled, etc., supplies are granted to His Majesty 'freely and voluntarily' by 'the commons . . . in Parliament assembled'. At first requests for laws took the form of petitions to the king, but later they were framed as bills.

Sources of Law

Even to-day the legislature is not the source of law-making. The five other sources of law, as analysed by Professor Holland, are:

(1) custom or usage;

(2) religion;

(3) adjudication or judicial decision;

(4) scientific commentaries; and

(5) equity.

Custom played a very important part in all early communities. There was no written law. The unwritten customs of the family, clan or tribe were interpreted and applied by the patiarch or council of elders. These customs for the most part were concerned with questions of life and property.

Religion was closely connected with customary law. Customs were not merely the ancient usages of the people, but they were also supposed to have divine sanction behind them. To disobey such God-given laws was to court Divine wrath, meted out by the village headman, council, priest, or priest-kings. History shows that while the religious basis of laws has continued for a long time in the Eastern countries, in the West it was soon replaced by the political.

Custom and religion did not always speak with the same voice. When the inter-mixture of tribes took place, there arose a complexity of customs, usages, and religious laws. In such cases, conflicts were referred to the wisest men in the community whose decisions were accepted as binding. These early judges not only adjudicated between differing customs and practices, but also applied common sense to the solution of problems of which these old customs were obviously unfitted or had made no provision at all. These legal decisions of judges were first transmitted orally, but were later committed to writing. 'Judge-made' laws even to-day constitute an important portion of legislation. Inasmuch as later decisions of judges are often based on the earlier decisions of the members of their fraternity, judges play an important, though indirect, part in law-making.

The next source of law is scientific commentaries which have acquired a reputation through the years. Lawyers and judges attach much importance to the opinions of great lawyers or jurists. Thus in countries where the English system of law prevails the legal opinions of men like Coke and Blackstone are received with great respect. Such opinions, to start with, are only arguments and not decisions. But to the extent to which they are accepted as sound, they in course of time are giving the weight of decisions. 'The authority of the commentator is established, just like a judge-made decision, by frequent recognition'. What the commentator does is to collect, compare and 'logically arrange legal principles, decisions and laws', and in so doing, to lay down 'guiding principles, for possible cases'. 'He shows the omissions and deduces principles to govern them. He provides the basis for new law, not the new law itself'.[3]

Another fruitful source of law is equity. By equity is meant 'anybody of rules existing by the side of the original civil law, founded on distinct principles and claiming incidentally to supersede the civil law in virtue of a superior sanctity inherent in these principles'.[4] Equity, in other words, simply means equality or justice. It is based on what earlier writers used to describe as the law of nature or nations. In cases where the existing law is altogether unsuitable or does not apply, the judge cannot wait till the law is altered or a new law is made. So what he does is to apply that law of 'intrinsic fairness' or 'equality of treatment', and this is known as equity. In England, the Court of Chancery is 'the supreme judicial organisation for equity jurisdiction'.

The final and most important source of law is legislation, which is an expression of the sovereign will of the people. In all modern States there is a tendency for legislation to supplant the other sources of law. Legislation more and more replaces custom and equity. The codification of law tends to limit the sphere of Judge-made laws, and scientific commentaries are used largely for purposes of discussion. In the making of new laws, well-established customs, religious opinions, and equity to play a part, but more as factors influencing legislation than as direct sources of law.

Laws made by Administrative Departments of Government

In the modern State the legislature alone does not make laws. The executive head in the U.S.A. for example, negotiates treaties subject to ratification by two-thirds vote of the Senate. The British Parliament does not have the time or the necessary knowledge to draft all the details of every legislative measure, and hence what it does in several instances is to content itself with passing the broad outlines of the measure, leaving the administrative departments to fill in the details by means of administrative orders, rules and regulations. Some of these are provisional in character and require the approval of Parliament, while others do not even require this formality. This species of 'delegated' or 'subordinate' legislation has assumed such great dimensions that Chief Justice Hewart describes administration in England by the telling title 'the New Despotism'.

Legislation by People

Switzerland, which is the home of political devices, has made experiments in direct legislation by means of referendum and initiative, and other States such as the Commonwealth of Australia and the constituent states of the American Union have followed suit. Referendum simply means that a piece of legislation after being passed by the legislature has to be approved by a specified majority of the voters before it can become valid. In certain cases, the referendum is optional depending upon a request being made for a popular vote by a specified number of voters or a specified number of the component units in a federation. In other cases, however, especially as regards constitutional amendments, as in the Commonwealth of Australia, the referendum is compulsory.

While the referendum is negative in character in that it approves or disapproves of legislative measure, the initiative is positive in that it enables the voters themselves to take the lead in law-making. According to this system a certain number of voters have to ask for legislation on a given question. They may themselves formulate the details of the legislation or give the general aim of the projected legislation to the legislature, and ask it to fill in the details. In either case it is submitted to the vote of the people and becomes effective if ratified by a majority voting at the poll. The Initiative is said to be more popular in the part states of America than is the referendum.

The Plebiscite is resorted to in ascertaining the wishes of the inhabitants of territory in transferring territory from one State to another or in creating new states. This practice has been in operation in Europe since the end of the 18th century. In 1935, the Saar region was restored to Germany as the result of a plebiscite. While on the surface it appears to be a democratic institution, in recent times there has been much intimidation under the name of plebiscite, as in Austria and Czecho-Slovakia.

Reviewing the value of direct legislation as a whole, it may be said that while small areas long accustomed to free democratic institutions, like the Swiss communes and cantons, can make it a success, it is likely to do more harm than good in large countries lacking the Swiss traditions of democracy and local-self government. According to Mr. Srinivasa Iyengar, direct legislation, instead of weakening the prestige of the legislature, is particularly valuable in times of crisis. It keeps down the excesses of party spirit, restores the national temper, and is unequalled as a method of practical instruction in politics.

The Organization of Legislature

Both in political theory and practice the organisation of the legislature has been a much-discussed question. Bi-carmeral legislature is the usual practice everywhere, especially as regards the centre. In provinces and component units of federation bi-cameralism is not uniformally found. Six out of the eleven Indian provinces possess bi-cameral legislatures. England has had a bi-cameral legislature more because of historical circumstances, than as a result of deliberate design. Countries which have copied the British system of Parliamentary government have copied her as regards bi-cameralism too.

Where there are two legislative chambers, it stands to reason that the should be organised differently, both as regards their compositions and powers and functions, in order to avoid conflict and jealousy. The lower house, which is also called the popular house, is usually elected by the people themselves, and representation is on the basis of population, and a wide franchise. The upper house, also known as the second chamber, usually represents interests in the community, or part states in a federation, and is usually not directly elected.

The British House of Lords is largely hereditary, and possesses larger numbers than the House of Commons. The Senate in the U.S.A. consists of 96 members, two from each of the 48 states, and has been directly elected since 1913. It is a continuous body, each member sitting for six years, one-third of the total number retiring every two years. It is one of the strongest, if not the strongest, second chambers, in the world. Second chambers in Switzerland and the Commonwealth of Australia are constituted on the same principle as the American Senate. Each of the Swiss cantons sends up two representatives and each of the six Australian States sends up six representatives to their representative federal second chambers. The Canadian Senate, like the American, consists of 96 members, but they are nominated by the Governor-General on the recommendation of the ministry. Representation is not on the basis of the provinces, but roughly on the basis of population. The Reichstag under the Weimer Constitution (1919) of Germany represented the states, as opposed to the people, both in legislation and administration but did not give them equal representation. The French Senate, another strong second chamber in the world, consisting of 314 members, is indirectly elected, and sits for nine years, one-third retiring every three years. The Union of South Africa combines the nominative and elective principles. In some of the Australian Provinces members of the upper chamber are nominated for life by the Governor. In some they are elected on a special and restricted basis. Turkey has a unicameral legislature.

Norway has a unique kind of a second chamber. The Strothing which is the popular house is elected every three years. As soon as it is elected it proceeds to elect one-fourth of its members to constitute an upper house known as the Lagthing, the rest constituting the Odesthing. The Lagthing has no power to initiate legislations, but it can suggest amendments to bills sent up by the Odesthing. If the amendments are not carried and the Lagthing refuses to yield, a joint session is held in which two-thirds majority decides the issue.

If second chambers are necessary at all, they should be distinctive from the popular house, act independently without being irresponsible, and possess the necessary capacity and impartiality to revise the work of the lower house effectively.

Are Second Chambers Necessary?

Just because second chambers are practically universal, it does not follow that they are indispensable. The usual reasons given in favour of second chambers are (1) that they are a useful check upon the hasty and ill-digested legislation of the lower house and (2) that in federal constitutions, they safeguard the interest of the component units. Both these arguments have been seriously questioned, and the last word on them has not yet been uttered.

Writing in the latter half of the last century, J.S. Mill feared that one house alone might become 'despotic' and 'overweening' and that a second chamber was necessary in order to prevent 'the corrupting influence of undivided power'. Sir Henry Maine went so far as to say that 'almost any second chamber is better than none', on the ground that a well-constituted second chamber provided not a 'rival infallibility' but an 'additional security'. According to Lord Acton, a second chamber, is the essential security for freedom: it provides the necessary balance of power in the polity, gives protection to the minorities, and a good revising chamber.

In England, the Rump of the Long Parliament did away with the second chamber and tried to make itself perpetual and independent of the electorate. But the result was so bad that Cromwell described it as the 'horridest arbitrariness that ever existed on earth'. The Convention Parliament voted that 'government is and ought to be by King, Lords, and Commons'.

France too experimented with a single chamber, but give it up as a fruitless endeavour. In our own day Greece tried the same experiment, but with no better results. From all this it would appear, as Marriot points out, that there is a singular uniformity in favour of two legislative chambers. Mr. S.S. Iyenger, on the contrary, holds that bi-cameralism in democracy is 'an outworn creed'. According to him, the institution of bi-cameralism is due to 'a hesitant faith in democracy, and a desire to conciliate minorities', and 'there is no valid reason why the popular will should seek two channels of expression, why democracy should speak in two voices.' In this view, second chambers are retained 'to provide scope for the ambitions of party men, who may not be accommodated in the first, to lessen rivalries in leadership within the party itself, and generally to enlarge the circle of party influence'. Their introduction in the Indian provinces, it would seem, is in order to bolster up vested interests and to put a brake on the possible radical tendencies of the lower house, especially as regards landed property.

The classical argument against bi-cameralism was stated by Abbe Sieyes when he said: 'If a second chamber dissents from the first, it is mischievous; if it agrees with it, it is superfluous'. The fitting reply to this dilemma which so paralyses thought is in the words of Finer: 'If the two Assemblies agree, so much the better for our belief in the wisdom and justice of the law; if they disagree, it is time for the people to reconsider their attitude'.

On theoretical grounds, there is no doubt whatever that a good case can be made out for a properly constituted second chamber. As a revising body, it can play a very useful part in legislation. On account of the nature of its composition, longer term of office, greater experience, and comparative freedom from the prejudices and passions of the popular house, it can consider measures in all their aspects in a more or less detached manner. But what practice shows is that is likely to become a bulwark of conservatism and even of reaction in politics More than once the British House of Lords had to be threatened with 'swamping' before it would yield to reason, and the Parliament Act of 1911 has rendered it almost powerless. It no longer has the right to meddle with money bills, and in matters of ordinary legislation it no longer enjoys a co-ordinate authority. The utmost that it can do is to hold up legislation for about 30 months or three successive sessions of Parliament.

The argument that a second chamber is necessary in order to check hasty and ill-digested legislation does not strike us as weighty. The various readings of a bill, submission to special committees, consultation of the public through the press and the platform, etc., seem to be sufficient safeguards against any hasty action being taken. Besides, on most urgent reforms, to give the power of delay to the upper house is perhaps to court disaster in the long run, and pave the way for popular revolution.

The further argument that a second chamber is a fundamental part of the federal principle, can also be questioned. Matters which are purely local are dealt with by the local legislatures, and a second chamber is not necessary to protect state interests as against national interests. Taking the U.S.A. as an example, we find that the Senate has not been any less 'national', or less progressive than the House of Representatives. It is wrong to assume that one house will think only in terms of provincial or state interests and the other in terms of national interests The likelihood is that in both houses there will be provincial-minded and national-minded men. We, therefore, consider Marriott's judgment an exaggeration, when he says that an upper chamber is a primary and effective guarantee for the preservation of the federal constitution.

To conclude, whether second chambers are necessary or not, our reply is that no uniform answer can be given which will be applicable to all cases. A great deal depends on historical antecedents. The U.S.A. and France will undoubtedly be the poorer if their Senates are abolished. Both of them have attracted to themselves men of mature wisdom and experience, who have played a notable part in law-making and policy-framing. Even Great Britain will be the poorer by the abolition of the House of Lords, which has been a reservoir of ministers, and a storehouse of knowledge and administrative experience, and has made possible unhurried and dispassionate discussion of some of the great questions of the day. Canada, on the other hand, is not likely to lose much if her Senate is done away with. So far as constitution-making for the future is concerned, a second chamber should be an exception rather than the rule. In order to avoid waste, it may be provided that controversial measures should be passed twice over by the lower house, with a general election intervening if necessary, before they take effect.

Powers and Functions of the Legislature

Law-making is not the only function of legislatures. They have to consider the budget, vote supplies, and exercise general superintendence over administration. In the matter of legislation, the usual practice is to give a more important place to the lower house than to the upper. Finance bills can only be introduced in lower house. Non-finance bills in many countries can be introduces in either house, but when there is a deadlock between the two houses, the upper house has usually to yield. In many constitutions arrangements are made for a joint sitting of the two houses or committees of the two houses, where the final decision is reached by a specified percentage of votes; and since the popular house is almost everywhere the more numerous body, the dice is loaded in its favour.

The British Parliament is one of the most powerful legislative chambers in the world. Its powers are as wide as public opinion and the will of the electorate would tolerate. It has both constituent and legislative functions. In the U.S.A. and Switzerland, on the other hand, in elaborate machinery is set up for changing the constitution. In Australia, too, constitutional changes require a special procedure. In France, while the constitution is technically not flexible, it can be changed by a relative simple process.

In countries where the parliamentary system of government prevails, parliament exercises control over administration through questions and answers or interpellations. While in England a vote of no-confidence cannot be moved in this connection, such a procedure is possible in France, and is frequently used in overthrowing ministries. Writers on public administration draw a parallel between the legislature and the board of directors of a business concern, in that both are responsible for the function or direction, supervision, and control, as against execution. In the U.S.A. it is the legislative branch of government which 'possesses the final authority to determine how the administrative branch of government shall be organised, how duties shall be distributed among the several parts, and what methods of procedure shall be employed by them'.

The legislature, particularly the upper house, also possesses a few judicial functions. Even to-day the Lord chancellor, the presiding officer of the House of Lords, is the highest judicial authority in England, and, together with the six law-lords constitutes the highest court of the realm. Though the judicial committee of the Privy Council consists of others besides these seven lords, its work is actually performed by the latter. In the U.S.A. the Senate tries cases of impeachment preferred by the House of Representatives. The French Senate is the high court of justice.

The upper house in certain countries has some executive functions. In the U.S.A. appointments of ministers, judges of the supreme court, ambassadors, consuls, and other such officers made by president require ratification by the Senate. In France the Chamber of Deputies may be dissolved by the President with the consent of the Senate. But convention has worked against this practice, and so the popular house enjoys practically a fixed term of years. In both the U.S.A. and France, the upper chamber is exceptionally strong enjoying almost the same power as the lower house. While the American Senate cannot initiate money bills, it can amend them. It exercises more influence in foreign affairs than does the House of Representatives. On account of its maturity of experience, longer term of tenure, its continuous nature, smaller size, connection with the political machine, and the powers conferred upon it by law, it enjoyed greater reputation in the country. In France, the lack of any strong party organisation linking the two chambers, and the bad conduct of the Deputies, have made the Senate strong. It has such great influence, that no cabinet dares to flout it: and as a matter of fact every cabinet has on it on an average three or four members from the Senate. It has the power to 'accept, reject, reduce, or increase the credits voted by the Chamber'.

Legislative Procedure

Law-making for modern times is not an easy process. It requires the service of expert draftsmen, and careful consideration of the general principles of the bill, as well as the details, clause by clause. In Great Britain, a bill has to go through the first reading, second reading, committee stage, report stage, and third reading. In order to prevent the dilatory tactics of the opposition, and to save the time of the House, recourse is has to 'guillotine' and various types of closure.

Political parties and 'pressure groups' exercise much influence on the course of legislation. Candidates have to promise to support the programme and policy of their party before they are officially accepted. At times groups of voters interested in some scheme or other obtain the written promise of a candidate as a condition of their support. In some constitutions, such as the part state constitutions of the U.S.A., when a legislator loses the confidence of his electorate in part or whole, he may be obliged to stand for re-election before his term is over by a protest known as recall.

The power of parties and 'pressure groups' and of public meetings is so great to-day that the old question whether the representative is a mere delegate, or one who can use his discretion, has lost much of its force. According to certain thinkers, the representative is only a human telephone, who has to record truthfully whatever his electorate wishes him to record. In this extreme form, the theory is unworkable. It is not only derogatory to the self-respect of an individual, but also one cannot foresee all the contingencies which may arise after the election is over. Besides, a representative has a duty to his own constituency as well as to nation at large therefore, he should be prepared to consider all sides of the question as presented by other representatives and different parties.

While there is no general rule regarding the circumstances when it should be obligatory for a representative to resign, it is generally agreed that he should resign and seek re-election when he changes his party, or adopts a line of conduct or policy totally opposed to the express wish of his constituency, or violates his election pledges.

Similar considerations apply also to a government in power in the parliamentary system. Finer discusses three circumstances in which dissolution is considered advisable in England:

(1) when it is proposed to launch upon a new policy of fundamental importance as Baldwin did in 1923 when he

wanted to introduce protection as a remedy for unemployment after Bonar Law, from whom Baldwin had taken the premiership, had promised at the general Election not to raise tariffs;

(2) when a government sees convincing signs that it is no longer trusted by the country;

(3) when the position of parties is such as to produce a deadlock preventing necessary legislation to be passed, and severe criticism of government so that it cannot keep itself in power with dignity.

The Committee System

Modern legislatures do much of their work through committees. In the U.S.A. all business in Congress is done by means of committees because of the separation of the executive and the legislature. The Committees deliberate in private. While both parties are represented on them, the majority party has the larger share, and the chairman belongs to that party. There is a tendency for the members of the party to act together. Ministers are sometimes asked to appear before these committees, but their advice need not be accepted. The chairman of some of the important committees practically occupy the position of a minister such as the chairman of the committees on Ways and Means, and on Appropriations. A similar system obtains in France, too, where the *rapporteur* of a commission can act as a rival to the minister even in financial matters. Under this system the chamber controls the administration as well as legislation. The chairmen of committees in the British House of Commons do not have the same prominence as in Congress. The ministers overshadow them on the floor of the House.

Duration of Parliament

There is no cut and dried answer to the question how long parliaments should last. In general, it may be said that the duration should be short enough to keep the representative close to the people, and long enough for the representative to gain experience, and not subject the people to frequent elections. In their zeal for popular control, the American people have made their lower houses very short in duration. One of the reasons for the comparative weakness of the House of Representatives is that its duration is only two years. In England, France and Germany a statutory period is laid down for the duration of the lower chamber, with the provision that it may be dissolved earlier under certain conditions. The statutory period of five years for the British House of Commons is really too long as the house is likely to get out of touch with the wishes, and desires of the electorate. Three years, on the other hand, as in the case of the provincial councils in India under the 1919 Reforms, is too short. A four year period with the right of earlier dissolution seems best for parliamentary governments. In Great Britain the Crown dissolves parliament, but the authority for dissolving it is located in the cabinet.

As regards second chambers, leaving aside hereditary bodies, bodies, which are directly or indirectly elected or bodies which are partly elected and partly nominated, as the provincial legislative councils in India, should not last for more than five years. Second chambers which are continuous bodies may last six years, one-third retiring every two years, as is the case in the U.S.A. The French practice of members sitting for nine years, one-third retiring every three years, does not commend itself to us. In the opinion of Mr. S.S. Iyengar, the provincial councils in India, just as much as the provincial assemblies, should be subject to dissolution. He further holds that no member should be eligible to be a representative of the people in any legislature for more than twice, in as much as it leads to professionalism in politics and encourages the operation of mercenary motives. Such restrictions, Mr. Iyengar believes, 'would prevent staleness and that dulled sense of responsibility and the tendency to run in grooves which are so conspicuous now.' Over against this point of view something can be said for experience and continuity in office. Besides, if a person is allowed to be a representative for only two terms, that will effectively shut out the non-leisured classes, and those who look forward to an honourable career in politics. The problem is to weed out the ineffective and hopelessly selfish and docile members of the legislature.

Salary of Legislators

Most modern governments pay salaries to their legislators. In the U.S.A., both senators and congressmen are paid $7,500 each per year. In France, too, members of both houses are paid. In Great Britain since the advent of Labour (1919), members of the House of Commons have been paid £400 a year. In India, under the present reforms members of the legislature receive a salary of Rs. 75/- a month. Mr. S.S. Iyengar thinks that this practice of payment is pernicious on the ground that it makes many of the legislators servile to the party. They look to pay rather than to service throwing aside the convictions for the same of an emolument. On the other hand, it must be said that if all classes of citizens are to take their proper share in the work of government, payment for service rendered is the only logical principle to follow. At the same time the salary paid should not be so large as to rule out motives of selfless service. The true reward of work in government, in all its branches, is the satisfaction of rendering public service, and the privilege given to one of moulding the destinies of millions.

Privileges of Legislators

Certain privileges are usually extended to members of the legislature in all countries. In their original form they were won by the British Parliament as the result of a struggle with the king. The important privileges are freedom of speech, and freedom from arrest for civil causes. Nobody can be punished for what he says on the floor of the house. This does not mean the use of unparliamentary language which is regulated by the Speaker of the House, nor does it mean endless speaking, which is restricted by rules relating to closure and 'guillotine'. Usually for 40 days before, and 40 days after the legislative session a member is given freedom from arrest in civil suits. In the U.S.A. this immunity extends to the period when the members attend the house and in going to and returning from the same. It does not include immunity from the service of summons in a civil suit.

Relation between the Legislature and the Executive

This takes four different forms. (1) According to the British Model, the cabinet is the streering committee of Parliament. It regulates 'the time, the policy, the law, and financial burdens of Parliament'. (2) In the French model, which is also of the parliamentary type, the cabinet is entirely dependent on the legislature even for its existence. The fate of the ministry depends upon the whims of the legislature, which has no settled principles in offering its co-operation or non-co-operation. (3) In the Swiss model, the executive is non-partisan and collegiates and enjoys a fixed term. If its measures or policies are turned down by the legislature, it does not go out of office, but makes the necessary adjustments to the legislature, (4) In the American model there is to legal relationship between the president and the House of Representatives. The legislature and the executive have no vital points of contact for close co-operation, but have several points (especially as regards the Senate) where they can come into clash with each other.

The Executive

The Executive plays such an important part in the modern State that very often it is described by the inclusive term 'government'. In non-democratic States, the executive authority is all-in-all. Even in democratic countries it exercises much greater authority than is generally believed. Finer says that the executive is the residuary legatee in government after other claimants like Parliaments and the law courts have taken their share. It performs many functions besides the execution of laws as laid down by the legislature and interpreted by the courts.

The Nominal Executive

It is usual to distinguish three aspects of the executive. These are the nominal or ornamental executive, the political executive, and the permanent executive. In England, the nominal executive is the monarch, the political executive is the Prime Minister and his Cabinet, while the permanent executive is the administration. In the self-governing British Dominions it is the same, except for the fact that the king is represented by the Governor-General. In the U.S.A. the line of demarcation is not so clear. The President is the chief of State as well as the political executive and performs several administrative functions. Several of the appointments which he makes are limited to his term of office. In France, the nominal executive is the President, but on account of the fact that he is elected for a term of 7 years and is often a party-politician, he does not command the same respect as the British King. The German President under the Weimar constitution occupied a place midway between those of the American and French Presidents, although he tended to approximate to the position of the latter.

In countries where the parliamentary system of government prevails the nominal executive has little to do with the actual governance of the country. While government is carried on in his name, all his acts have to be countersigned by a minister, who is responsible to the cabinet to the legislature, and to the people at large. Many of the functions performed by the nominal executive are ceremonial in character, as in the case of the king of England. He summons Parliament, prorogues and dissolves it, but all this is done in accordance with the arrangements made by the ministry of the day. The king is a titular sovereign. He reigns, but does not govern. It is true that he does play some part in the choice of the Prime Minister, especially when there is more than one recognised leader of a party or when no party has an absolute majority in the lower house. But even here his discretion is restricted to narrow limits. No ministry has been dismissed by the King since 1784 although he has the legal power to do it. The power of veto has not been exercised since 1707. The force the king has in the country is the result of is influence and the non-party position occupied by him, and not the result of authority directly enforced by him. He breeds a respect for government and a readiness to obey laws. His constitutional rights are, in the words of Bagehot, 'the right to be consulted, the right to encourage, and the right to warn'. As far as the British Empire is concerned, he is the visible symbol of unity and the most important link which holds together countries and peoples scattered over the different parts of the world.

The nominal executive in France is the President, who is elected for a term of 7 years by the two houses of legislature sitting together for the purpose. In theory he has all the powers of the American President except the veto, as well as many powers which belong to the king in England. But in actual practice he neither reigns nor governs. As has been well said, he is a prisoner in an iron cage. Every act of his has to be countersigned by a minister, who in turn is dependent on parliament. Therefore, the real governing authority in France is parliament, and not the President. The only function which he can perform without the consent of a minister is to preside ever national festivals. He is a mere-figurehead and Parliament can compel his resignation before the expiration of his term, as happened in the case of Millerand. He can be impeached for high treason by the Chamber of Deputies and tried by the Senate.

The nominal executive in Germany under the Weimar constitution was the President. Unlike the French President he was elected by the people who also had the power to recall him. He was given wider powers than those enjoyed by the French President. He could submit to a popular referendum bills passed by the Reichstag, but which did not meet with his approval. He had no power of veto. He could also declare a state of siege, suspend various constitutional rights of the citizen, and govern virtually as a dictator. In France, on the contrary, a state of siege could be declared only by the legislature. Whereas in France the President could dissolve the lower house only with the consent of the Senate, the German President could do it on his own authority. This power, however, did not mean much in practice, as the acts of the German President, like those of the British King and the French President, required the countersignature of some responsible minister or other. The legislature could not reduce him to a position of subjection and compel him to resign, as in France. What it could do was to suspend the President by a 2/3rd vote of the popular house, and submit him to popular recall. If the popular recall resulted in a vote of confidence in the President, the Reichstag was to be dissolved and a new house elected the President himself getting another term of office, presumably 7 years. He could be impeached by a 2/3rd vote of the Reichstag, and tried before the supreme judicial court for 'wrongful violation of the constitution of laws of the Reich'.

The Political Executive

Turning from the nominal to the political executive, we find at least four distinct forms: the English, the American, the Swiss, and the French. In England, the Prime Minister and the Cabinet constitute the political executive. They can remain in office only so longs as they command the confidence of Parliament. They are members of one or the other house of the legislature and play a leading part in initiating legislation. They are also administrative heads of departments and, in that capacity, are responsible to Parliament not only for policy but also for the details of administration. They work together as a team and, in their relation to Parliament, stand or fall together. They are the 'energising, responsible center of government'. The Prime Minister is not the master of his Cabinet. In this respect he is quite unlike the American President. He is 'the first among equals' and is responsible to the king and country for the work of the Cabinet as a whole. It is his business to act alone or with the other members and make the necessary adjustments.

The British system of government works for smoothness and harmony between the executive and the legislature. By their personal day-to-day contact with parliament and their responsibility to it, the Cabinet ministers are kept in the strait and narrow path. Whatever praise or blame they deserve is administered to them at the time it is deserved, although the general election is the real testing time. Parliament in turn cannot afford to be irresponsible, because the Cabinet can always threaten it with dissolution before its normal term of five years is over and can actually carry it out. In spite of all these merits, what we find in actual practice is that when the party in power has an overwhelming majority in the Commons, it tends to become indifferent to the criticism of the opposition and to public opinion in general. It even becomes lethargic and self-satisfied, resting on its oars.

Summing up the importance of the British Cabinet, Finer writes: 'On the whole . . . the British Cabinet system offers quick, vigorous, thoughtful and responsible leadership; it is controlled, but not *stultified; threatened but not executed; questioned, but* not mistrusted; politically partisan, but not personally malicious; restrained as much by the spirit of responsible power as by its institutions and sanctions; and Janus like, it looks, at once to the people and to the Senate'.[5]

In the American system of government, the President is the political as well as the ornamental executive. Even to-day in form he elected by a body of electors representing the various states in the Union. In actual practice, however, he is popularly elected. His term of office is four years, and he cannot be removed before that time except for treason. He is *not* a member of the Legislature, and so whatever legislative programme he wishes to carry through he can do only with the help of individual legislators or committees of the Congress. He also sends periodical messages to the Congress outlining his policy and legislative programme. In the nature of the case, this is an unsatisfactory method, and is conducive to lack of harmony and friction between the executive and the legislature. The President is almost entirely independent of the legislature. He possesses the power of suspensive veto, which is not used unless there is reason to think that there is popular support behind the action of the President. When the party which has the majority in the legislature happens to be different from the party to which the President belongs, there is endless trouble, as during the second term of President Wilson. Good measures are at times thrown out by the legislature, in order to discredit the President.

The President nominates his own Cabinet ministers who are directly responsible to him and not to Congress. They are not members of the legislature, and as such their responsibility is to the President alone. In the absence of Parliamentary Questions and Answers or Interpellations, which are a prompt and effective way of checking administrative irregularity and of eliciting information on matters of current importance, the American Congress depends upon resolutions of enquiry, which are a round about way of securing the desired end.

In spite of the fact that the President's power is some what weakened on account of his lack of contact with the legislature, he is one of the greatest political officers in the world. Wilson considered the office to be almost unlimited in its influence. As the executive or administrative head of the government, as the leader of his political party, and as the guide of nation in legislation and policy- framing the President enjoys wide powers and influence. He is the only one who can be regarded as the spokesman of his country and the platform from which he can address the country his the national platform. In times of emergency he is given wide powers'.[6]

The Swiss executive is indeed of a very unique kind. It consists of a board or council of 7 members elected for a fixed term of three years by the two houses sitting together. It is controlled by the legislature, and there is no question of resigning because of 'no-confidence' motion or vote of censure. If the legislature does not approve of the policy or measures of the Council, the Council, makes the necessary adjustment and goes on with its work. It is not a party government and there is no prime minister at the head of it. One of the seven is elected annually as the President.

He is only a chairman and is not the 'first among equals' as the British Prime Minister. He has no more power than his colleagues. He performs the ceremonial duties of the executive. The work of the Council is divided into departments and each member is in charge of a department. Since the final control of the Council does not belong to a single individual, the Swiss executive council is usually described as a collegiate or Plural executive. Although a plural executive generally means lack of unity, direction, and swifting of action, the people, for long accustomed to plural executive in their cantons, have made a success of the Council. Besides, the Swiss temperament does not run along strong party lines.

The French executive is a parliamentary executive. On account of the group system it is almost always a coalition of some kind and is more dependent on the legislature than is the British Cabinet. The French ministers have the right of entry to both Chambers and may speak in either. French ministries are notoriously unstable, the average life of a ministry between 1878 and 1928 being nine and a half months. In the works of Finer there is no Ministry in France; there is only a collection of ministers. And these have no real administrative control on account of their precarious tenure. The commissions play a large, and even a rival part in the legislative, financial, and administrative work of government. The Council of Ministers presided over by the President deliberates on *policy*, while the Cabinet presided over by the Prime Minister deliberates on *tactics*.[7]

The Governor-General of India and governors of the Indian Provinces are in a totally different category from their counterparts in the British Dominions. They are still far from being nominal executives, possessing as they do powers which they can exercise in their discretion or individual judgment, and being the custodians of the interests of certain classes of peoples and of public officials.

Mr. S. Srinivasa Iyengar and others to-day advocate a non-party political executive for India, elected by the legislature. Some others want an executive representative of the different parties in the legislature. Having secured communal representation in the legislature—often of a weighted kind—they seem to think that such representation in the executive is the next logical step. In our judgment, neither a non-party nor an all-party executive in the present circumstances prevalent in India will really be a satisfactory solution. An all-party executive will mean continuous conflict and friction both within the Cabinet and outside. So long as the various parties in the country are not agreed on their political objective and everything is viewed from the communal range, an all-party executive will mean lack of unity and cohesion, vacillation, and constant wrangling. Instead of allaying communal feelings, it will intensify them, even as communal representation in the services and the legislatures has done. As for a non-party executive, it seems to be outside the range of practical politics at a time when communal feelings are at their worst. Accustomed as we are to British parliamentary tradition, the safe course will be not to launch upon untried and novel experiments.

Single and plural executive

It is agreed by all reputed thinkers that a single executive is preferable to a popular executive. As Napoleon has well said, one bad general is better than two good ones. In ancient Athens, the executive power was broken up into fragments. The Romans for a long time had two consuls with no clear division of powers between them so that one could veto the actions of the other. In modern times, Switzerland alone has a plural executive, but even there, one does not find an overlapping of powers and functions among the members of the executive council. The Commission form of municipal government in the U.S.A., which divides responsibility among the commissioners, is being replaced by the City Manager type, where there is one strong city administrator.

Plurality in the executive means a division of responsibility. It tends to conceal faults and militates against promptness of decision and singleness of purpose. It lacks unity and energy. In its favour its may be said that it is a check upon the abuse of power and the possibility of a *coup d' etat*. It may also bring to the service of the State a higher degree of ability than is possible under the single executive. But the fact that it lacks unity, directness, and swiftness of action is enough to condemn it. It is possible, however, to combine the principles of single and plural executive. Modern administration is so complex that no individual, however gifted he may be an expert in every branch of administration. What is wanted is responsibility at different levels of administration working up to a single executive at the top.

Tenure of the Executive

In the case of a hereditary executive, it stands to reason that tenure should be for life. The question is as regards elected or nominated executives whose tenures at present vary from 1 to 7 years. In a majority of the American States thee governors are elected for 2 years. The U.S.A. President is in office for 4 years, while the French and German Presidents are given a long period of 7 years. In Great Britain and the Dominions the maximum period is five years, subject to the confidence which the Cabinet commands in the lower house and earlier dissolution. In India the Governor-General and the governors were appointed for 5 years.

Under modern conditions a short tenure of one to two years is worse than useless. It is detrimental to a continuity of policy. The executive is not given enough time to gain experience or to plan in a large way and execute big schemes. Frequent selections have disturbing effect on public life. Very often they lead to abuse and corruption. The executive is placed at the mercy of the people, especially when it is entitled to seek re-election. It becomes weak and vaccinating and is afraid to act boldly and independently.

A period of 7 years is, on the other hand, too long a period for an elected executive, even for a nominal or ornamental executive. If the executive is to play a ceremonial part, the tenure should be short so that the ambitions of many may be satisfied. From this point of view the annual election of the Mayor of Madras has something to commend it. For political executives as well as for many nominal executives a period of four to five years seems to be the proper duration. It is interesting to note that among the framers of the American constitution, Hamilton advocated good behaviour for the President.

Whether the chief executive should be eligible to succeed himself is a debated question. In India the Governor-General and the Governors are seldom re-appointed to the same or similar posts. In the U.S.A. according to convention the President is re-eligible only once, but this convention has been set aside by the election of President Roosevelt for a third consecutive therm. In favour of re-election it may be said that it secures the continuance of good polity'. Against it, it is said that it leads to pandering to the public, the executive being too timid to act independently. In general, what we find is that a selfish individual will behave selfishly whether he is eligible for office only once or many times. The question really to decide is whether a tried chief executive is a man of outstanding ability, still in full possession of his powers with a determination to carry through much-needed changes or progressive programmes and policies. When the electorate come by such an individual there should be no legal restriction to electing him as many times as the people choose to.

Powers and Functions of the Executive

The legislature expresses the will of the State, and the executive carries it out. Garner classifies the powers of the executive under five heads. These are the diplomatic power, the administrative power, the military power, the judicial power, and the legislative power.

(1) ***Diplomatic power***—The diplomatic power includes the conduct of foreign relations. The executive appoints diplomatic representatives to foreign States and receives representatives from them. This latter power is construed to mean the right to recognise or refuse to recognise the independence of foreign States and their governments.

Treaties and other international agreements are concluded by the executive alone or in conjunction with one or both houses of legislature. In order to secure secrecy, the legislature is kept out of the negotiations, at least in the early stages. This policy was severely criticised in England during and after the Great War of 1914-18. It was said by some that the secret bungling diplomacy of Great Britain had led her into war with Germany. The Labour Government was willing to place all treaties before Parliament for its assent, but there has been a setback since it went out of office. A battle cry in America at the end of the war was for 'open treaties openly arrived at'.

In Great Britain even to-day the treaty-making power is largely in the hands of the executive. Parliament has no share in it except 'where legislation may be necessary to perfect the treaty or carry it into effect'. The executive both negotiates and concludes treaties. In many of the other States, ratification by the legislature is required. In the U.S.A. certain classes of international agreements, such as reciprocal, trade agreements, may be concluded on the authority of the President alone. As regards other treaties, the rule is that they should be ratified by the Senate. This power has been interpreted by the Senate to mean not only the right to ratify or reject the draft submitted to it, but also to amend it. The House of Representatives has only an indirect share in treaty-making through the power of the purse. It may refuse to sanction the appropriations necessary to put the terms of a treaty into operation. It may also refuse assent to treaties which deal with the regulation of foreign commerce. In the German Republic, treaties and alliances, except minor agreements, required the approval of the lower house. The practice in France is for ratification by both House of most classes of treaties. The houses have the power only to approve or to reject treaties, but not to amend them. In Switzerland, provision has been made for submission to popular referendum of treaties of more than 15 years' duration. In the U.S.A., there is a proposal to substitute for the present practice ratification by both Houses by a simple majority.

(2) ***Administrative power***—The administrative power means the execution of the laws and the administration of the government. In some countries this latter power is exercised in a detailed manner, and in others in a general way. The administrative power of the executive is described by some as Internal, and by some others as Home powers. It includes financial, commercial, agricultural and educational administration. In France, a useful distinction is made between the *political* or governmental functions of the executive and the purely *administrative* functions. In many States appointments made by the executive are to be ratified by one or other of the two Houses. In the U.S.A. they require ratification by the Senate, but the president alone has the power of dismissal. Ordinarily this power of appointment by the chief executive extends only to the appointment of high political, judicial and military functionaries. In Czeecho-Slovakia, even university professors are appointed by the chief executive. In the part-states, cities, and counties of America a great many public offices are filled by popular election. In Switzerland, on the other hand, choice by the legislature is a common practice.

As for the power of direction, we find that it varies in different

States, and sometimes in the same State itself. In countries where the monarchical tradition has persisted the power of the Ministry is very great. In the U.S.A., the President's power of direction is often restricted by legislative acts. He had, however, the power to issue instructions and order to departmental heads. In great Britain, the permanent civil service works in close contact with the Ministry.

(3) ***Military Power***—In countries with the monarchical tradition like England, the military power of the executive includes the right to declare war. In France, the assent of both houses of legislature is required for the declaration of war. In the U.S.A. the Congress alone can declare war, but in the conducting of foreign relations the President may bring the country to such a pass that declaration of war becomes inevitable. The President has the supreme command of the army, navy and air forces. In times of emergency he may declare martial law and suspend the constitutional rights of citizens, including such an important right as the writ *of habeas corpus.* He can suppress newspapers. During the world war a series of Congressional Acts practically gave him dictatorial powers. Similar powers were conferred upon the executive of other belligerent countries too.

(4) ***Judicial Power***—One of the important powers of the executive under this head is the right of pardon or clemency. Montesquieu considered it as quite out of place in republics. But considerations of justice and humanity demand that in every constitution, whether monarchical or republican, there should be room for pardon because of the imperfections of law and too rigid administration of justice. The existing law and its processes which the judge applies may be defective or the extenuating circumstances under which the crime was committed may not have been fully considered or new facts may have come to light since judgment was delivered. In all these cases justice demands that a condemned person should have the benefit of the doubt and the person who can best exercise this prerogative is the supreme executive. In Great Britain this power is exercised by the Crown on the advice of the Home Secretary. In many of the component states of the U.S.A. the Governor is assisted by an advisory board in the discharge of this function. According to many constitutions, the right of pardon cannot be extended to the offence

of impeachment. The American President has the power of pardon before as well as after conviction. He can remit fines and forfeitures, grant reprieves and commutations, and exercise the right of amnesty to large numbers of persons convicted of crime.

Under democratic constitutions departments of government acting under the general supervision of the executive are given wide powers of a semi-judicial character. Thus the Ministry of Health in England in the exercise of its administrative functions can impose fines, recover costs, etc.

(5) ***Legislative Power***—In all constitutions, both the legislature and executive have control over each other. In parliamentary countries the executive has the power to summon, open, adjourn, and prorogue sessions of the legislature. This power of the executive is limited in the presidential systems of government, where regular sessions of the legislature meet automatically. In parliamentary constitutions the executive has the power to dissolve the legislature and call for new elections; it also has a ceremonial opening. All this is found lacking in the presidential form.

The power of the executive in the sphere of legislation is strictly limited in countries with the presidential system of government. It 'consists in furnishing the legislature with information concerning the legislative need of the country; in recommending measures for its consideration; sometime, though rarely, in the initiation of legislative projects, in approving or disapproving its acts and in promulgating those which are approved'.[8]

An extraordinary power of the executive in the presidential system is the power of veto. In the U.S.A. it is a suspensive veto, which can be over-ridden by a 2/3rds vote of each house. It is considered to be a check on hasty and ill-digested legislation. In declaring his veto, the president is required to state his reasons for dissent, and the legislature is given an opportunity to reconsider its decision. In France the power of suspensive veto is practically a dead letter.

In most modern States the executive is given the power of subordinate legislation known as the Ordinance power. This power takes the form of decrees, orders, rules, and regulations, some of which require parliamentary approval. The usual qualification in the exercise of this power is that it should not modify or suspend statutory law but should be calculated to promote the execution of statutory law or fill in the details. Occasionally, extraordinary power is given to the executive in times of emergency, as in the present war, to issue regulations for securing the public safety and the defence of the realm. This power is practically unlimited. Under it the country may virtually be placed under a martial law.

German writers make a distinction between 'law' ordinances and 'administrative' ordinances. The effect of the former type is 'to create new law or to modify the existing law'. 'Administrative' ordinances, on the other hand, take the form of orders or instructions to the administrative authorities concerning the conduct or functioning of the services under them. Consequently they do not bind or affect the people directly.

Garner distinguishes three types of ordinances. The first of these consists of 'laws promulgated by the chief executive in pursuance of a general power of legislation conferred upon him by statute'. The governance of the French colonies by the decrees of the President falls under this category. A second class of ordinances comprises those which are 'issued by the executive in pursuance of legislative authority to regulate specific matters'. The third group is made up of ordinances issued upon the 'invitation' of the legislature to fill in details and pass regulations for the execution of a particular law. This form of ordinance is much in use in France, where Parliament contents itself with passing the general outlines of legislation, leaving the details to be supplemented by ordinance. Up to 1907 the supreme administrative court of justice refused to interfere with the legality of ordinances even when they seemed to contradict existing statutes. An important decision given in 1907, however, has brought the ordinance power under judicial control.

In the U.S.A., there is not much scope for ordinances since the Congress frames statutes in great detail. Nevertheless, there are a large number of presidential proclamations and executive orders and regulations governing the transaction of business in each of the executive departments, besides a large body of specialised rules, regulations, and instructions issued by the various departments.

In England the King no longer enjoys the inherent power of law-making by means of proclamations and ordinances. Nevertheless, the power of issue regulations may be conferred on the servants of the Crown for the proper conduct of public affairs. Ordinances are made in the form of 'statutory rules and orders', and these have the same binding effect on the community as statutory laws. The filling in of details is often left to administrative departments, especially in such matters as education and public health.

Tests of a good Executive

The tests of a good executive are promptness of decision, unity, finality, and sometimes secrecy of procedure. In the very nature of the case, the executive should be small in size. Otherwise quickness of decision and promptness of action become impossible. It is here that modern dictatorships score over democracies. It is a significant fact that in times of emergency the American President is given extraordinary powers. Such powers have recently been given to the Governor General of India for the duration of the war. In England a War Cabinet of six has been formed to ensure promptness of decision and action.

Immunity of the Executive

From judicial process it is considered to be necessary in the interest of good government. In England the theory is 'the king can do not wrong'. The American President is not subject to the jurisdiction of the ordinary courts during his terms of office. For his criminal acts the Senate may try him acting as a court of impeachment and remove him from office, if found guilty. After that he may be tried for criminal acts by the ordinary courts. During the term of office the President cannot be arrested or compelled to appear in person before a court o · obey any judicial process. Such immunity is enjoyed by the Governor-General and Governors of India too.

The Civil Service

Definition and History

The Civil Service constitutes the permanent executive in the modern State. While the Parliament, the Cabinet, and the President may reign, it is the civil service which really governs. Doctrines of popular sovereignty, parliamentary supremacy, and cabinet control have a theoretical value to the academic students of political science. But the doings of administrative officials concern him as well as the ordinary citizen in his daily life and contacts.

Finer defines the civil service as 'a body of officials, permanent, paid and skilled'. All these features are essentially modern in character. For a long time, even in some of the advanced States of the world, the task of administration was performed by amateurs in the intervals of their occupations. This was the case in England up to the end of the eighteenth century, but since then public service has become a skilled profession.

The civil service is so called in order to distinguish it from military and judicial services. There is evidence to show that some form of civil service existed in ancient Egypt both under the Pharaohs and the Ptomaines. Ancient Athens did not possess a professional civil service on account of its extreme democratic theory that A was as good as B for public service. Offices were for the most part elective. Sometime the system of election was combined with the system of lot. Republican Room, too, like Athens, had no civil service. But Imperial Rome was obliged to engage the services of special classes of administrators. Members of the aristocratic classes alone were preferred for responsible administrative posts. Inferiors were employed as spies and subordinate officials, and as chief officials in the remote corners of the Empire. Similar bureaucracies existed in ancient China and India, too.

Alongside of the various guilds and crafts, public service as a profession was developed during the Middle Ages in Europe. The emphasis was upon the honour and prestige attached to public office rather than upon emoluments. Recruitment was more from the middle classes and less from the feudal aristocracy.

In modern times Prussia has been a pioneer in organising public services. Infinite care was bestowed in that country upon the proper methods of recruitment and training of public servants, and elaborate rules were framed to make the service as efficient and useful as possible. Even to-day Germany has the best system of rights and guarantees for civil servants. On the side of liabilities, it must be said that the German services still carry with them an authoritarian tradition, but everything possible was being done, until the advent of the Nazis, to smooth the rough edges, convert officiousness into good service. The Bourbon kings of France did something to build up public-service traditions in Europe, but appointments and dismissals remained arbitrary.

One of the finest public services in the modern would is found in England, dating from the middle of the last century. Finer describes the British Civil Service as the envy of the world. It combines 'technical efficiency and humane serviceability as no other civil service does'. In the words of Graham Wallas: 'the creation of this Service was the one great political invention in nineteenth century England'.

In its origin and development, it is necessary counterpart to the amateurishness of the British cabinet government. In nine cases out of ten the British Cabinet Minister who is placed in charge of he administration of a department knows little or nothing of the inner working of the department. He brings to his task a fresh mind free from preconceived notions and bureaucratic inhibitions, while the civil servant brings expert technical knowledge. A combination of the two results is good government. But writers like Lord Hewart, Ramsay Muir and C.K. Allen condemn the system saying that it makes the permanent civil service too important. According to Ramsay Muir, in legislation, administration, finance, and enunciation of policy, the body which really directs affairs, though from behind the scenes, is the civil service. He is alarmed to find that bureaucracy thrives under the cloak of ministerial responsibility.

Whatever may be the element of truth in the above criticism, there is no gainsaying the fact that England is one of the best administrated countries in the world because it has an efficient, dependable, and impartial civil service to attend to the day-to-day work of administration.

In India under the British rule administration has played a very notable part. It has been so very comprehensive in its activities as to include almost all that we describe under the term 'Government'. In addition to performing its legitimate task of administration, it has had an important share in the enunciating of policy and the framing of legislation. The administrative officials in India are often described as belonging to a bureaucracy, meaning thereby that as a body they are accustomed to the exercise of irresponsible power, uninfluenced by public opinion. But this state of affairs is gradually disappearing with the extension of responsible government.

Conditions of public service in America have been unsatisfactory on account of the prevalence of the 'spoils system', according to which hundreds of civil service posts were filled up at the end of every Presidential election by supporters of the victorious party at the polls. The person who was responsible for this policy of rotation of offices, and of giving a political colour to public offices was Andrew Jackwon who, as President (1821-37), declared: 'the duties of all public officers are so plain and simple that men of intelligence may readily qualify themselves for their performance; and I cannot but believe that more is lost by the long continuance of men in office than is generally to be gained by their experience. No one man has any more intrinsic right to official station than another'. The result of this vicious policy laid down by Jackson was inefficiency, partisanship, corruption, and bribery. The evil reached such a climax that in 1888 the country was forced to move in the direction of the principle of permanent civil service by competitive examination. Public service commissions were set up, but their usefulness was greatly diminished by making them representative of two main political parties in the country. Another wave of reforming enthusiasm spread over the country in 1905, but even that has not been able to abolish the spoils system, altogether. By 1916 more than half the civil service posts were filled by competitive examination. Even to-day the prevailing rule is short-period appointments for several posts, although much is being done to keep party politics and nepotism out of the picture.

Recruitment and Training of Civil Servants

One of the most important questions to consider in evolving a right type of civil service is recruitment and training. Till the middle of the last century, both in England and India, patronage played a dominant part. A Scottish member of the Board of Directors found posts under the East India Company for most of his 19 children. In his capacity as president of the Board of the Control, Dundas sent out a great many Scotsmen to India. As late as 1858 John Bright said that 'England's foreign policy was nothing more than a gigantic system of out-door relief for the aristocracy of Great Britain'.

The evils of patronage became so great that some other way of selection had to be found. The first step with regard to the Indian Civil Service was to limit patronage by a qualifying examination and by a thorough training at Haileybury. In 1853 when the East India Company's Charter came before Parliament for revision, Macaulay secured the complete abolition of the patronage system and substituted for it the competitive system. He said: 'It seems to me that there never was a fact proved by a larger mass of evidence or a more varied experience than this; that men who distinguish themselves in their youth above their contemporaries almost always keep to the end of their lives the start which they have gained'. Macaulay did not favour any technical or professional training for admission into the civil service. He insisted on mental alertness and capacity tests by competitive examination. Technique, he said, could be acquired later. What he wanted was a liberal rather than a specialised education.

The reforms of Macaulay in India bore fruit in England in the report of Northcote and Trevelyan in 1853. They too recommended competition, and the elimination of party politics in the selection of candidates. The recommendations were given partial effect to in 1855 by an Order-in-Council and the first Civil Service Commission was created in the same year. Other reforms were adopted in the succeeding years.

According to the system prevalent in England and India to-day, recruitment for the most part is by open competition supplemented by an interview, both conducted by a Public Service Commission. For recruitment to certain departments, the competition is 'limited', as in the case of the Foreign and Diplomatic Service in England. The *viva voce* test which was established in England in 1917 is given a prominent place in all competitive examinations.

Civil servants as a rule are recruited at an early age because of the pliability and receptiveness to new ideas of youth. The Civil Service Commission in England consists of three members directly appointed by the Crown by an Order-in-Council. This means in practice appointment by the Cabinet after consultation with the highest authorities in the Treasury. It is free from outside, and especially political influence. Its decisions are never questioned. It is considered to be the guardian of honest efficiency. It does arduous work. In 1935 it filled nearly 23,000 posts. Similar Commissions function in India both at the federal centre and in the provinces.

Admission to the Indian Civil Service is largely by means of competitive examination. Simultaneous examinations have been held in England and India since 1922. A certain number of vacancies are filled up in India by nomination with a view to redressing communal inequalities. Recently the Secretary of State for India was allowed to recruit directly European candidates holding good honours degrees without their having to go through competitive examination. This practice may lead to patronage. Competitive examinations have been suspended in India for the present, on account of war conditions.

After selection the successful candidates are required to undergo a year's probation in England, during which period they are to study some special subjects and some of a general character—subjects such as codes and acts, history, vernacular, riding and hygiene.

At the end of the period of probation there is an examination. During the probationary period each British candidate receives £300 and the Indian candidate £350 a year. Government pays the candidate's passage to India. Further examinations are held in India at the end of six months by the department concerned.

The age of recruitment in Germany is even lower than in England and India. 'The weight is still given to learning in Germany, but the tendency is in the English direction (*i.e.* towards a liberal education)'. Stress is laid on a study of law and social sciences. A period of preparatory service has always been a part of the training given to German civilians. One chief criticism is that the German method devotes too long a time to preparation.

While the examinations in England are designed to test general ability, in the United States they test technical efficiency. For many appointments there is a qualifying examination, rather than a competitive examination with the result that the American Civil Service is not sought after by capital and highly educated men. For many classes of posts one does not require much more than 'the ordinary high school education, together with some practical efficiency'.

Conditions of Service

If the State is to secure the best possible service from its servants, it should provide them an adequate salary, and relieve them from the fear of insecurity and want, especially in old age. Security of tenure till the time of superannuation is a recognised rule in England and India. When a civil servant has successfully completed his period of probation, and passed what departmental tests there may be, he has nothing to fear so long as his work continues to be satisfactory, and he is in full possession of his mental and physical powers. Such security enables in individual to enter government service as a 'career service', giving to it the best years of his life. In the U.S.A. where civil service traditions are still in the making, it is not uncommon for civil servants to be on the look out for openings outside. There is no satisfactory arrangement in that country for superannuated pensions.

Salaries for public servants in England are low compared with the abnormally high salaries and allowances in India. The maximum pay for administrative heads in England (about 40 of them) is £3,000 a year, although many of them can easily command 10,000 a year in the city. The modern Indian Collector receives a maximum of Rs. 2,650 per month including overseas pay. But there are a number of posts 'above the time scale'—divisional, financial, and judicial commissionerships, the posts of provincial Chief Secretary, posts of Secretaries to Government of India etc., the salaries for which posts range from £27,00 to £3,600 a year. In a great many provinces the post of Governor is open to civil servants, although a change in this direction is very urgent. The Madras civil servants are given a higher maximum since there are no commissionerships in that province. A civil servant, early in his career, can become a judicial officer climbing up to the High Court. He can become a member of the Board of Revenue, which is the final revenue court of appeal, or become a financial commissioner. A considerable number of special posts are open to him such as audit, customs, posts and telegraphs, political department, tariff board, membership on the public service commission, etc.

Overseas pay after the first four years of service can be turned into sterling at the rate of Rs. 10 to the pound. A liberal pension is provided for at the time of retirement. The Indian Civil Servant can retire before time and draw proportionate pension. He also enjoys very liberal leave privileges.

Besides security of tenure, adequate salary, and liberal leave privileges, the civil servant should be given a reasonable chance of promotion, work suited to one's capacities and protection in the faithful performance of one's duties. In Great Britain manipulative and clerical services are distinguished from the executive and administrative services, and different types for entrance examinations are held for the two types of services. Superior services are recruited not only by direct recruitment but also by the promotion of the most capable from the lower grades. Since 1920 it has been possible for transfer and promotion from one department to another.

Promotion according to seniority is a sound policy for many situations. It as least saves considerable administrative inconvenience. But seniority alone is not enough. There should be opportunity for men of capacity to rise rapidly from one grade to another. Finer claims that the least amount of evil in State service is produced by the best classification of civil servants according to efficiency and by correlating efficiency with rises and falls in salary, promotion, demotion, and dismissal. The U.S.A. had made rapid progress in the technique of rating. The Report Form used by the various departments in England seeks to establish competitive records of past efficiency. The Report calls for information on knowledge (a) of branch and (b) of department, personality and force of character, judgment, power of taking responsibility, initiative, accuracy, address and tact, power of supervising staff, zeal and official conduct. It is true that personal equation is bound to play a part even in filling up a report of this kind, but still it keeps down favoritism at as low a level as possible.

The civil service is a silent and anonymous service. In the nature of the case, it cannot come out in the open and defend charges made against it. Such being the case, it is necessary to give to the civil servant the necessary protection for the faithful performance of his duties. France and other continental countries, recognising this fact, have set up special administrative courts for the trial of cases in which public officials are involved. In the English-speaking countries, on the other hand, the same system of law and the same system of courts obtain for both private wrongs and wrongs in which officials are involved, although Australia in recent years has departed from this practice. They fail to recognise the public and, in some cases, the political character of the task entrusted to government servants. In this respect it seems to us that a great deal is to be said in favour of the continental, as against the English system. Contrary to expectation, the administrative courts are far from lenient. They take into account the administrative side of the question, and have often given good judgments. The State accepts liability for the wrongs done by its servants.

According to Finer, the civil service in Germany has a well-defined body of right accorded to it by law and by the ultimate assent of the people. There are also ways whereby the civil servant can challenge any but the smallest amount of disciplinary measures against him.

The civil service is not only a silent service, but it is also subjected to strict discipline. In England particularly it is expected to serve whichever political party may come into power with equal respect and equal earnestness. In order to attain this end, civil servants are forbidden to take an over part in public political affairs. They are not allowed to stand as çandidates, although they have every right to vote as they please. A great deal of political activity is allowed to civil servants in France. This is rather unfortunate. The Weimar constitution of Germany allows civil servants to contest seats.

Practice varies on the question of the right of association and the right to strike which civil servants may claim. In Great Britain up to 1917, individuals and associations in the civil service could get their grievances redressed mainly by means of memorials which had to go through various hands before reaching the Head of the Department and finally the Treasury. The negotiations were all conducted in writing and personal discussion was almost entirely excluded. Since 1917, with the adoption of the recommendation of the Whitley Report for non-public industries, a modified form of Whitley Councils is allowed to civil servants in the lower grades, drawing a salary of less than £700 a year. England provides a special court for interpreting the clauses relating to the pay and working conditions of the civil servants under this category. But the final interpreter of the terms of the judgments of the courts is the Treasury. A civil servant in England has no legal action against his dismissal inasmuch as the ultimate interpreter of the Superannuation Rights is the Treasury, and not any law court.

If civil servants require to be protected against the public, the public in turn requires protection against the arbitrary use of authority by civil servants. Such protection is provided by a system of checks and balances by certain legislative controls over administration, and by certain judicial controls, namely through the issue of such writs as mandamus, injunction, *habeas corpus, quo warranto* and *certiorari* which are orders by courts to public officers commanding them to do or not to do certain things. In this respect of affording protection to the public, Finer considers that France and Germany occupy the most enviable place, while England occupies the least enviable place, with the U.S.A. occupying somewhat of a middle position.

Function of Civil Servants

It is the business of civil servants to carry out the law entrusted to their care. In this respect they are literally the servants of the legislature and the supreme executive. Whatever indirect share they may have in framing policy in their personal contact which the political executive, direct share they have none, at least in fully self-governing countries.

In the nature of the work performed, the British and Indian civil servants differ fundamentally. Though a collection of experts, the British civil service does not determine the political policy of the country. That is done by the ministry of the day. The Permanent Under-Secretary and his assistants give all the necessary advice and suggestion, but they do not dictate. Specialists are not consulted directly by the ministers. A weak minister may easily be led by the civil servant. But a strong man can always have his way.

The Indian Civil Service has occupied an entirely different place. As Governors in most provinces, as members of the Executive and Legislative Councils and now as Advisers to the provincial Governors, the civil servants have exercises a decisive influence in the framing and executing of policy. But since the Montagu-Chelmsford Reforms, and especially since the coming in of provincial autonomy, this power has been considerably curtailed. Speaking of the modern Indian civil servants, Sir E. Blunt rightly says: 'Where his predecessor gave orders he must advise' 'The civilian who used to serve by ruling, must learn to rule by serving'. It is not too much to hope that in the not long distant future what policy-making power the I.C.S. still possesses will disappear. Its chief function will be to advise and administer. Practice of sound parliamentary government requires that ministers should decide the policy, while official should carry it out faithfully whether they agree with it or not.

While the British civil servant spends most of his time at the desk in the midst of files and folios, his counterpart in India has a very varied life. As a district officer, he spends there to four months in the year in camping, establishing contacts with the people. He is a collector of revenue as well as a district magistrate. He is 'the Government on the spot'. He is the *Sarkar.* Under him there are the sub-divisional officer, the deputy collector, the tahsildar, etc. He tries revenue and criminal cases and hears appeals from magistrates with second and third class powers.

Whether it be in India or elsewhere, pure administration is not the sole task of civil servants. They are given semi-legislative and semi-judicial powers. Officials of departments are empowered to make tules and regulations binding upon their subordinates and the general public. Some of these, especially in war time, take effect even before Parliament has given them its formal approval. The permanent executive fixes in detail the manner in which the requirements of parliamentary statutes are to be met and how the rights created under them are to be enjoyed. In the matter of delegated legislation, England stands midway between France and the U.S.A. Summing up the causes for the increasing amount of delegated legislation given to administrative departments, Marriott writes: Partly owing to the increasing complexity of industrial and social conditions, partly under the subtle influence of Fabian Socialism, partly from the general abandonment of the principle of *laissez faire* and the growing demand for governmental guidance and control in all the affairs of life, partly from sheer despair of the possibility of coping with the insistent cry for legislation, parliament has manifested a disposition to leave more an more discretion to administrative department'. (*Marriott*, Vol. II, p. 233).

As Marriott observes, while the delegation of quasi-legislative functions is convenient, legitimate, and even inevitable, it is liable to be abused. To avoid this danger, Marriott suggests three safeguards: (1) the power to which the authority is delegated should be in the most literal sense trustworthy; (2) representatives of interests which are affected should be consulted; (3) in every case the limits of the delegated authority should be defined. In the famous *Zomora* case of 1916, the Privy Council declared that the Crown had no power to alter the law of the land by Order-in-Council, unless such power was specifically delegated by statute. The Supreme Court in the United States recently set aside some of the provisions of the N.R.A. on the ground that the legislature had gone beyond its province in giving too wide and unspecified powers to the executive, and had failed to lay down standards to guide executive actions.

Administrative departments in many countries enjoy semi-judicial functions e.g., the Inter-State Commerce Commission in the U.S.A. They are given the power to investigate into the truth or justice of the complaints made by the public against the official acts of their subordinates. Thus the 'Income-Tax Commissioner alone is empowered to hear complaints raised by a private individual over the assessment made by a subordinate of the Department'.

Similarly, a high official of the Industrial Department decides cases of compensation to workmen in factories for injuries sustained in the course of their work.

One further question which merits our attention in connection with the work of administration is the chaotic way in which departments and their sub-divisions have been allowed to grow. If economy and efficiency are the touchstones of sound public administration, it is necessary that departments of government should be carefully organised so as to avoid overlapping and bring together closely-related departments under common control. Undue centralisation, as in France, as well as undue-decentralisation are defective. Integration offers a *via media* in that it calls for co-ordination at different levels of administration, working towards a final head.

The machinery of Government Committee of 1917 presided

over by Lord Haldane was in favour of differentiation according to service. It recommended a reorganization of the departments of governments under I Finance, II and III National Defence and External Affairs, IV Research and Information, V Protection (including Agriculture, Forestry and Fisheries), Transport and Commerce, VI Employment, VII Supplies, VIII Education, IX Health and X Justice. Some of the large departments would require more than one Minister. The Cabinet of the future should be a small one, comparable to a war cabinet, concerning itself with supervising and co-ordinating functions rather than with administrative functions.

A suggestion made by the Haldane Committee which is receiving more and more attention to-day is the need for a permanent planning or 'thinking' commission attached to each department of government or to administration as a whole, doing research into questions of administration and planning for the future so as to make the whole machinery of administration efficient, economic, progressive, and serviceable to the people.

Tests of a Good System of Civil Service

Public administration, unlike business administration, is not a money-making concern. Its chief aim is to render service wherever it is most needed. In doing that, civil servants must be fair to everybody. They should not favour one individual or one class of individuals above another. They must be guided only by the application of equal law to everybody. They should consider themselves as servants of the people in the real sense of the term. One of the charges frequently levelled against the Indian civil servants is that they are supercilious and overbearing in their attitude to the public.

Finer holds that the civil service should possess life, inventive power, ability to serve the needs of the population and enterprise. A besetting sin of civil servants is to fall into a rut, to rise out of which they do not have the necessary disposition or ability. A certain amount of routine and red tape is no doubt essential in the management of public affairs, but it should not be allowed to occupy the foreground. Care for human values should be given the first place in all planning and execution of official tasks.

The civil servant should do everything possible to remove

the attitude of fear and hostility which the public often has towards government servants in general. Speaking in general terms, Finer says: 'The public is hostile to the official, it is afraid of him, misunderstands him, occasionally admires him'. In England, says the same writer, the general public is on the whole mildly indifferent to the existence and work of the civil service. In India, the illiterate villager has a superabundant faith in the ability of the civilian to work wonders, coupled with a profound fear that his destinies are placed in the hands of the civilian.

While the administrator should act without fear or favour, he should not purposely defy public opinion because of his exalted position. In no circumstance should he usurp the powers of the political executive or of the legislature. He should rid of the temptation to become self-opinionated. He should not multiply correspondence, adore prestige, and adopt dilatory formalities.

Communal representation is insisted upon as a condition of a good system of administration in a country like India with its rival communal groups. All that needs to be said is that public administration should not become a plaything of politicians, if its honesty and efficiency are to be kept unimpaired. Other things being equal, there should be a due proportion between the strength of any one community in the country and its representation in the services. But it must be remembered that the right of the citizen to be safeguarded against inefficient and worthless officials is much greater than the right of every caste and community to have its mathematical percentage in the various services.

The duties of the civil servant in Germany, as stated by Finer, are:

1. The civil servant must discharge is duties in accordance with the constitution and the laws and obey the official orders of his superiors, in so far as they are not contradictory to the law.
2. He must carry out the duties of his office with the greatest sincerity and probity without regard to private advantage, with the greatest impartiality, with all industry and care. He must be especially on his guard against partiality.
3. He must keep punctually to the hours of arrival at and leaving his work.

4. Without claiming extra pay, he must be prepared to undertake additional duties or other duties to which his training and capacity fit him.
5. He must be truthful in his official doings. He must not pass over in silence important facts the disclosure of which is of concern to the Department.
6. Respect for superiors is demanded, outside as well as inside the office, even when the superior is objectionable in character and demeanour.
7. In their intercourse with the public, officials must always be courteous.
8. The civil servant must not allow insults to pass unnoticed, lest the Service should suffer degradation.
9. No official may take on any additional offices or employments, other than those for which he has asked and obtained permission of the appropriate departmental authority.
10. The civil servant must observe official secrecy.

The Judiciary

The Importance of the Judiciary

A country may have a very good legislature and an excellent executive, but if it does not have an independent and impartial judiciary, its constitution is not worth much. Protection against arbitrary rule is a condition which every citizen expects a civilised government to provide for him; and a properly constituted judiciary is one of the best means by which this condition can be secured. It is for this reason that it is often said that the excellence of a country's judiciary is a measure of the excellence of its government.

That the judiciary has always occupied an eminent place in the thinking of people is proved by the fact that something of divinity has often been attributed to the judicial function. Justice is considered to be one of the divine attributes and the judge has been pictures as a blind-folded person who administers even-handed justice without fer or favour. In the olden days the function of the judge was considered to be a part of the function of the priest.

While people greatly value the importance of the judiciary, its evolution has indeed been slow. The kind of justice which prevailed in early times was a tribal conception of justice. It did not matter whether the guilty person was punished or not. The ends of justice were supposed to have been met when punishment was inflicted upon members of the offending clan or tribes. Very often the punishment inflicted was out of all proportion to the offence committed. It was therefore, a distinct step forward when the idea of exact retribution, an eye for an eye, and 'a tooth for a tooth', came to prevail. A little later came the idea that compensation in goods or money known as Wergild could be substituted for physical injury.

All through this period justice was personal and private. The aggrieved individual or tribe had to take whatever action it was possible to take. Besides, in many cases there was no way of enforcing a decision. A drastic remedy which was often resorted to was one of expulsion from the community, as seen in the story of Cain in the Old Testament. Fear of God and spirits of various kinds also played a part in keeping early man to the narrow and strait path.

Gradually there developed the idea of the King's peace. It first included 'bootless' crimes, *i.e.*, crimes for which atonement could not be made by money payment. Later on, theft and other such crimes came to be included under King's peace. Feudal lords and the Church continued to administer their own kind of justice for a long time, and it was not without a struggle that they gradually gave place to the King's justice.

In the modern State all crimes are crimes against the State, although we speak of private law and public law. While various social organisations may use persuasion, moral pressure, and social ostracism in reference to their members in enforcing a certain line of conduct, they have not right to imprison people, award capital punishment or do the like. *Justice is a function of the State.*

The greatest enemy of an independent judiciary has been an all-powerful executive. Under the first two Stuarts in England endeavour was made to subordinate the judiciary to the executive and even some of the judges of the time were a party to this unholy endeavour. The judges were indeed to be lions, but 'lions under the throne' (Bacon). They were to be, in other words, the handmaids of the executive. The independence of the judiciary in England was finally secured by the Act of Settlement; and it was laid down that judges could be removed only upon the address of both Houses of Parliament.

Conditions required of an efficient judiciary

The first condition required of a good system of judiciary is independence. The manner in which a judge is appointed and the terms of service under which he works should all be such as to enable him to act in an independent manner. Fear of the executive or of the people at large should not influence him in any way in the performance of his duties.

Impartiality in the administration of justice is as important as independence. It is commonly said that in England 'there is one law for all' and that 'all men are equal before the law'. Differences in wealth, influence, and social position should not weigh with the judge. Under no circumstances the executive should be allowed to dictate to the judiciary the kind of judgment to give, especially when it is one of the interested parties.

Besides being independent and impartial, the judge should be learned and skilled in his profession. An incompetent judge is bound to reduce the popular regard for the judiciary. A judge should be absolutely incorruptible, upright and fearless in the discharge of his duties.

Passing from judges to courts, it must be said that justice should be swift and sure. To the attainment of this end, the number of judges should be large enough to prevent delays. In the U.S.A. it is said that justice is neither swift nor sure. There are so many loopholes in the law and its processes that it is possible for a clever lawyer or client to delay justice unduly, if not to thwart it altogether. If the poor people are to benefit by the judiciary, it is necessary that justice should not be as costly as it is today in many countries. The judicial process should be simple, direct, and inexpensive. While ample provision should be made for the correction of judicial errors by a well-organised system of appeals, every thing possible should be done to prevent prolonged and vexatious litigation. Strenuous efforts should be made by courts to effect reconciliation and arbitration wherever possible. In this matter of the amicable settlement of disputes the lower courts in India might be instructed to play a useful part which they are not playing to-day.

Functions of the Judiciary

(1) The primary function of the judiciary is to apply the law to specific cases, both in civil controversies and in cases where persons have been accused of crime. This function is not as easy at it may seem on the surface. There are many cases where the law is not clear, altogether free from ambiguity. Therefore, the judge is asked to interpret the meaning of laws, and in so doing judges have built up a great body of 'judge-made' or 'case law'. In Anglo-Saxon countries, in dealing with cases which are not covered by statute law, judges declare what is the common law. In France, 'almost the whole body of administrative laws has been built up by he decisions of the Council of State, the supreme administrative court of the country'.

While precedents are not binding on future decisions, much respect is attached to them. Both lawyers and judges make use of them. In the Anglo-Saxon countries precedents are not merely an evidence of the law but are a source of law. In France, Germany, and on the continent generally, however, judicial precedents do not bind even the inferior courts.

Precedents, says Garner, are of two kinds; precedents which *create* law for the future and precedents which merely *declare* the pre-existing law. The later are more numerous but less important. Another form of classification is the division between *authoritative* and *persuasive* precedents. As the name itself implies, an authoritative precedent binds future judges. This is true in the relation between superior and inferior courts. Even an authoritative precedent may be overruled by the judge of a superior court, if he considers it to be contrary to reason or law. A persuasive precedent is not obligatory and the judge gives to it such weight as he thinks it deserves.

(2) A second important function of the judiciary is the protection of the individual against the encroachment of the State. No special provision is made for this purpose in the English-

speaking countries and in Beligum where the rule of law prevails, according to which there are the same laws and same courts for both officials and private individuals. What special courts there may be are subordinate to the ordinary courts. In France, Germany, Italy and other continental countries there are special administrative courts applying administrative law.

Controversy has raged over the question as to whether the rule of law is superior to administrative law or *vice versa*. A.V. Dicey is largely responsible for the exaggerated importance given to the rule of law and for the prevailing opinion in English-speaking countries that the rule of law alone can adequately protect the liberties of the individual against public officials. More intimate knowledge of the special administrative courts of France than was available in the days of Dicey has convinced thinkers that administrative courts and administrative law do not necessarily mean arbitrary rule. There is no solid foundation for the popular belief that in administrative courts justice is perverted for the sake of administrative convenience of in order to oblige those in authority. Judges of the administrative courts are not only well-versed in law but also have had administrative experience which enables them to take into account both the public and private aspects of a case in which State officials are involved. In course of years they have become the protectors of the individual against the arbitrary and illegal acts of government and its administrative agents.

One respect in which administrative law is superior to the rule of law is that, in a country like France, the individual can sue the State and obtain an indemnity if he has suffered injustice at the hands of its officials. In England and America, on the contrary, the individual cannot generally sue the State. He has to sue the officer concerned for damage which may not be forthcoming if he is insolvent or it unable to pay. When some high official is to be sued, permission has to be sought by means of a petition of right, and this is not always easy to obtain.

A significant development in recent years is that both the rule of law and administrative law have undergone changes in the direction of each other, thus minimising the sharp differences between two. As seen earlier, a great many administrative departments in England such as Health and Labour enjoy semi-judicial powers, and in some cases there is no appeal to a higher authority. Continental administrative courts, in their turn, have become more and more judicialised with a definite procedure regarding evidence, judgment, etc. There is no country in the world where the public official is on a footing of absolute equality with the private citizen as regards his privileges and immunities. This being the case, it seems best to accept frankly the French view that the public official in the performance of his duties is in a different category altogether from the private individual in his relations with other private individuals. It is an English writer, C.K. Allen; who says: 'The remedies of the subject against the State in France are easier, speedier, and infinitely cheaper than they are in England to-day. It has become a maxim of constitutionalists, and a bulwark of French democracy that the *Counseild' Etat* is the great buffer between the public and the bureaucrat'.

The Council of State, the supreme administrative court of France, is presided over to-day by a non-political head, instead of by the Minister of Justice, as before. In some respects, says a recent writer, it is like the Public Service Commission in India, issuing rules for the civil services, investigating their grievances and hearing their complaints. The Council of State further exercises the function of judicial review over the ordinances and rule which do not have their source in the legislature.

(3) An important function of the judiciary in federal constitutions is the interpretation of the constitution and declaring invalid of statutes which are at variance with the constitution. As has been well pointed out, there are in the U.S.A. four kinds of laws possessing various degrees of authority. There are (a) the Federal constitution, (b) Federal statutes, (c) States constitution, and (d) State statues. Of these the first prevails against all the rest. 'Federal Statutes, if within the competence of the Federal Legislature, prevail alike over State Constitutions and State Statutes; the State Constitutions prevail over State Statutes'.[9]

The Supreme Court Judges are the guardians of the federal constitution. This does not mean that they scrutinise the constitutionality of every statute law before it can become operative. It is for the aggrieved party to bring the alleged violation of the constitution to the notice of the Supreme Court. As a recent writer observes: 'The court has no authority to interfere until its office is invoked in a cause submitted to it in the manner prescribed by law'.

The power of judicial review given to the Supreme Court enables the judiciary to act as a guardian of the constitution against the possible inroads of the Executive or the Legislature. On the whole, the system has worked admirably, in spite of the fact that there have been occasions when the class prejudices of the judges have contributed much to the rejection of essential social legislation under the pretext of defending the constitution. Thus, as Prof. Ramaiyar points out, the Employers' Liability Act, Workmen's Compensation Act, Minimum Wages Act, Act to Prevent Child Labour, etc. passed by the Federal Congress and approved by the President, have been rejected by the Supreme Court under the pretext that they contravened the 14th Amendment.

(4) Other functions of the judiciary as summed up by Garner are (a) the issuing of writs and injunctions of various kinds; (b) the pronouncing of declaratory judgments regarding what is right or what the law requires when such opinions are requested by interested parties; (c) the giving of advisory opinion on questions of law when requested by the executive or the legislature; (d) the adjudication of disputed cases of jurisdiction in federal constitutions; (e) the appointment of certain local officials of the court, the choosing of clerical and other functionaries, the granting of licences, the appointing of guardians and trustees, the admission of wills to probate, the administering of the estates of deceased persons, the appointing of receivers, etc.

Organisation of the Judiciary

The judiciary is organised differently from the legislature and executive. As Garner points out: 'The judicial power . . . is exercised neither by a single magistrate nor by an assembly, but by a series of magistrates or collegially constituted tribunals usually hierarchically organised one above another with a supreme court of review or cassation at the apex'.[10]

In the Anglo-Saxon countries, except in the case of the courts of an appeal, the usual practice is for each court to consist of single judge. In France, Germany, and several other European countries the collegiate principle generally prevails. Plurality of judges, it is believed, is a protection against arbitrariness. But it is very expensive. In Great Britain and the U.S.A., the number of judges in the lower courts is relatively small.

Another difference between the Anglo-American and continental courts is that in the former judges go 'on circuit' from country to country, holding court in different places for the convenience of litigants. On the continent of Europe, on the contrary, courts are 'sedentary' or localised; and litigants are to go them.

A valuable feature of the continental courts, when contrasted with the part-state courts of America, is that their judicial system is unified and integrated. It is highly desirable that all the State courts should be organised into one system so that there will be one great court with several branches under it.

In federal States, such as the U.S.A., 'there are usually two separate and distinct series of judicial bodies, one to exercise national or general jurisdiction, the other local jurisdiction'.[11]

Such diversity is not necessary, as can be seen in the case of Germany under the Weimer constitution where there was 'a single uniform system for the federation and the States'.[12]

No division of jurisdiction was observed between the federation and the states; nor was there any diversity of law. In the U.S.A., on the other hand, in spite of a certain degree of uniformity and similarity as regards essentials, the different states possess different systems of judicial organisation and law procedure. This does not mean that the courts of the various states regard each other as foreign. On the contrary, they give full faith and credit to the records and judicial proceeding of each other.

The two general types of courts, as distinguished by Garner, are the ordinary of regular courts and extraordinary or special courts such as administrative courts, military, commercial, and industrial courts, labour arbitration courts, courts of claims, conciliation courts, probate courts, customs courts, courts of impeachment, consular courts, etc. Many of the courts under the second category exercise only voluntary or non-contentious jurisdiction.

The federal judicial system of the U.S.A. consists of District courts, the Circuit Court of Appeals, and the Supreme Court in addition to several special courts. The Supreme Court consists of a Chief Justice and eight associate justices. Six form a quorum. The original jurisdiction of the Supreme Court is 'determined by the Constitution and includes only cases in which either ambassadors or States are parties; its appellate jurisdiction is determined mainly by statute, and includes all cases from state courts involving conflicts between Statute Law and Federal Law, all cases involving conflicts between Statute Law and Federal Law, all cases involving the interpretation of the Federal Constitution or any Federal law or Treaty, cases involving a conflict between a State Constitution and the constitution of the United States, and all cases where the decision of the Circuit Court of Appeals is not final'.[13] There are other kinds of appeal also received by the Supreme Court, which need not detain us. While in England judges are never called upon to interpret the constitution, in the U.S.A. the Supreme Court judges are frequently called upon to do it. They have the right to declare the legality of the law itself and are, in a literal sense, the guardians of the constitutions. Their appointment rests with the president, subject to the approval of the Senate. Once appointed they hold office for life, there being no statutory age of retirement. They can be removed only by impeachment.

'The Federal courts, like the Federal Laws, operate directly upon the individual citizens'.[14] In Switzerland on the other hand, the execution of the laws and decrees made by the Executive Council is left to the cantonal administrators and courts of justice.

'The State courts are wholly distinct from the Federal courts, the bifurcation of judicial administration being absolute and complete. Each State has its own series of courts, and appeals from those courts to the Federal courts of the United States lie.......only in cases involving Federal Law, or in cases where one of the parties to the suits belongs to a different State'.[15]

The British courts consist of the central courts located in London and Local courts scattered throughout the country, such as Country Courts, Coroner's Courts, Assizes, and Quarter Sessions. The High Court of justice in London consists of 25 judges. It does not sit as one body, but meets in three branches, viz., the King's Bench, the Chancery, and the Probate, Divorce, and

Admiralty Division. These courts have both original and appellate jurisdiction. 'The Court of Appeal is solely concerned with the hearing of appeals from persons all over Britain and cases tried in the first instance at other subordinate courts'. The judicial Committee of the Privy Council tries appeals coming from different parts of the Empire.

For purposes of local judicial administration, Britain is divided into 8 circuits and sub-divided into several counties. Offences which are non-indictable, also known as 'petty' offences, receive a summary jurisdiction. There is not jury trial in such cases. The presiding officer of such courts is very often an honorary Justice of the Peace, assisted by a clerk well versed in law. Indictable offences are tried by Assizes and Quarter-Sessions, the jury acting as a complement of the judge. Rigorous proof of crime is required before a person standing the trial is condemned.

While in criminal cases the State appears as the complainant, in civil cases both sides appear in their private capacity. The Circuit Courts or Assizes deal also with civil disputes, but with different procedure and in a different hall.

In France there is a hierarchy of ordinary courts as well as administrative courts. They combine original and appellate jurisdiction. The highest administrative court is the Council of State. Below it are the Councils of Prefecture which deal 'with complaints regarding direct taxation and transactions of the lower public officials with private individuals'.[16] Administrative courts deal also with election petitions.

The High Court for ordinary law in France is called the Court of Cassation. It is the supreme court of appeal as well as the court which annuls all decisions contrary to the laws of the land. Cases where disputes of jurisdiction arise as between the ordinary courts and the administrative court are decided by the Court of Conflicts. The French Justices of the Peace in the cantons are concerned more with persuading parties to arrive at an amicable settlement of disputes than with delivering judgments.

The federal judiciary in Switzerland does not occupy the high place occupied by the Supreme Court of America. It has the power of judicial review only over cantonal statutes and cantonal constitutions and not over federal statutes and the federal constitution. It can compel the obedience of the cantons, but not of the citizens of the cantons, to the federal constitution and federal statutes. It can approach the citizens of the cantons only through the cantonal administration. There is no hierarchy of federal courts in Switzerland, as in the U.S.A., but only a single federal court of 24 judges at Lausanne.

In Canada and Australia no distinction is made between the federal judiciary and provincial or state judiciary. There is only one judiciary which is under the control of the Federal Government. It has no power of judicial review, as in the U.S.A. It has 'original jurisdiction in all disputes between the component states or provinces, and appellate jurisdiction over cases coming from the subordinate courts established in the states, or provinces and the right of judicial review over laws passed by subordinate law-making bodies'.[17] Since the passing of the Statute of Westminster in 1931 no Dominion allows appeals to the Privy Council from the decisions of the Dominion Courts. The British judicial system including the rule of laws the jury system, and the system of honorary magistrates has been extended to India with the necessary alterations. The High Courts of India do not possess the same powers and functions as those possessed by the High Court in England. The Judicial Committee of the Privy Council is the highest judicial authority for India and various kinds of appeals are allowed to it from the High Court.

The Collector of the Indian District is at the same time at a Magistrate. In this capacity he is responsible for the maintenance of law and order as well as for the criminal jurisdiction of the district. He is also responsible for the administrative control of the subordinate magistracy. He seldom tries criminal cases, but is responsible to see that the trying magistrates do their work properly.

The Sub-divisional Magistrate for each division of the districts all important cases with are not sufficiently serious to be sent up to the Court Session. He also hears appeals from the Subordinate Magistrates under his administrative control. Appeals from his own decisions lie to the Court of Session.

The Tahsildar is given magisterial powers, but he seldom exercises them. The Sub-Magistrate in each *taluk* tries criminal cases which are not sufficiently serious to be committed to the Sub-divisional Magistrate or so petty as to be tried by the village court. Where there is a Deputy Tahsildar he tries cases which would otherwise be tried by the Sub-Magistrate at the Tahsildar's headquarters.

The High Court is the highest court of civil as well as criminal jurisdiction in the Province. Under the High Court there is the District and Session Judge, who tries both civil and criminal cases. The Subordinate Judges have jurisdiction of original suits and proceedings of a civil nature. Ordinarily they have no appellate jurisdiction. Below the rank of the Subordinate Judge on the civil side are District *Munsifs* and Village Munsifs. 'Small Causes' are dealt with in summary way by District Munsifs and Sub-Judges, although the High Court has the power of revision.

More recently a Federal Court has been established with a limited jurisdiction. Provision is made for transferring to it some of the powers now enjoyed by the Privy Council in civil litigation. 'At present its jurisdiction is limited to cases involving the construction of the provisions of the Government of India Act and to disputes between the various Provinces in their sovereign capacity or between the Provinces and the Central Government in their respective spheres. There is also a certain amount of advisory jurisdiction conferred upon the Federal Court at the instance of the Central Government'.[18]

A point of departure from the British judicial system is that in India when the State encroaches upon the property of a private person or enters into a contract with a private person, a regular suit can be filed in the ordinary way against the Crown. In England, on the contrary, the aggrieved party has to proceed by means of a Petition of Right, which is an appeal to the good will of the Sovereign. The difference in India is due to the fact that as the government has succeeded to some extent the old East India Company, the liability of the Company is continued under the present system of law.

Discussion of the organisation of the judiciary cannot be complete without a word about the part assigned to laymen in the judicial system. For petty cases laymen are employed as unpaid, honorary judges for short periods. In England this function is performed by Justices of the Peace and in India by honorary magistrates. On the whole, the system has not worked satisfactorily. There is a lack of uniformity in the decisions given.

In Britain the 'justice of the Justice of the Peace' is rather slipshod, lacking in uniformity. On the other hand, this system gives opportunity to well-to-do citizens with leisure for political education and social service, although there is a possibility of the power given being abused.

Akin to the system of Honorary Magistrates is the jury system which is used widely in many countries. Its object is to help the judge to appreciate the facts of a case. It originated in England and has been widely adopted in other lands. In favour of the system it is said that it acts as a check upon bribery and other corrupt motives influencing the judges. It is also said to be a valuable means of education in civic duties and responsibilities. By its spirit of disinterestedness and application of commonsense, it is argued that the jury can help the judge in a proper appreciation of the facts of the case.

In actual practice, however, the jury system has not been a great success. There are many cases where an upright judge has been hindered in his work by a partial and prejudiced jury. This has notoriously been the case when Negroes in the United States had to be tried before juries composed exclusively of white men. An unpaid jury is reluctant to give its time when the case prolongs for days and weeks together. In cases where technical issues are involved, an ordinary jury is worse than useless.

The jury system was introduced into India in 1861. In spite of its trial for 60 years in the Madras Presidency it must be said that it has been more a failure than a success.

Another practice which has even less justification than the jury system is the system of trial by assessors. In the criminal courts of India the system of assessors has not served any useful purpose. As a well-known judicial authority puts it: 'The assessors are not anxious to be there. Judges are not anxious to have the assessors'.

Appointment, Tenure, and Removal of Judges

There are three principal forms of appointment of judges, *viz.* (1) election by the legislature, (2) election by the people, (3) appointment by the executive by itself or under certain conditions such as appointment from a list of nominees submitted by the courts or on the basis of a competitive examination or with the approval of an executive council or the upper house in the legislature.

(1) *Election by the legislature*—Appointment by the legislature prevails in Switzerland. The judges of the federal court who number 24 are elected by the two houses of the legislature at a joint session for a period of six years and can be re-elected any number of times. This system was popular in the U.S.A. for some years after the Revolution. Since then all but four states have abandoned it. The defects of the system are that the judiciary is made unduly dependent on the legislature and appointments are made by the party caucus. Political and geographical considerations are given greater weight than technical qualifications. Notwithstanding these defects which particularly apply to America, the system has worked well in Switzerland on account of the small size of the legislature and the comparatively lack of partisanship in politics.

(2) *Election by the People*—This system was first introduced in France in 1790 and was much abused in 1793 when stone-cutters, clerks, gardeners, and common labourers were elected as judges. Napoleon abolished it so far as France was concerned.

The system prevails to-day in the cantons of Switzerland and in many of the States of America. It is the worst method of securing good and efficient judges. Judges who are popularly elected are likely to be lacking in independence and legal knowledge. The masses do not possess the necessary discrimination or knowledge to elect efficient judges. When judges can stand for re-election, the system becomes infinitely worse. Judges have to give popular judgments in order to win votes. Able and distinguished jurists, are often defeated. Condemning the system, Garner writes: 'it lowers the character of the judiciary, tends to make a politician of the judge, and subjects the judicial mind to a strain which it is not always able to resist'.[19]

The evils of the system have been partially overcome in the U.S.A. by non-partisan primaries nominating candidates and by the bar recommending suitable candidates to the electors.

(3) *Appointment by the Executive*—This seems the best method. It prevails on Great Britain and the British Dominions as well as in the Federal Government of the United States and in six of the part-states of America. Though political considerations play a part in making the selection, when once appointed the judges are independent and are not under the influence of the executive. In France the executive is not given a free hand. A competitive examination is held to fill up vacancies in the lower grades, and from there promotion is by seniority. In England and the U.S.A. practising lawyers the often chosen to judgeships.

Appointment by the executive is the best method on the whole. The executive is a better judge of the merits of those appointed than either the legislature or the people can be. The method makes for the independence of the judiciary since the tenure is 'during good behaviour'. In France it is complained that the Minister of Justice is influenced to frequently by the Deputies in making appointments. To overcome this and other defects in the method under consideration, it is suggested by some that the executive selection should be from a list of nominees made by the court in which the vacancy is to be filled.

Tenure of Judges

Short-term tenure is the usual practice in the part-states of America. The term varies from 2 to 21 years, while the average is from 6 to 9 years. In Switzerland the federal judges are elected by the two houses of the legislature for a period of six years, but can be re-elected any number of times. Outside the U.S.A. good behaviour tenure is almost universal. This is a sound practice because it secures 'a steady, upright, and impartial administration of the law'. It also secures experience and knowledge of judicial precedents.

The U.S.A. practice of fixing no age limit for the retirement of the Supreme Court judges is indefensible. It keeps in the saddle too many old men who are terribly conservative and incapable of adjusting themselves to new conditions.

Removal of Judges

In every constitution there must be provision for the removal of corrupt and inefficient magistrates. In England judges can be removed by the Crown upon an address of both houses of Parliament. The usual practice in the U.S.A. is impeachment whereby the lower house makes the charge and the upper house tries it. The process is rather cumbersome. It is capable of being used for party purposes. But this abuse can be checked by requiring an extraordinary majority of votes for the removal of judges. In 12 of the American states judges can be removed by the legislature, while in 9 they can be removed by the Governor upon address by the legislature. Several states have adopted the popular recall of judges, which is altogether indefensible. It destroys the independence and dignity of the judiciary. It is worse as regards criminal justice than as regards civil justice. In many of the countries of continental Europe 'judges may be removed only by the court of which they are members, or by the supreme court sitting as a disciplinary tribunal, and after a regular trial, and for reasons expressly stated in the laws'.[20]

Even worse than the popular recall of judges is the popular recall of judicial decisions adopted by one state in America, *viz.*, Colorado. There is, if the judiciary sets aside a law on the ground that it contravenes the constitutions, the matter is to be submitted to a popular vote and the decision of the people stands. The exercise of this power, as pointed out by an eminent American jurist, Ehihu Root, cuts at the very root of the whole system of American Government.

NOTES

1. *Introduction to Politics*, p. 63.
2. 'The Lord Chancellor, who is at once a member of the Cabinet, of the House of Lords, and the head of the judiciary is a standing refutation of the doctrine *of* separation of powers' (Gilchrist: *op. cit.*, p. 254).
3. Gilchrist: *Principles of Political Science*, pages 166-7.
4. Sir H. Maine.
5. H. Finer: *Theory and Practice of Modern Government*, p. 994.
6. According to Lindsay Rodgers, legislation which was the President's minor role has become his major role. He is now the

chief legislator and the country judges him on the basis of his success as a legislator rather than his success as an executive.

7. Finer: *Theory and Practice of Modern Government*, p. 1063.
8. J.W. Garner: *Political Science and Government*, p. 726.
9. Marriott: *Mechanism of the Modern State, Vol. II*, p. 306.
10. pp. 780-1.
11. Garner, Ibid., p. 783.
12. Ibid.
13. Marriott, Vol. 2, p. 301.
14. Marriott, Ibid, p. 307.
15. Marriott: Ibid, p. 308.
16. Ramaiyar: *Politics*, p. 356.
17. Ramaiyar: Ibid, p. 361.
18. Sir S. Varadachariar.
19. pp. 795-6.
20. Garner, p. 802.

REFENENCES

Blunt, E., *The I.C.S.*

Dicey, A.V., *The Law of the Constitution.*

Finer, H., *The British Civil Service.*

Finer, H., *Theory and Practice of Modern Government*, Vol. 2.

Garner, J.W., *Political Science and Government.*

Get tell, R.G., *Introduction to Political Science.*

Gilchrist, R.N., *Principles of Political Science.*

Iyengar, S.S., *Problems of Indian Democracy.*

Marriott, J.A.R., *The Mechanism of the Modern State, Vol. 2.*

Ramaiyer, *Politics.*

3

Classification of Governments

MEANING OF FORMS OF GOVERNMENT

Forms of Government and not Forms of State

In common usage, many a time the terms 'state' and 'government' are used carelessly and indiscriminately as if the two terms are synonymous. Several books speak of forms of state, which really means forms of government. Scientifically it is incorrect to speak in terms of forms of state, as all states have territory, population, government and sovereignty as the essential elements. All states in the world, whether the people in them subscribe to liberal principles, communist theories or autocratic shibboleths have all these four essential elements; if any one of them lacks any of these elements, it does not deserve to be called state The U.S.A., the U.K. and the U.S.S.R. are all states with the same essential elements.

Differences in Government

While all states are similar, there is difference between one state organisation and another. The organisation of a state is its government. A state formulates its policies and expresses its will through its instrument known as government. Governments are organised or built up in different ways, and hence we speak of different forms of government. Owing to the prevalence of diversity in socio-political factors, different forms of government are found in different countries. The political scientist, who has to be careful in using various terms, should not speak of forms of state, when the correct expression is "Forms of Government." Stephen Leacock says on page 108 in *Elements of Political Science*

(1938): "Some writes have held that we ought not to speak of a classification of states, since all are identical in the essential attributes. They prefer to classify instead the different 'forms of government' seen in the state." Leacock says that we may "either speak of the various *forms of government* or *forms of state*." (*Ibid*, p. 109). J.W. Garner is in favour of using the phrase Forms of Government. "...in the last analysis such a classification is nothing more than a classification of governments and not of states . . . consistency and scientific logic therefore require that such classifications be placed in their proper category and labelled as classifications of government and not of states." (See *Political Science and Government* (1955), p. 22).

Meaning

We may note the meaning of Form of Government. Karl Lowenstein says: "The term *form of government* usually describes the functional arrangement—co-ordination or subordination of the various orangs in the process of determining the will of the state. Here the post-war constitutions did not add anything new to the traditional repertory." [See Eckstein and Apter (Ed.), *Comparative Politics*—1963, p. 153].

Complex Topic

"Forms of Government" is a complex topic on which much study has been conducted by various scholars at different times and ages since the birth of political science. But even now the topic is not easy for study, as the classification of governments cannot be made in a simple ways according to one principle only. For instance, a government like that of Britain or India may be classified as democracy according to one principle; but the classification is not complete, as it is also parliamentary. In the same way, the government of the U.S.A. is democratic and also presidential. In judging the governments of England and the U.S.A., we make use of more than one criteria. To make the problem more confusing, England has a monarch in a democratic set-up. Therefore, it should be remembered that forms of government have to be studied by taking into consideration various principles of classification.

CLASSIFICATION OF GOVERNMENTS BY SOCRATES AND PLATO

Greek Thinkers

To have a comprehensive view regarding the topic "Forms of Government" we have to peep into the dead past and fix our eyes on the studies conducted by thinkers of ancient Greece. The names of philosophers that strike our mind first are Socrates, Plato and Aristotle. The views of these thinkers can be understood and appreciated fully only when we take note of the circumstances in which these seers found themselves, and the influences in which the environments worked on their minds. Greece produced small city-states and not large territorial nation-states as we see today. Socrates, who valued virtue, justice and goodness, was the teacher of Plato, and Plato the great idealist was the master of the master-mind, the mobile one-man university, Aristotle.

Greek political thinkers did not draw a line of difference between state and government, as we do in modern times.

We are concerned here chiefly with Aristotle's views, though a brief reference may be made to those of Socrates and Plato.

Socrates

Socrates spoke of three main forms of government: monarchy, aristocracy and democracy. He believed in the principle that "only those who know shall rule." The classification is made on the basis of two principles; (1) the number of people who rule, and (2) the principle of knowledge.

Plato

As with Socrates, with Plato also knowledge weighed very much, and he classified governments applying the standard of knowledge. Plato believed in a political cycle, which brought about changes in government, which resulted in the good becoming bad or the best becoming second best. Plato speaks of three kinds of states:

1. States of Perfect Knowledge

This is an ideal state, as great ideas or reason is sovereign. Herein one notes the sovereignty of reason or wisdom, and not the sovereignty of one or of a group of people.

2. States of Imperfect Knowledge

In these states men are imperfect, and therefore laws are necessary; but the laws are obeyed by the people.

3. States Wanting Knowledge

These re states of ignorance, in which laws exist but are not obeyed by the people.

Plato's classification cannot be accepted fully, because imperfect men live in this world, and a state with sovereignty of reason does not exist. Hence it is needless to examine the first type of Plato's state.

Taking the two remaining types into consideration, we may divide them into two categories: (1) states in which laws are obeyed, and (2) states in which laws are violated.

A state in which one man rules and in which laws are obeyed is called monarchy; a state in which laws are obeyed is called aristocracy, and the rule of the few in which laws are disobeyed is called oligarchy. Similarly the rule of the many in a state in which laws are obeyed is called moderate democracy, while the rule of the many in a state in which laws are disobeyed is called extreme democracy. Plato gives the highest place to monarchy, the next place to aristocracy and the lowest place to tyranny. As regards democracy he says that it is better is non-law states and worse in which law prevails.

Plato lays great emphasis on the type of mind which exercises power in the state. His ideal state of perfect knowledge is called ideocracy. According to the political cycle, as the mind degenerates, democracy makes room for timocracy, the rule of honour or spiritedness, which is synonymous with military rule. Reason finds a place in timocracy, but the rise of selfishness and private property brings down the state. In course of time, timocracy shades off into oligarchy, which is the selfish rule of the few. Then people rebel against oligarchy, and democracy is set up; but in democracy, as conceived by Plato, there is the rise of the ordinary man in the street. As the ordinary man and not the ideal man rules, there is no order, freedom or justice in democracy. Democracy enables demagogues to seize power, and thus tyranny rises.

ARISTOTLE'S CLASSIFICATION

Aristotle's Views

Classification according to Number and Aims. Aristotle's views on this topic merit greater attention than those of Plato, as they are realistic and provide a reasonable basis of classification. While Plato's state of perfect knowledge cannot be realised anywhere on this planet, it is possible to apply Aristotle's principle of classification to a world of reality.

Aristotle classifies governments according to two criteria: (1) the number of persons wielding power or the location of sovereignty in the state; (2) the purpose (good or bad) for which supreme power is wielded, or the ends for which it is exercised.

Governments are normal, if they have good aims of promoting the welfare and happiness of the people, and if they bend their energies in realising these aims. But whin governments ignore these noble aims and work in an evil way for promoting the ignoble and selfish ends of those wielding supreme power to the detriment of the larger interests of the community, they are perverted.

Empirical and Normative Criteria

Aristotle blends empirical and normative criteria in his classification. The classification not only describes, but also lays down instruction regarding what ought to be.

Table of Aristotle's Classification

First Principle: Number of Persons Exercising Supreme Power	Second Principle: Purpose of Exercising Supreme Power	
	Normal Form of Government	Perverted Form of Government
One	Monarchy	Tyranny
Few	Aristocracy	Oligarchy
Many	Polity	Democracy

The form of government is monarchy or tyranny, if supreme power is vested in the hands of one man. A government by one man is regarded as monarchy, if it aims at the realisation of good life. Normally a monarch keeps before his mind a high and unselfish aim to promote the good of the people. When the ruler forgets the public good and aims at promoting his own good, he degenerates into a tyrant. Thus one man's rule is monarchy; but its perversion is tyranny.

The form of government is aristocracy or oligarchy, if power is vested in the hands of a few. The normal government of a few people aiming at public good is aristocracy; its perverted form is oligarchy.

The form of government is polity or democracy if power is vested in the hands of many or a large proportion of the population. The normal rule of the many is polity; in its perverted form it is democracy .

As in Plato's classification, in Aristotle's classification too, we discern the political cycle. Aristotle not only classifies, but also explains the cyclic political changes. He philosophically elucidates how one form of government yields place to another. In Plato we realise that the lowering of the mind leads to desegregation. The movement is from ideocracy to timocracy, timocracy to oligarchy, oligarchy to democracy, and finally from democracy to tyranny. Here the word 'democracy' is used not in the modern sense, but in the Platonic sense.

In Aristotle's classification, the lowering of the aims of the state results in perversion, whether it is the rule of one, few or many. Monarchy degenerates into tyranny; aristocracy deteriorates into oligarchy; and polity becomes perverted to form democracy, not in the modern sense, but in the Aristotelian sense. Today we do not talk of polity; what was polity to Aristotle is to us democracy. What was democracy to Aristotle is to us mob rule or ochlocracy. In democracy there is no certainty or stability, and intolerable disorder prevails. Among normal forms of government the best is monarchy and the worst is polity. But among perverted forms, democracy is the best and tyranny is the worst.

The difference between the classification to the two great Greek philosophers is obvious; in Plato we find and idealist approach; in Aristotle the approach is relatively scientific or rational.

Evaluation of Aristotle's Classification

We may briefly consider the merits and defects of Aristotle's classification.

Merits

The following are the merits of Aristotle's classification:

1. *Earliest Thinker to Classify.* Credit should be given to Aristotle for his classification which was the earliest or one of the earliest. In fact it was Aristotle who set the course for traditional classification of governments. Aristotle's approach was scientific and systematic. He classified governments, after making a thorough and exhaustive study of all the types of government known in his days. We cannot judge Aristotle by modern standfars; but when judged by the contemporary standards, that is of the 4th and 3rd centuries B.C., Aristotle's views on classification have to be appreciated.
2. *Provided Historical Basis with Survival Value.* Aristotle's qualitative and quantitative classification is of practical value. As R.N. Gilchrist says, it has provided the historical basis of practically all classifications made hitherto. It was Aristotle who set the ball of classification of governments rolling. Even though his classification became outdated after some time, he provoked political scientists to think about the problem of classification seriously and make their own contribution. Aristotle's historical basis has survival value. Robert A. Dahl says on page 26 in *Modern Political Analysis* (1963): "Aristotle's classification has, however, proved so useful for so many different purposes that it has survived the political vicissitudes and transformations of 25 centuries. Indeed it or some thing like it is as much a part of the habitual thinking of the student of politics today as it was to the observant Greek in Aristotle's day."
3. *Perversion in Government.* The degeneration that Aristotle outlines in his political cycle, one can actually see in some of the ancient, medieval or modern states of the world. Being a product of his times, Aristotle could not be blind to the degeneration of monarchy into tyranny, of aristocracy into oligarchy, and of policy into democracy. The trend in the lure of power, as we find in some of the modern states, may not be exactly similar as given in the Aristotelian pattern, but the evil spirit of degeneration is one and the same.

4. *Systematic Classification.* Aristotle had a definite scientific method to classify governments. He undertook the task bearing two clear-cut principles in mind.

Demerits

The following are the chief demerits in Aristotle's classification:

1. *State and Government not Separated.* Aristotle does not distinguish between state and government. This flaw is serious, because this difference is one of basic importance in political science.
2. *Inadequate.* His classification is very simple, and it may be useful only in the study of the ancient city-states of Greece, but as far as modern territorial states are concerned, the classification is totally inadequate. For instance, a proper study of states like India today cannot be made with the application of Aristotle's simple classification. The study of the British constitution is not possible with this classification. England has a monarch, yet England is a democracy. Aristotle uses terms, whose meaning does not fit into modern political and constitutional context. While we value democracy as the most desirable form of government, Aristotle regards it as the perverted form of polity. To us, democracy is people's government, which is highly valued, but to him it is mob rule. Forms like Tyranny and Polity are not found anywhere in the world today.
3. *Distinction Difficult.* It is difficult to draw a clear line of difference between aristocracy and democracy. Hence again England's example can be taken to show how the two are mixed. Distinction between aristocracy and oligarchy is also difficult.
4. *Several Factors Ignored.* Aristotle's classification is overloaded with ethical values. He speaks of citizen's partnership with the state in a life of virtue and happiness. That is not the case with the modern citizen. While ethical values should be given the importance due to them in modern states, it is incorrect to ignore other factors. Aristotle ignores the various social and economic factors,

which influence the growth of the state. Greek philosophers like Aristotle give an ethical or qualitative basis to the state. Modern thinkers speak of a legal basis of state. Instead of a qualitative or moral basis, they mention a quantitative basis.

5. *Complex Structure.* The structure of modern governments is highly complex. Aristotle's classification presumes governments to be in pure form, which is not the case today. No form of government anywhere in the world is pure at present.

Classification by Other Writers

We now consider briefly the views of modern writers like Machiavelli, Jean Bodin, John Docke, Motesquieu, Rousseau, Bluntchli, Von Mohl, Jellinek, Burgess, Marritt, Leacock and Mac-Iver.

1. Machiavelli on Aristotle's Classification and Mixed Form of Government

Machiavelli, the author of *The Prince* and the relentless advocate of absolute monarchy, accepts Aristotle's classification. Besides, Machiavelli puts forth the mixed form of government as found in the works of the ancient Greek historian Polybius and the Roman writer Cicero. The Stoics in Greece and Aristotle mention mixed types of states. Strictly speaking, there is not such as thing as a mixed state. It is ridiculous to divide states into Pure States and Mixed States. Those who speak of mixed states do not clearly distinguish between state and government. What they mean to say is that elements of monarchy, aristocracy and democracy are blended in a particular government (not state).

While Aristotle's classification belongs to the ancient times, that of Machiavelli belongs to the modern; in fact, it is Machiavelli's writings that draw the line of separation between the medieval times and the modern.

While ancient thinkers like Socrates, Plato and Aristotle lay emphasis on ethical values, Machiavelli separates the ethical principles from the political. As a practical-minded thinker, Machiavelli believes that the form of government should be according to the circumstances. Mostly he expresses his chief concern for monarchies and democracies.

2. Bodin on Monarchy, Aristocracy and Democracy

The first comprehensive classification of forms of government in modern times is given by Jean Bodin. He speaks of three forms: (1) monarchy, (2) aristocracy, and (3) democracy.

3. Bodin Followed by Hobbes

Bodin's classification is followed by Hobbes; but Hobbes does not distinguish state from government.

4. Locke's Emphasis on Legislative Powers

Locke speaks of the highest importance of legislative power in a state and classifies governments as democratic, oligarchic, and monarchical according to the location of the supreme law-making power. Unlike Hobbes, he clearly distinguishes state from government.

5. Republics and Monarchies in Montesquieu

Montesquieu classifies governments into three forms:

(1) Republics which may be aristocratic or democratic;

(2) Monarchies of the Western type; and

(3) Monarchies of the Eastern type, that is, Despotism.

6. Monarchy, Aristocracy and Democracy in Rousseau

Rousseau speaks of three forms of government: (1) monarchy, (2) aristocracy, and (3) democracy. He gives the concept of the General Will, which is the basis of popular sovereignty.

7. Aristotle's Classification and Theocracy in Bluntchli

The German-Swiss writer Bluntschli adopts Aristotle's classification and adds one more form of government, that is, theocracy. The perverted form of theocracy is idolocracy.

Strictly speaking theocracy cannot be a separate form of government, and it can be easily brought under one or the other category in Aristotle's classification.

In a theocracy, it is believed that the ruler's will gives expression to God's will, and God Himself is supposed to rule. In contrast to the democratic state, there is the secular state. In a theocracy, government has an official religion of its own, whereas a secular government like India is neutral in religious matters, and it neither favours nor penalises any religion. The balance of religions is held evenly by a secular government like India. On the other hand, Israel, which is a Jewish state, and Pakistan and Iran, which are Islamic states, are not secular. The other Muslim countries of the Middle East are also not secular.

There is a difference between theocracy of ancient times and that of the modern times. In ancient times, theocracy meant a government in which the ruler said that he represented the will of God, whereas in modern times it means a government in which religion plays an important part in public affairs.

Modern political scientists clearly separate religion from politics.

8. Patriarchal, Theocratic, Patrimonial, Classic, Legal, and Despotic States in Von Mohl

Robert Von Mohl, a German publicist of the nineteenth century, having for his background the canvas of history classifies states as follows:

(1) Patriarchal states;

(2) Theocracies;

(3) Patrimonial states;

(4) Classic states of Greece and Rome;

(5) Legal states functioning according to law; and

(6) Despotic states.

The cardinal defect in Von Mohl's views is the lack of difference between state and government; moreover his classification is not made according to any clear-cut principle, and there is overlapping in his classification.

9. Monarchy and Republic in Jullinek

George Jellinek of the Heidelberg University in the nineteenth century rejects the classifications of all writers since Aristotle "as being arbitrary, unscientific, confusing and valueless." (See J.W. Garner, *Political Science and Government*—1955, p. 230).

He classifies governments into two types: (1) Monarchy, and

(2) Republic.

10. Burgess Supports Aristotle

In his *Political Science and Constitutional Law* (1896), Burges regards the Aristotelian classification as "correct and exhaustive and that no additional forms could be made out of a combination of these three (*i.e.* monarchy, aristocracy and democracy) or by a union of several states." (*Ibid.*, p. 233).

11. Three Types of Classification by Marriott

J.A.R. Marriott says that Aristotle's classification, though fundamental and useful is inadequate to meet modern requirements. Today there are various forms of government, which do not yield to the simple and outdated classification of Aristotle.

Marriot classifies governments in three ways as follows:

(1) Unitary and Federal,

(2) Those with Rigid constitutions and those with Flexible constitutions; and

(3) Those with Presidential form and those with Parliamentary form.

Unitary and Federal

In a unitary state, which has only one set of government, the different units into which it is divided (whether they are Provinces or Countries) are the creations of the central government. England has a unitary form of government; the central government can change the countries or abolish them, if it so desires. On the other hand, in a federal state in which there are two sets of government, both the federal and provincial or state governments enjoy powers as given in a written constitution. The federal government cannot treat the state governments as its creatures. Both the federal and state governments drive their powers from the constitution. The USA is a federation, in which the units known as States derive their power from the constitution and not from the federal government. (See Chapters 43 and 44 for details).

Rigid and Flexible Constitutions

The second classification of Marriott is on the basis of constitution. Constitutions are of two types: flexible or rigid. A flexible constitution can be amended easily; the procedure of amendment is very simple and the legislature in its ordinary course can amend the constitution in the same way in which ordinary laws are amended or passed. On the other hand, it is difficult to amend a rigid constitution, as a special and complicated procedure is laid down in the constitution itself. England has a flexible constitution, whereas the United States of America has a rigid one.

Monarchical, Presidential and Parliamentary

The third classification is according to the relations between the executive and the legislature. Marriott draws the line between the monarchical and the presidential governments on one side, and parliamentary, cabinet or responsible governments on the other. Here the question of the position of the executive *vis-a-vis* the legislature rises. In a despotic monarchy, the executive is superior to the legislature; in the presidential system, the executive is co-ordinate with the legislature; and in the cabinet system the executive is subordinate to the legislature.

As despotic monarchies do not form the general order at present, we are concerned chiefly with the presidential and cabinet systems.

In the USA, there is the presidential system; the president cannot be removed from power by the legislature before his term of 4 years expires.

England and India have the cabinet system. The cabinet is responsible to the legislature, and can remain in power only as long as it can command the confidence of the legislature.

12. Leacock's Classification into Despotic and Democratic, Limited Monarchy and Republic, Unitary and Federal, Parliamentary and Non-parliamentary

Stephen Leacock's classification of governments is broadly into despotic and democratic. A despotic government is one in which power is vested in a single person, who uses it according to his own will. For instance, in the medieval times, the Sultans of Delhi ruled as despots.

A democratic government is one in which power is vested in the people. At present, India has a democratic form of government.

Leacock divides democratic government into two categories: (1) Limited Monarchy, and (2) Republic.

Each of these categories is divided into Unitary and Federal. Both Unitary and Federal forms are divided into Parliamentary and Non-Parliamentary .

The following is the table as given by Leacock in *Elements of Political Science* (1933):

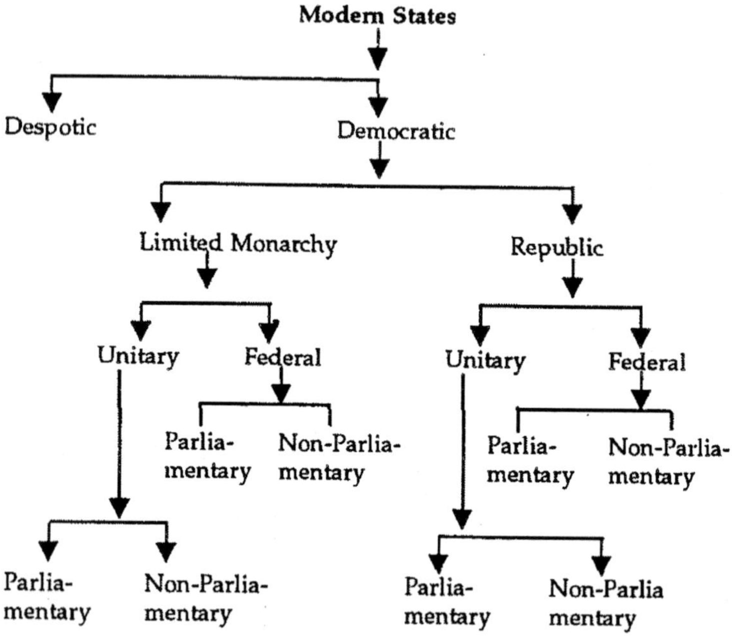

13. MacIver's Classification on Four Bases—Constitutional, Economic, Communal and Sovereignty Structure

MacIver says in *The Web of Government* 1959: 149): "No specific form of government endures, though there are certain major type forms that have at least a relative prominence." While he agrees that the traditional classification has stood the test of time, as it is based on a primary differential between types of government, he criticises it as inadequate to classify certain forms of government as found in feudal states, city states, republican states and limited monarchical states. To meet the requirements of the modern times, MacIver, as given in his conspectus, classifies governments on four bases: (1) Constitutional, (2) Economic, (3) Communal, and (4) Sovereignty Structure.

1. Constitutional

On the constitutional basis, governments come under two types—(a) Oligarchic, and (b) Democratic.

(a) Oligarchy takes different external forms. In dictatorship, theocracy and plural headship, power may actually lie in the hands of oligarchs. The same may be the case with a dictator. Monarchy is hereditary; dictatorship may originate in a *coup d'etat;* and the theocratic ruler is elected by a priestly college or caste. MacIver observes: "Of all theocracies that of Judea was the most potent in consequences for the modern world. It differed from most others in its completeness and in its intransigence. Its theocratic spirit subordinated considerations of class and gave an unusual unity to the people as a whole." (*Ibid.*, p. 153). Dual headship is found in primitive society. Pre-imperial Rome (of co-equal Consuls) and the medieval city states like Florence are examples of plural headship.

(b) Democracy can be under limited or constitutional monarchy as in Britain. It can also exist under a republican constitution like that of the USA or India.

2. Economic Basis

Governments can be divided into four types according to the type of economy followed by them:

(1) In ancient times there was folk economy in the primitive governments.

(2) In the medieval period in Europe, there was the feudal economy, in which the feudal estate or manor was the economic unit.

(3) In the modern times, with the outbreak of the Industrial Revolution during the period 1750-1850, Western countries like England developed a capitalist economy.

(4) As a reaction against capitalism, there arose socialism in the 19th century, and several countries developed a socialist economy.

3. Communal Basis

On a communal basis, there are different types of government:

(1) In very ancient times, government was in the hands of the tribal leader. This was a primitive type of government.

(2) In countries like Greece, city-states were organized.

(3) In several states, monarchy or any other types of government gave peace and order to the people of the whole country. In the modern times, with the rise of nationalism, nation-states emerged.

(4) Under the same government, there can be several nationalities.

(5) World government is yet to be formed.

4. Sovereignty Structure

MacIver speaks of three forms of government, according to sovereignty structure:

(1) Unitary government;

(2) Federal government;

(3) Empire, Colony and Dependency.

The following is the Conspectus of Forms of Government as by MacIver, *The Web of Government* (1959: 151) (see Table 1):

5. Obstacles in the Way of Classification

With all the forms of classification of governments furnished by modern writers like Marriott, Leacock and MacIver, we are not in a position to surmount the numerous difficulties that confront us in bringing about a real and complete classification of modern governments.

The following are the difficulties coming in the way of classifying governments:

1. Difference in Form and Spirit

A particular form of modern government may not yield to one particular type of classification. For instance, there is much difference between the form of government and the true spirit that animates it into action; and so also the difference between the apparent and the real may be noted.

Table 1: Conspectus of the Forms of Government

1 Constitutional Basis	2 Economic Basis	3 Communal Basis	4 Sovereignty Structure
I Oligarchy a1 Monarchy	b1 Folk Economy-Primitive Government	c1 Tribal Government	d1 Unitary Government
a2 Dictatorship	b2 Feudal Government	c2 "Polis" Government	d2 Empire, Colony, Dependency
a3 Theocracy	b3 Capitalist Government	c3 Country Government	d3 Federal Government
a4 Plural Headship	b4 Socialist Government	c4 National Government	
II Democracy		c5 Multi-national Government	
a5 Limited Monarchy a6 Republic		c6 World Government	

England in actual practice shows the spirit of a democratic republic, while it is a limited monarchy in external form. Theory indicates England as a monarchy though actually the monarch exercise only nominal power, and every action of his has to bear ministerial responsibility.

Another example can be given to show the difference between form and spirit. France has no king; the President, the head of the state is elected. Hence, in form the government is a republic; but in actual practice French political institutions appear to be as in a monarchical state, and the spirit that animates the government is the imperialist spirit and not the spirit of a republic. The conduct of the French government in recent times bears ample testimony to the truth of the allegation. The nature and attitude of the French people, who are regarded as unrealistic and emotional, quite contrary to the sober and realistic British people contribute much in keeping the gap between the form and the spirit rather very wide.

India today can be given as a third example. Some would like to ask the question whether India is truly federal or unitary. The constitution does not use the word 'federal'; according to the written word of the Constitution of India, it is a "Union of States." Even then, India is a federation; but the difficulty is that residuary powers are not with the units as in federations like the U.S.A., but with the Centre. India combines unitary features and federal features. It is better to regard India as quasi-federal.

2. Rapid Changes

Very rapid changes take place in this age in which scientists envisage inter-planetary travel. In 1969 American astronauts landed on the moon. Political situations change rapidly, and it is almost impossible to apply the same foot-ruler of classification. While in ancient times thinkers like Plato and Aristotle used to speak of political cycles according to which governments change or degenerate in a particular pattern, the same cannot be said about modern times. It is absurd to says today that monarchy degenerates into tyranny, and aristocracy decays to become oligarchy and so on. R.H. Soltau observes in *An Introduction to Politics* (1969: 113): "We must . . . not be deceived by the outward forms of a particular state; the old classifications of monarchy, aristocracy and democracy have become practically meaningless, for they give no clue to the real purposes of the state."

3. Forecasting Changes Difficult

Governments do not behave in a particular way or change their forms according to a set principle. In modern times, many factors are at work in various states, and particular political effects cannot be precisely forecast. Government cannot be dealt with in the same way as substances are handled by the chemist. That is why modern thinkers cannot evolve particular laws or principles pertaining to succession of governmental forms.

4. Emergence of New Factors

In modern times, particularly in the nineteenth century, in which political and economic forces emerged and grew rapidly, the problem of classification of governments has become more complex. Nationalism, liberalism and democracy are powerful political forces of the modern times. According to the basis of liberal ideas or their absence governments may be regarded as democratic or totalitarian. With the rise of industrial capitalism and its antithesis socialism, economic factors also play an important part in shaping the form of government. The economic factor is so important that MacIver makes it a separate basis of classification, and calls governments primitive, feudal, capitalist or socialist. The communists desire to speak of two types of governments only, that is, communist and capitalist.

6. Solution to the Problem of Classification

SINGLE-BASIS CLASSIFICATION IMPOSSIBLE

The problem cannot be solved by having one basis of classification, for, as it has been already noted, the complex nature of modern governments defies a single-basis classification. The only way out is to study modern authors like Marriott, Leacock, MacIver, Bryce, Jenks and Strong, and classify governments according to the following bases :

(1) the sphere of the state;

(2) the nature of the state;

(3) the nature of the constitution; and

(4) the nature of (a) the executive, (b) the legislature, (c) the judiciary, and (d) the electorate.

C.F. Sronge points out in *Modern Political Constitutions* (1958: 61): "Our classification does not pretend to be exhaustive, because much of subject-matter of comparative constitutional politics defies classification. But it does adequately cover sufficient ground."

The following tables give classification of governments on various basis:

1. Sphere of the State

Governments

With liberal ideas	With totalitarian ideas
Examples: England, France, the U.S.A. and India.	Examples: Nazi Germany, Fascist Italy, Soviet Russia and Communist China.

2. Nature of the State

Governments

- Unitary type
  Examples: England and France.
- Federal type
  Examples: the U.S.A., Canada, Australia and India

3. Nature of the Constitution

Governments

- With Flexible Constitution
  Example: England
- With Rigid Constitution
  Examples: the U.S.A. and France

4. Nature of the Organs of Government and the Electorate

(a) Nature of the Executive

Governments

- Parliamentary or Responsible
  Examples: England, France and India
- Non-Parliamentary
  Example: the U.S.A.

(b) Nature of the Legislature

Governments

- With Unicameral Legislature
  Examples: Some states like Kerala and Gujarat in India, State of Nebraska in the U.S.A., State of Queensland in Australia.
- With Bi-cameral Legislature
  Examples: the U.S.A., England, France and India

(c) Nature of the Judiciary

Governments

- With Rule of Law
  Examples: England and India
- With Administrative Law
  Example: France

(d) Nature of the Electorate
Governments

With Adult Suffrage Examples: England, France and India	With Limited Suffrage Example: England in 19th Century and British India.

Pluralist and Monolithic Regimes

Maurice Duverger classifies regimes into Pluralist (as in Britain, France and the U.S.A.) and Monolithic (as in the U.S.S.R. and Communist China).

Classification of Political Systems

Alan R. Ball while speaking of classifying political systems rather than types of government points out in *Modern Politics and Government* (1971: 12): "David Easton published *The Political System* in 1953 claiming that he was attempting to construct a theory to embrace all the social sciences.... He defines the political system as "that system of interactions in any society through which binding or authoritative allocations are made. Authoritative allocations may be roughly translated as policy-making." There are in this political system inputs and outputs. Inputs are the demands and supports from the various environments, and these are converted into outputs *i.e.* authoritative decisions." It may be mentioned here that David Easton uses the term Political System instead of state in discussing the scope and methodology of political science.

Political systems can be brought under the following three categories:

1. Liberal Democratic Systems

In such systems, political parties function freely and openly. Elections are free and are based on liberal franchise. The judiciary is independent. People enjoy civil liberties, and the mass media like newspapers, radios and television are not government monopolies. The U.S.A., Britain, France, West Germany, Sweden, Canada and Australia have liberal democratic systems.

2. Totalitarian Systems

In a totalitarian system there is only one powerful political party. All aspects of individual's life are brought under government control. All political activity shall remain subordinate to one elaborate ideology of those in power. The mass media like newspapers are regulated and controlled. The judiciary is committed and cannot function independently. Mussolini's Italy, Hitlerite Germany, Soviet Russia and Communist China have totalitarian systems.

3. Autocratic Systems

In an autocratic system, people are subjected to force and coercion without being compelled to follow any dominant political ideology like Nazism or Communism. Political parties cannot function freely. Periodical elections based on adult franchise or wide franchise are not held. People do not enjoy civil liberties as in a liberal democratic system Political power is vested in a traditional political elite or a modern elite or the army. This group monopolising power controls the mass media and the judiciary. Saudi Arabia, Egypt, Ethiopia, Nigeria, Algeria and Nepal and among the countries having autocratic systems.

REFERENCES

Ball, Alan R., *Modern Politics and Government*, 1971, Macmillan.

Barker, Ernest (Tr. and ed.), *The Politics of Aristotle*, 1946, Oxford.

Dahl, Robert A., *Modern Political Analysis*, 1963, Prentice Hall, New Jersy.

Easton, David, *The Political System*, 1959, Alfred Knopf, New York.

Eckstein and Apter, *Comparative Politics*, 1963, Free Press of Glencoe, London.

Garner, J.W., *Political Science and Government*, 1955.

Gettel, R.G., *Political Science*, 1956.

Leacock, Stephen, *Elements of Political Science*, 1938.

MacIver, *The Web of Government*, 1959.

McIlwain, *The Growth of Political Thought in the West*, 1932, London.

Soltau, R.H., *Introduction to Politics*, 1959, Longmans, Green & Co.

Stewart, M., *Modern Forms of Government*, 1960.

Strong, C.F., *Modern Political Constitutions*, 1958.

Weldon, T.D., *The Vocabulary of Politics*, 1953, Penguin Books, London.

Willoughby, W.F., *The Nature of the State*.

4

Monarchy and Aristocracy

1. MONARCHY

Meaning of Monarchy

Supreme Power in Hereditary King

Monarchy is a form of government in which supreme power is vested in the hands of a king. The king is the source of all authority, and all the organs of government and the officers therein function under the orders of the king and carry out his will. All laws in the state are his commands. The king is the maker of law. He enforces it and interprets it. Lawmaking, law enforcing and law-interpreting are functions performed by persons working under the king's orders. Aristotle says that monarchy is a normal form or government in which supreme power is located in one person, who rules for promoting the welfare and happiness of people. It is the oldest form of government which emerged almost everywhere in the world. R.G. Gettell says on page 195 in *Political Science*: "While monarchy is generally considered as a form of government in which the head of the state derives his office through hereditary succession, any government in which supreme and final authority is in the hands of single person is a monarchy, whether his office is secured by usurpation, by election or by hereditary succession." Alan R. Ball links monarchy with basic laws. "Monarchy is a system of government in which power, although in the in the hands of single person, is regulated by fundamental laws and the powers of other groups in society." (See *Modern Politics and Government*, 1921, p. 40.)

Universal Form of Government

Monarchy is the oldest form of government. Hundreds of examples of monarchy all over world can be given, as it was found everywhere in the ancient, medieval and early modern world. Even now it survives in Britain, Japan, Arab countries and possibly in some other parts of the world.

2. Fortunes of Monarchy

Setback in Modern Times

Monarchy had a serious setback in modern times with the rise of nationalism, liberalism and democracy. However, absolute monarchs in many countries (including the Czars of Russia, the Ottoman Emperors and the Hohenzollerns of Prussia) continued till the First world War (1914-18). Few states in the world have monarchs at present. Among the important states today, England and Japan have monarchy. In these countries, too, monarchy survived, as it was brought under legislative control. The British monarchy is strictly limited or constitutional. The English people have tolerated the continuation of monarchy but strictly within the framework of parliamentary or responsible system of government in which the monarch does not have a will of his own. The cabinet in England exercises *de facto* power, though the government is in the name of His or Her Majesty. France, Germany, the USA, the USSR, India, China, the Latin American countries and many other states do not have monarchy; they are all republics.

We may briefly review here the factors which were favourable and unfavourable to monarchy.

Favourable Factors

For a long time several factors were favourable to monarchy. These were the following :

(1) Almost everywhere in the world, obedience to the authority of the king was habitual, as religious and other factors prompted the people to submit to monarchical government.

(2) Monarchy provided the most stable type of government at a time when people were desperately in need of peace and security.

(3) In Europe under feudalism, people suffered much at the hands of the nobles, and felt that kings with all their drawbacks were far better than barons.

(4) The record of some great kings in the different parts of the world and the golden age ushered in by monarchs in their respective countries were highly in favour of monarchy.

Unfovourable Factors

Certain factors were unfavourable to monarchy. There were the following:

(1) The misuse of power by many power-drunk and oppressive monarchs in modern times utterly discredited monarchy. Monarchy lost all the sympathy and support, which were originally in their favour.

(2) With the end of the age of faith and with the dawn of the age of reason, climate in Europe became very uncongenial for the continuation of monarchy. Many of the monarchies became stay in Europe.

(3) The rise of the spirit of nationalism, liberalism and democracy in the nineteenth century gave a further setback to monarchy in Europe. The new spirit spread in the Afro-Asian countries in the next century.

(4) Revolutions like the American (1775-83), the French (1789) and the Latin American (1800-25) became fatal to monarchy. In the later modern times, the spirit or republicanism triumphed all over the world, and monarchy lost its hold almost everywhere. Big countries chose the republican system of government, and their example was followed by other countries too.

(5) In the 20th century, nationalism and democracy spread in the Afro-Asian countries, where monarchies were swept aside. In India with the end of British imperialism and the.abolition of princely rule, the death knell of monarchy was sounded.

3. Kinds of Monarchy

Monarchy can be classified in two ways : (1) Absolute and

Limited; and (2) Elective and Hereditary.

1. Absolute and Limited

In an absolute or despite monarchy, supreme power is exercised according to the will of the monarch, who is not responsible to any one. Louis XIV (1643-1715) who was a model to the absolute monarchs of Europe exclaimed: "I am the state and laws of the state are in my breast." An absolute monarch exercises real power without any hindrance or restraint. He can do whatever he likes, good or evil, without being questioned by any one. People are helpless, if the governs cruelly and capriciously, as they have no means of controlling him.

Some absolute monarchies have a theocratic colour. The king exercises political and religious power. The ancient Pharaohs of Egypt and the priest kings of ancient Sumeria enjoyed unlimited political and religious authority. Many of the kings all over the world ruled according to the principle or Divine Right of Kings. They regarded themselves as agents of God and were not answerable to any human being.

A constitutional or limited monarch cannot govern arbitrarily according to his whims and fancies. He is bound by constitutional principles and conventions and is directly answerable to the legislature and indirectly to the people. While Louis XIV of France could rule despotically, Queen Elizabeth II of England today has no political will of her own. She exercises only nominal power and real power is exercised by the Council of Ministers with the Prime Minister as head.

Monarchies, which continue today in Europe, are all limited or constitutional. Similarly most of the surviving monarchies in other parts of the world are limited. J.W. Garner says on page 280 in *Political Science and Government* (1959): "What is usually described as limited monarchy is one in which the power of the monarchy is restricted by prescriptions of a written constitution or by certain unwritten fundamental constitutional principles, such as the British monarchy." R.N. Gilchrist says that there is hardly any difference between a limited monarchy and a republic. "Limited monarchy is thus a constitutional type of government. . . . The only difference between the limited monarchy and a republic is that in a republic the chief executive is selected, whereas in monarchy the chief executive is hereditary."

2. Elective and Hereditary

In the case of elective monarchy, succession is governed by election, whereas in the case of hereditary monarchy, succession is governed by hereditary principle. Monarchy is hereditary in England. In early Rome monarchs were elected; so also were monarchs in Poland. In ancient India too there were elective monarchies. Generally monarchies are hereditary. Monarchy is governed by the principle of primogeniture (succession by the first born) or succession by the eldest male, or some other law of succession. Generally, the eldest son succeeds a king as laid down by the constitution or law. Gradually elective monarchies yielded place to hereditary monarchies. MacIver's observation on monarchy and dictatorship is worth-noting. "Hereditary monarchy is very different from dictatorship in structure and *limited monarchy* belongs in the area of democracy, whereas absolute monarchy is at the opposite pole." (See *The Web of Government*-1959, p. 149.) Monarchy should not be mixed up with dictatorship, because by no stretch of imagination the dictatorship or Hitler or Mussolini can be put on a par with the monarchy of Akbar the great or Queen Elizabeth II.

4. Merits and Defects of Monarchy

We may make a brief evaluation of monarchy.

Merits

History gives several examples of eminent writers singing the praise of absolute monarchy. Though it is true that these writers indulged in excessive flattery, it is incorrect to suppose that monarchy did no good to the people. Monarchy did render valuable service and has distinct merits of its own.

Monarchy may claim the following advantages:

1. *Acts Promptly.* Monarchy has unity of command, singleness of purpose and simplicity of organization. Quick decisions can be takin, and in times of ;war or emergency great secrecy can be maintained. Laws can be enforced easily. Merit in wise and capable men can be easily recognised by the monarch, and they can be put in authority. Inefficient, dishonest and other undesirable incumbents can be speedily eliminated from the administration.

2. *Benevolent.* A country can reap great benefits if it is governed by a capable and benevolent monarch. Kings like Ashoka and Akbar, Charlemagne and Harun Al Raschid ruled the people of their respective empires efficiently and well.

3. *Good for Primitive Societies.* Absolute monarchy is the ideal form of government of primitive societies. Even in the case of advanced societies, there have been cases, when monarchs acquitted themselves creditably. Even Rousseau, the champion of popular sovereignty, uttered a word; of praise for monarchy. J.W. Garner says: "Rousseau went on to compare a skilful monarch governing his people throughout a vast state to and engineer, seated tranquilly on the shore of a sea and setting in motion without difficulty, a huge vessel upon its water." (See *Political Science and Government*-1955, p. 340.) R.G. Gettell also refers to the advantages of monarchy. "Monarchy was well suited to the needs of early states, when it was necessary to impress discipline and habits of obedience on uncivilised people and when political consciousness and the ability to take part in government were not yet developed." (See *Political Science* -1956, p. 196.)

Defects

The following are the main drawbacks of monarchy:

1. *Inefficiency.* The world has seen many weak and inefficient monarchs, who presided over chaotic conditions. Capable monarchs are few and far between. Perhaps for one Akbar, there may be hundreds of inefficient, unenlightened or oppressive monarchs.

2. *Curse to People.* An absolute or oppressive monarch devoid of wisdom, and understanding can be a curse to the people, who in their, misery may not be able to do anything against the king. Unbridled power of a monarch can he a continuous nightmare to the helpless people. There is no limit to which foolish and selfish kings cannot go in misgoverning.

3. *Evil of Heredity.* Hereditary monarch may become an evil.

If succession is hereditary, there is the possibility of a good and enlightened king being followed by a weak stupid or oppressive monarch. J.W. Garner says on page 342 in *Political Science and Government*: "......There is always the possibility that an imbecile or a fool rather than a sage or a statesman may succeed to the throne and be charged with governing and determining the destinies of millions of people." Stephen Leacock says that "a hereditary ruler seems on the face of things as absurd as the hereditary mathematician or hereditary poet-laureate."

4. *No place for Worthy Men.* In an absolute monarchy, there may not be any scope for worthy men, as appointments may be made according to the whims and fancies of the absolute ruler. Sycophants and flatterers thrive in courts of despotic kings, while honest and worthy persons may find it difficult to get appointments, and even if they to get them, they will find the court atmosphere quite uncongenial.

2. ARISTOCRACY

1. Meaning of Aristocracy

Rule of Elite

Aristocracy is a form of government in which the final or ultimate authority is vested not in the hands of the king or of the people, but in the hands of a group of nobles, who rules by virtue or their birth, wealth and experience. It is a form of government in which political power is exercised by the elite. Elitism may be based on birth, wealth or competence. The Greeks regarded aristocracy as the government by the best. In Greek *aristos* means the best and *kratos* means power. Greek thinkers regarded aristocracy as government *par excellence* or government by the best citizens as it was based on virtue, intellectual power and ability. Aristocrats were entitled to rule by superior intellectual qualities, wisdom, administrative ability, experience and wealth. All power is monopolised by the rich, and the poor are completely excluded. R.G. Gettell says on gage 197 in *Political Science* (1956): "Aristocratic government places political power in a comparatively small part of the population of the state. This class may be based on birth, wealth, age, military power. Priestly power, education, or a combination of these and similar distinctions."

Aristocracy all Over the World

In the various parts of the world aristocracy rose, but it was never so widespread as monarchy. In Greeks city-states like Athens one of the forms of government was aristocracy. In Rome, with the abolition of monarchy power fell into the hands of Patricians (Roman nobles). The ancient Roman Republic was not democratic but aristocratic. For some time, at least, all power was vested in the hands of Particians. In many countries aristocrats enjoy power behind the throne. In fact monarchy depended much on aristocrats, who were the bulwarks of the king's power. For instance, aristocrats were supporting pillars of the despotic monarchy of Louis XIV of France. In modern times all over the world, the voice of the aristocrats has been predominant. In England even after Parliament came to the forefront, all power was in the hands of landed aristocracy, and with the outbreak of the Industrials Revolution, power was monopolised by the industrial magnates. In certain states, aristocracy, landed or industrial, actually governs under the cloak of democracy. In all modern democracies, power that really counts is in the hands of the rich.

2. Kinds of Aristocracy

Birth, Wealth and Culture

Most of the writers do not try to classify aristocracies, but some writers have spoken of different kinds. Rousseau speaks of natural, elective and hereditary aristocrats. J.W. Garner mentions "aristocracies of birth or birth or family; aristrocracies of wealth; aristocracies of culture and education; aristocracies of elder statesmen; military and even priestly aristocracies; natural and artificial aristocracies."

3. Decline of Aristocracy

Attacks from Democracy and Socialism

There was a time when aristocrats wielded great power almost all over the world. As the aristocrats were linked with those of monarchy, the decline of monarchy also led to the decline of aristocracy. In modern tomes, the forces of socialism and dem ocracy have been harmful to the interests of the blue-blooded people. In the Age of Revolutions in Europe (1750-1850) along with monarchy, aristocracy also got rude shocks. With the onward march of democracy, and with the triumph of the principles of liberty and equality, aristocrats lost the privileges which they once enjoyed and jealously guarded.

Aristocracy as a form of government in the technical sense is almost extinct now, but big business talks loudly even in a democratic set-up.

4. Merits and Defects of Aristocracy

We may briefly discuss the merits and drawbacks of aristocracy.

Merits

As a form of government, aristocracy can claim the following merits:

1. *Emphasis on Quality.* Aristocracy lays emphasis on quality rather than quantity; it recognises the principle that all pe ple in society are not competent to govern. Only a few people are capable of governing by virtue of their birth, family background, wealth and experience. Thus only men with quality or those capable of doing full justice to the task of governing should be allowed to exercise power. The record of several aristocracies in the world bears ample evidence to the value of quality.
2. *Curbs Passions.* Owing to their conservative outlook and desire to wait, watch and examine, aristocrats are in a position to curb unreasonable or passionate tendencies in a state. The moderation exercised by aristocrats on government is a stabilising influence in the state.
3. *Stability.* Aristocrats have been responsible to give a good measure of strength, efficiency and stability to governments all over the world by upholding customs and traditions.

Demerits

Aristocracy suffers from the following drawbacks:

1. *Wealth not Synonymous with Wisdom and Goodness.* Aristocrats may boast of their birth, wealth and experience; but not in all cases these have value from thee point of view of the public. A wise aristocrat's son need not necessarily be wise; yet by virtue of his birth he wields authority to the detriment of the people. Similarly, the qualification of wealth also can be called for scrutiny. Wealth can never be synonymous with wisdom or goodness, and it is dangerous to give power to the people merely because they are born in aristocratic families. The experience of aristocrats may not suit the times, and actually it may be synonymous with reaction.
2. *Conservative and Reactionary.* Aristocrats have generally sympathy for their own rank and status, and have little sympathy for the common man. This explains why aristocrats who are selfish are against any radical changes and refuse to move with the times.
3. *Extravagant and Wasteful.* Aristocracy is inevitably linked with pomp and splendour to maintain which public money may be extravagantly spent or wasted.
4. *Exclusion of Ordinary People.* Aristocracy is based on the power of the nobles, and ordinary people are excluded from sharing power. The interests of the poor are likely to be neglected. Moreover, the ordinary people have absolutely no scope to have political training.
5. *Want of Integrity.* It is also not correct to say that aristocracy and good character go together. Governments run by them are characterised by inefficiency and corruption.
6. *Against Democracy.* Aristocracy stands for a privileges few and are contrary to liberty and equality, the basic principle of democracy. Aristocracy is of little values in modern times in which new values have been evolved. The values of aristocracy are antagonistic to those of democracy. Aristocracy tries to uphold distinctions between one class and another, whereas democracy wants to do away with invidious political, social. Economic and other distinctions.
7. *Rigidity.* Aristocracy which is rigid is unsuitable to , meet the needs of a changing society. A government, which

blindly respects traditions and customs in the name of stability, remains rigid, and it can hardly be expected to show the necessary dynamism to serve the interests of the people.

REFERENCES

Ball, Allan, R., *Modern Politics and Government*-1971, Macmillan.

Garner, J.W., *Political Science and Government*-1955, The World Press, Calcutta.

Gettell, R.G., *Political Science*-1956, The World Press, Calcutta.

MacIver, *The Web of government*, 1959.

Sabine, S. H., *A History of Political Theory*-1957, George Harrap & Co., London.

5

Democracy and its Rivals

1. DEFINITION AND MEANING OF DEMOCRACY

Multi-headed Concept

We live in an age in which democracy enchants people. It is politically fashionable to speak of it and sing about its charms. The term 'democracy' is known to all; but it is difficult to define democracy precisely and satisfactorily in a sentence or two. Here is a term, which is apparently easy to understand but actually very difficult to be defined and explained clearly and comprehensively. Freeman observes that "it is commonly very hard to make out what modern writers mean by democracy." Though we are familiar with the term 'democracy', we cannot present all the implications of democracy in a single sentence definition. Democracy is a multi-headed concept and a compound of several elements *viz.* political ideas, economic and social forces, ethical principles, a form of government and a way of life.

Different Interpretations.

Much has been written on democracy; perhaps few subjects in political science have commanded the attention of such a large number of thinkers as democracy. Yet, it is not easy to have a clear image of democracy, for democracy does not connote the same ideas to all, and it has been interpreted differently by different writers. It stands for many ideas and principles, and has various facets. Herman Finer says on page 67 in *Theory and Practice of Modern Government* (1960): "Democracy has come to mean so many different things; some very hostile to each other that it needs careful analysis if misunderstanding and idle controversies are to be avoided, and, if the possible and quite legitimate differences of connotation and its varied institutional arrangements are to be revealed," C. D. Burns says on page 9 in *Democracy* (1935): "Democracy is a word with many meanings and some emotional, colour. It is not an algebraical symbol but a flag or the call of a trumpet for some; and for others an obsolete mythology, which has undesirable connections with capitalism and imperialism."

All things to all Men

E. M. Burns says on page 9 in *ideas in Conflict* (1960): "Few words have been more loosely and variously defined than democracy. It has almost literally meant all things to all men," The confusion is increased, because not only Western democracies, but even communist countries like the USSR and Communist China speak of democracy. Communists argue that perfect democracy is found only in communist states, while western countries have democracy in which there is exploitation by capitalists and imperialists. It is interesting to note that Ayub Khan (1958-68) introduced "basic" or "controlled" democracy in Pakistan, while Sukarno (1945-66) gave "guided' democracy to Indonesia. Here it has to be noted that Western democracy based on liberal ideas and communist "democracy" are diametrically opposed to each other.

Several Ideas and Principles

The concept of democracy has been expanded steadily in recent times. What was originally a political principle has been enlarged to include social, economic and political ideas. Democracy embodies the following ideas and principles:

1. Principles of Liberty

Democratic government is understood in the Western countries aims at securing a maximum of liberty for its citizens. The laws or rules of government, which restrict freedom should be self-imposed, that is, they should be in accordance with the will or consent of the people. Self-direction implying maximum of liberty is the basic principle of democracy. This stands against the imposition of decisions made by others.

2. Principle of Equality

The principle of equality goes hand in hand with the principle of liberty under a democratic government. Democracy, it is claimed, stands for an egalitarian society in which the individual has equal status with others. W. F. Willoughby says on page 321 in *The Government of Modern States*: "The word democracy is unfortunately used in popular discussion, and indeed in much political literature, in two different senses: as designating a society or community in which class distinctions are absent or relatively unimportant, and as designating a distinct form of government." Here the emphasis is on the doctrine of equality. In the words of Sir John Seeley, democracy is "a government in which everyone has a share." A democratic government gives opportunities to all to take part in political matters. Every citizen has the right to vote and right to stand for election. The word 'democracy' was first used in ancient Greece in the *History* by Herodotus in connection with the concept of *isonomia* (equality before the law).

3. Government of the People

The term democracy which is derived from the Greek words *demos* (people) and *kratos* (government) means power or government of the people. Does this mean that democracy is government run by all the people or by a few people only? In the ancient Greek city state of Athems all citizens took an active part in the governance of the citizens. Hence it was direct democracy. Direct democracy is not possible in the modern nation-states having a large territory and population. All the people in a modern democratic state do not take an active part in the affairs of the government. The people elect their representatives, who are supposed to think, speak and act on behalf of the people. Hence in modern times, there is indirect or representative democracy, which means government by elected representatives. In his Gettysburg speech in the USA, President Abraham Lincoln defined democracy as government of the people, by the people and for the people. Power is vested in the people, and hence it is government by the people. Government is run by the people through their elected representatives. Government is also run for promoting the welfare and happiness of the people. A democratic government as conceived by Lincoln is not something which is separate from the people. The government, which is of the people, is not alien to them. Government exists for representatives of the people and are ultimately responsible to the people. Ministers are the servants of the people and not their masters. John Stuart Mill says that democracy is a form of government in which "the whole people, or some numerous portion of them, exercise the governing power through deputies periodically elected by themselves." Here the emphasis is on the political aspect of democracy. In the words of Mazzini, government of the people stands through "the progress of all through all under the leading of the best and the wisest."

4. Rule of the Majority

Democracy stands for a rule of the majority with adequate safeguards to the minorities. Every state has political parties. One of them comes to power by capturing a majority of seats in the legislature. This means democracy is a system of government based on the principle of majority rule. It is believed that what the majority says has greater validity than what the minority says. Moreover, taking a realistic point of view, the majority is stronger than the minority. These are two basic reasons justifying majority rule. In a democratic constitution, linguistic, racial, religious and cultural minorities are guaranteed basic rights.

5. Freedom Rights, Abundance and Public Welfare

Merriam underlines the importance of people's welfare in explaining democracy. He enthusiastically, spells out the ideals and benefits of democracy to the people in modern times. E. M. Burns says on page 23 in *Ideas in Conflict* (1960): "In defending democracy Merriam wrote with evangelical zeal. Transformed in accordance with modern intellectual discoveries the ideal the maintained, world have virtually limitless possibilities for leading mankind into Promised Land of Freedom and Abundance. Under the aegis of democracy, science would have the power to lift the burdens of war, famine, poverty and disease from the brows of man." R. M. MacIver says: "Democracy is not a way of governing whether by majority or otherwise, but primarily a way of determining who shall govern and broadly, to what ends."

F.D Roosevelt enlarges the ideas of democracy in upholding the concept of social welfare. To him, democracy "was not a mere matter of universal suffrage and unhampered expression of the popular will. It must be a positive and constructive force in the daily lives of the people, and provides not merely for political but economic needs. If men were forced to choose between liberty and bread, he asserted they will choose bread." (See E. M. Burns, *Ideas in Conflict*—1960, p. 20.) E. M. Burns observes: "The function of interpreting democracy during the World War II was performed by Roosevelt's Vice-President, Henry A. Wallace. Wallace conceived of democracy partly in terms of social welfare and partly as a defence of the dignity and rights of the individual. (See Ibid., p. 21.) The people of the United States of America have not only spoken eloquently on the great ideals and principles of democracy, but have also showed it as a positive and constructive force. Americans reaped a rich harvest of democracy a form of government and a way of life in terms of principles and material benefits. However, it is true that few democratic governments in the world have come up to the description given by Lincoln and Roosevelt, and in several countries democracy exists in theory on paper only.

6. Government by Consent of Public Criticism

Democracy means government by discussion. Sir Stafford Cripps lays emphasis on freedom of expression. He says: "Democracy is a system of government in which every adult citizen is equally free to express his views and desires upon all subjects in whatever may he wishes and to influence the majority of his fellow citizens to decide according to those views and to influence those desires." In a democracy there is free discussion instead of intellectual slavery.

Democracy is sometimes regarded as government by consent or by public criticism. It is said no man has the right to be governed except by his own consent. By consent we mean not consent to every law but consent to persons who make the law. Every person should have the right to take part in electing legislatures. In a democracy one man or a group of men cannot rule as they please without the consent of the people. Governmental machinery shall move according to the wishes of the people and for meeting the requirements of the people. Government has to be responsive to public opinion, and in the light of genuine and responsible public criticism, it may have to change its course for the benefit of the people. An unpopular and inefficient government, which has lost the confidence of the people is likely to be overthrown by the pressure of public criticism and through the ballot box. A. D. Lindsay observes on page 134 in *The Modern Democratic State*

(1961): "Modern democracy stands or falls with the right of discussion and with the existence of a recognised opposition. That implies that the sincere expression of differences is essential to political wisdom."

Democracy shows hospitality to all kinds of ideas, and it is possible in a democratic state for several parties to function freely. In authoritarian and totalitarian states people have to believe in ideas "manufacture" by those in power.

7. Democracy, Form of Government and Way of Life

Democracy is not only a form of government but also a way of life. Popular sovereignty and freedom to live as one pleases go together. Under a democratic government, the dignity of the human personality is fully recognised. Every individual is free to live in his own way, think freely as he likes, express his opinion freely, move about freely, enjoy the company of people he likes and become a member of associations and parties of his choice. In a democratic country, the individual enjoys liberty and equality. He is given certain minimum rights called the fundamental rights, on which nobody can encroach. He can follow a religion of his choice, speak the language of his choice and have a culture to which he is accustomed. Thus, not only in the political sphere, but in other fields too the individual enjoys complete freedom. In this connection we may refer to C. C. Maxey's definition of democracy on page 690 in *Political Philosophies* (1936) : "Democracy as reinterpreted in the twentieth century is thus seen to be more than a political formula, more than a system of government, more than a social order. It is a search for a way of life in which voluntary free intelligence and activity of man can be harmonized and co-ordinated with the least possible coercion, and it is the belief that such a way of life is the best way for all mankind, the way most in keeping with the nature of man and the nature of the universe." Dewey emphatically says that democracy is much more than a form of government. He observes that "to say that democracy is only a form of government is like saying that home is more or less geometrical arrangement of bricks and mortar, or that church is a building with pews, pulpit and spire."

8. Against Imperialism and War

Democracy goes beyond the frontiers of democratic country

to enter the realm of international affairs. In the international sphere, democracy stands for the principle of self-determination and for the regulation of inter-state relations on the basis of equality, justice and reason. Democracy is against aggressive nationalism, imperialism and war.

In an international society or organisation of states like the UNO, certain democratic procedures are followed, and these are accepted by all democratic states. All sovereign states regardless of their size and power are treated on the basis of equality. It is significant to note here that the principle of equality is followed in the UN General Assembly, but not in the Security Council.

9. Communist View on Democratic State

Communists speak in terms of a democratic state as a against a democratic government. To them a democratic state is a socialist state with the dictatorship of the proletariat; such a states is free from exploration. Giovanni Sartori says on page 417 in *Democratic Theory* (1962); "Marx declared and thought himself a democrat. He used the name democracy and ended by stating clearly enough what he meant by it. In the *Communist Manifesto* (1848), Marx had limited himself to asserting that it was the task of the proletariat as a dominating class to arrive victoriously at democracy—a democracy referred to as an association in which the free development of each is the condition for the free development of all"

In Soviet Russia, Lenin, Stalin and others ruled ruthlessly with an iron hand. In Communist China, Mao Tse-tung and others claimed that they succeeded in establishing New Democracy. Whatever may be the professions of communists, the actual working of communist governments shows that communism is totally anti-democratic. While democracy stands for peaceful and persuasive methods, communism advocates the use of violence to pull down the capitalist structure of society.

Conclusion about Basic Democratic Principles

With reference to the foregoing paragraphs, we may draw the following basic principles by way of conclusion on the meaning of democracy:

(1) Democracy allows all individuals the right to speak, criticize and disagree with each other.

(2) It allows plurality of ideas and ideologies, and stands firmly for the principle of tolerance.

(3) It is wedded to the methods of persuasion and peace both in the internal and international spheres.

(4) It is clearly opposed to coercive methods, even if they are for the social good. A government cannot be called democratic, if it uses illegitimate coercion in the name of social welfare.

(5) It upholds the dignity of the human personality and gives various kinds of rights to the individual.

(6) It is built on the foundations of liberty and equality.

(7) It is a form of government in which sovereignty is vested in the people.

(8) In actual practice, democracy means the rule by the majority with full safeguards for the rights of racial, linguistic, religious, cultural and other minorities.

(9) It is government by the representatives of the people; and these are elected by adults, who are free to vote as they please without being coerced or pressurised by any one. Voting is not open, but secret.

(10) A democratic government functions strictly according to the principles of a constitution (whether written or unwritten) which has been accepted by the people.

(11) A democratic government gives adequate opportunities to all, and makes every one feel that his existence is recognized and that full justice is being done to him.

(12) It is government aiming at the welfare of all.

(13) Democracy provides for a peaceful change in government according to constitutional principles, and it is against any change by violent or revolutionary means.

(14) Democracy has various aspects—political, social and economic. Politically it is people's government. Socially it stands for a way of life. Economically it stands for social welfare and freedom from exploitation.

Presumptions in a Democratic State

Philosophically speaking, democratic theory is based on

certain presumptions.

(1) The individual is rational. Every person has the capacity to think about the problems of the community and is capable of taking his own decisions.

(2) The human being is fallible, and is likely to commit mistakes.

(3) Society is democratic, and invidious social distinctions of high and low are absent. Social relations are democratised.

(4) There is no conflict between the individual good and the good of the community.

(5) The use of physical force or violence in solving problems is entirely ruled out.

2. ORIGIN AND GROWTH OF DEMOCRACY

In Ancient Greece and Rome

W. F. Willoughby says on page 74 in the *Government of Modern States* (1936): "The origin of this doctrine (of popular sovereignty) is to be found in the early Greek and Roman republics. In a very true sense their governments may be said to have rested on this principle." Sartori says on page 250 in *Democratic Theory* (1962): "The term 'democracy' was coined twenty-five hundred years ago. It first appeared in Herodotus's *History* in connection with the notion of *isonoima*, equality before the law. From than on even though it was eclipsed for a very long interval, it has remained part of the political vocabulary." Democracy did not prevail on a vast scale in the ancient times. In ancient Greece it was found only in city states, and here too it was restricted to citizens only. (Women and slaves were not citizens and had no share in democracy.) Aristotle regarded democracy as a perverted form of polity. It was to him mob rule with its intolerable confusion. In the Roman empire, the will of the people in the field of actual governance, though in theory the emperors were elected by the people, who were represented by him.

In Ancient India

In ancient India, some states followed the principle of *swarajva*; but by and large democracies had no scope for survival, particularly when powerful kings or emperors rose. Except perhaps with a few small exceptions, democracy could not flourish on a large scale in ancient Indian States.

In Medieval Age

With the fall of Rome and the coming of the dark age, democracy had no scope at all in Europe. In the feudal structure of the medieval period in Europe, the barons were very powerful, and people were powerless. In the early modern times in Europe in spite of the movements like the Renaissance, democracy could not rise, as conditions were favorable to absolute monarchy.

In Modern Times

The misuse of power by the absolute monarchs in European countries brought about a strong reaction against tyrannical and oppressive rulers. The new ideas given by philosophers like Voltaire and Rousseau weakened the hold of monarchs over their subjects. In England, the authority of the Stuart kings, who were ruling by the theory of Divine Right, was challenged by Parliament. As the Stuart did not change their autocratic attitude and policy. Parliament drastically reduced their power with the aim of making monarchy constitutional. Ultimately, parliamentary democracy triumphed. England showed the path of parliamentary democracy to other countries. Here democracy was not established by a single stroke by a band of revolutionaries. The British people proceeded slowly and cautiously mile after mile along the road of democracy with the help of Parliament. England set up democratic traditions, which became the envy of countries, which valued democracy as a form of government and a way of life.

British colonies in America revolted against the autocracy of England and won their independence. The United States of America provided a fertile soil for the principle of popular sovereignty and individual rights. Americans drafted a written democratic constitution, and like England chose to walk along the democratic path; but unlike England, they had a federal and republican constitution. In France, too, people abolished monarchy and set up a democratic republic.

Golden Age of Democracy

In the twentieth century, democracy seemed to have entered its golden age. In European countries democracy which moved hand in hand with nationalism became almost a passion. The leading statesmen of Britain and the USA said that World War I (1914-18) was fought to safeguard democracy and uphold the principle of self-determination. After the war, new nation states were carved out on the basis of self-determination, and in several countries democratic forms of government were established. Countries suffering under the imperialist yoke wanted to free them selves and set up democratic institutions. F. W. Coker says on page 303 in *Recent Political Thought* (1947): "Many of the transformations that arose from the upheavals of the World War seemed to strengthen the traditional faith in some sort of heroic law of democracy. Popular revolutions, peaceful or bloody, swept away—by assassination, deposition and forced abdication—a Tsar, a Sultan, three emperors and nearly a score of minor kings, grand dukes, dukes and princes." But the golden age of democracy came to an end soon, and democracy had to face the rough seas. Unfortunately the developments in the inter-war period (1919-39) were highly unfavourable to the very existence of the new democracies, and dictators, who capitalised on the misfortunes of the people could have their own way and destroy democratic institutions.

After the end of World War II many countries in Asia and Africa became independent.

In August 1947, India was granted complete independence and in 1950 she became a Sovereign Demoeratic Republic. In running democratic institutions, so far at least India has done fairly well.

In Pakistan, Ayub Khan's military dictatorship in the garb of "Controlled Democracy" lasted for ten years (1958-68). Early in 1969 Ayub was forced to step down and power fell into the hands of the army Chief Yahya Khan. Z. A. Bhutto came to power, when Yahya Khan fell in December 1971 after facing a humiliating defeat in the Indo-Pakistan War and after the emergence of independent Bangladesh. Bhutto also misused power and governed as a dictator. He was overthrown by General Zia-ul-Haq, who proved to be more ruthless as a dictator than his predecessors. In July 1977 Pakistan came under military rule. He go Bhutto executed on April 4, 1979, at Rawalpindi after the latter's conviction in a murder case.

In Indonesia, President Sukarno's dictatorship under the label of "Guided Democracy" lasted for 21 years (1945-66). During the period 1966-67, Sukarno was stripped off all his powers and was disgraced. In 1970 he died.

3. FORMS OF DEMOCRACY

As stated already, democracy has two forms: Direct and Indirect.

1. Direct Democracy

The concept of direct democracy has been defined in many ways. James Garner conceived of it as a form in which the will of the state is directly or immediately expressed through the people. (See J. S. Roucek and Others, *Introduction to Political Science*—1954 p. 205.) Direct democracy was a success in the Greek city-states, particularly Athens, which was regarded as the School of Hellas. Though the Greeks have been praised for conducting an experiment in direct democracy and making contributions in the political field, one wonders whether democracy as found in Athens was democracy in the real sense according to the modern concept. Democracy makes no distinction between one individual and another; there is equality before the law; and persons enjoy the same rights, and no individual is made to suffer from any disabilities owing to his birth, race, language, caste, creed or colour. But in the Athenian Democracy, there was the ugly institution of Slavery, which is repugnant to modern democracy. Moreover, only about 40,000 persons were citizens in a population of 280,000. The number of slaves was as large as 100,000. Women, slaves and foreigners were not citizens. In spite of these real blemishes on Athenian democracy, Western writers have praised it to the skies. Devices of direct democracy are found in some of the Cantons of Switzerland in which all laws are passed, and all important policy decisions are made in the assembly of all male citizens.

Merits. Direct democracy has certain advantages.

(1) Citizens who are highly devoted to the state take pride in participating directly in the affairs of the state.

(2) Every citizen some time or the other gets a chance to serve the state in some capacity. Such opportunities are not at the disposal of citizens in an indirect democracy.

(3) It was direct democracy that enabled citizens in Athens to have a partnership in life of virtue and happiness, and enjoy the fruits of a higher life.

Drawbacks. Direct democracy, however, suffers from, serious drawbacks.

(1) The fruits of direct democracy in Greece were enjoyed only by a few people. Aliens, women and slaves were not regarded as citizens, and they reaped no benefits of the privileges of citizenship.

(2) Liberty and equality, which are so very essential to make democracy real, were absent in ancient Greece.

(3) Direct democracy can work well only in very small states, and it can never hope to succeed in the large territorial states of the modern times.

2. Indirect or Representative Democracy

Meaning

In Britain, the USA, France, India and several other states there is indirect or representative democracy, which is of two forms: Presidential and Parliamentary. W. F. Willoughby says on page 94 in *The Government of Modern States*: "A representative government, we have seen, is that form of government, which results where a legally sovereign electorate, instead of itself attempting to act as the directing head of the machinery of government, brings into existence an organ or organs to represent and act for it in this capacity." Modern states are very huge and the population is too large and unwieldy to have direct democracy. Conditions in modern times make the introduction of direct democracy an impossibility.

Evaluation

We have already referred in the earlier pages to the great advantages of representative democracy prevailing in modern states. We may now turn to the disadvantages.

Disadvantages. The following disadvantages may be mentioned:

(1) Very few people have real interest in political affairs. Only a few enterprising and keenly interested persons study

political questions. It is only these men and women who stand for election.

(2) Most of the people have practically no interest in political activities. This is particularly true in the case of underdeveloped countries. In such countries, few people who become leaders can exercise power as they please and exploit the poverty and ignorance of the people in the name of democracy.

(3) The art of government at present is a thousand times more difficult and more complicated than what it was once upon a time. Governments now have to face many knotty problems, which require great technical skill, sagacity and calibre for being solved.

(4) It is not possible for every individual in a state to be the President or Prime Minister or Member of Parliament. Most of the people have to rest satisfied as mere electors of members of the legislature.

Direct Democratic Devices

The drawbacks in representative democracy have made states like Switzerland have a mixed type of democracy having features of direct and indirect types of democracy. Even in such countries, only direct democratic devices like the Referendum, the Initiative, the Plebiscite and the Recall have been introduced. American and Swiss people are similar with such devices. After the First World War, these were tried in Germany, Ireland, Latvia, Estonia and other countries. (See Chapter 58 for these: devices.) Direct participation of all citizens in governmental affairs is not possible today.

4. ESSENTIAL CONDITIONS FOR THE SUCCESS OF DEMOCRACY

The Best but the Most Difficult Form of Government

Democracy is regarded as the best form of government. At the same time, it is the most difficult form, and certain minimum conditions are essential for its successful working. In certain countries democracy has been a great success, while in others it is a total failure or walks like a cripple. Other forms of government do not require so many essential conditions for their successful working.

The following are the essential conditions for the success of a democratic government:

1. Urge and Thirst for Democracy

Democracy can succeed only in states, in which the vast majority of the people have a genuine urge and thirst for democracy as a form of government and a way of life, and desire to have the principles of liberty and equality. A passion for a democratic form of government creates a strong basis of democracy and enables people to overcome hurdles, however great they may be. The feeling among the people that the government in their country should function according to their own wishes and not as desired by few people at the top will prepare a good ground for democracy. In highly advanced countries like England and the USA, the people and an urge to participate activity in the affairs of government; they refused to be led by the nose, and themselves wanted to have a say in governmental matters. If a strong desire for democracy can be taken for granted, democracy can be easily successful. The desire for democracy rises from the mental habit and temperament of the people. H. V. Kamath aptly says: "It is well to remember that democracy has worked fairly successfully only in those countries—some in Western Europe, and some others in North America—where there has been a tradition of ethical liberalism, a strong middle class, widespread education, where civil liberties have been cherished and where sustained regard for political dissent exist." (*The Illustrated Weekly of India,* Sept. 10, 1961, p. 45.)

2. Eternal Vigilance and Will to Act

Democracy needs eternal vigilance and will to act. Citizens should always be active and should not remain as mere silent spectators satisfying themselves in only watching political activities. Even elected representatives are likely to misuse their power, if they neglect their duties and tyrannise over the tax-payers. If the rulers know that they will be over-thrown by an active and intelligent electorate, they will govern with a sense of duty and will ever be cautious to ensure that the electorate is happy. If citizens are eternally vigilant, persons in power will always remember what Abraham Lincoln said: "You can fool part of the people all the time, and all the people part of the time; but you cannot fool all the people all the time." A democratic form of government established in a state cannot last long, if the people are not prepared to protect it as a priceless treasure at all costs with their eternal vigilance. Democracy is not something, which can be imposed from outside on unwilling people. It is something which should be born spontaneously within the minds and hearts of the people and for which they are ready to pay an adequate price, make the necessary sacrifice and protect it from internal and external dangers. If people slumber, autocracy or dictatorship may rise; or a foreign power may commit aggression. More important than the armies, navies and air forces maintained by a state is the spirit of the people to cherish the principles of democracy and keep alive the flame of democracy.

Obedience is a virtue in a democracy, if it is rational. Citizens should obey all good laws and cooperate with rulers. But at the same time, they should be watchful and resist, if government misuses power. Citizens should not surrender their right to protest and resist. It would be dangerous to obey blindly, when bad laws are put on the statute book. Bentham's principle: "While I will obey punctually, I will censure freely" should be always remembered.

3. Conflict of Ideas, Co-operation, Tolerance, Sympathy and Understanding

Democracy can thrive only in an atmosphere of peace. People should have nothing to do with violent methods, but should settle their controversies peacefully. Democracy believes in a peaceful conflict of ideas as against violent conflicts. It can be successful, if people have sympathy for one another and try to understand one another in a spirit of tolerance. Modern democracy, which means majority rule, needs fairness on the part of the majority and tolerance on the part of the minorities. The members of the majority party in power should be just, fair and sympathetic to the minorities, which in turn should co-operate with the majority and not oppose the majority merely for the sake of opposition. A democratic country will gain much, if the majority and the minorities understand each other. H. B. Mayo says on page 219 in *An Introduction to Democratic Philosophy* (1960): "A democracy is unique in recognising the political expression of such conflicts as legitimate and in providing for their peaceful adjustment through the negotiations of politics, as an alternative to their settlement by force of fiat." People must understand that they have to solve their problems through arguments and discussion and not through violence. Corecion has no place in a democracy. Y. R. Simon says on page 194 in *Philosophy of Democratic Government* (1951): "Democracy implies, then, that every government has a duty to seek the maximum of voluntary co-operation, to explain its purposes and methods to educate the governed, to appeal indefatigably to whatever element of good will can be found in them, and never to resort to coercion unless persuasion proves impossible."

4. Public Consent and Criticism

People should realise that a democratic form of government is based on public consent and criticism. Government is under public control. If government deviates from the right path and tyrannises over the people, they should criticise it and force it to go back to the path of rectitude. People who should be public-spirited should not hesitate to expose a bad government. Countries in which people lack the necessary qualities to control the government will be incapable of having democracy, and even if the leaders prepare a democratic constitution, it will remain a dead letter. In modern democracies, political parties work on the basis of the principle of consent. C. D. Burns says on page 41 in *Democracy* (1935) : "In practice.... democracy is a form of government in which the organised public power is maintained by a tacit agreement between groups, who want to use that power for their advantage—an agreement not to fight, if each can have a turn." Political parties in the opposition should be active and vigilant. They should criticise the government whenever it goes wrong and make it aware that it is being watched all the time.

5. Intelligent, Educated and Enlightened Electorate

Democracy succeeds only where the electorate is educated and well informed and is capable of actively participating in political activities. As democracy is people's government, people should be educated and enlightened so that they are fully aware of their obligations and rights. They should have the will and ability to exercise power. An educated and well informed electorate will choose its leaders intelligently, will co-operate with the government fully, and when necessary criticise the leaders.

An intelligent and educated electorate cannot be misled by the government, which will be always compelled to feel the pulse of the people. That education is an asset to democracy has been amply borne out in advanced countries like Britain and the USA. When there is widespread literacy and education good leaders and representatives of the people emerge. Ignorance and illiteracy are the worst enemies of democracy. As Beni Prasad says on page 95 in *A. B. C. of Civics*: "Democracy is suited to a state of society in which the people want to exercise power, are capable of sinking minor differences and co-operating for the general good and have acquired knowledge and judgement enough to elect suitable representatives and to judge as to the propriety of general lines of policy."

6. Good Leadership

Good leadership is another condition essential for the smooth working of democracy. England and the USA with their far-sighted, enlightened and effective leadership could easily make a success of democracy. In backward countries, poor leadership is a great stumbling block. Good leadership should work hand in hand with an educated electorate to make democracy meaningful. Great leaders like George Washington, Abraham Lincoln, Winston Churchill, Jawaharlal Nehru and Lal Bahadur Shastri can lead democracies to success.

7. Reasonable Standard of Living

Democracy can succeed in a country, if it has a reasonable standard of living, and people by and large are free from poverty and all its evil corollaries. Economic conditions have much to do with democratic institutions. While prosperity is conducive to the growth of democracy, poverty is one of the most obstacles. Poverty keeps people uneducated, backward and timid. Poverty-stricken people are more concerned with their bread than with anything else, and democracy is a luxury to them. In economically backward countries, a few rich people at the top capture power and wield it as they like.

8. Democratic Society

Democratic politics can be successful only in a democratic society, in which there are democratic non-political associations. In the words of Wolff, "a democratic society is a society of free, equal, active and intelligent citizens, each man choosing his own way of life for himself and willing that others. Should choose theirs." It is only in a democratic society that people value equality and liberty. Unless people have the feeling of fellowship or fraternity, democracy will fail. In a country, where nonpolitical associations do not allow liberty, equality, discussion, opposition and tolerance, the democratic political machinery cannot function satisfactorily. Robert A. Dahl says that democratic society is a "social system that not only has democratic (sub) systems but also a number of other sub-systems that operate so as to contribute directly or indirectly to the strength of the democratic political processes."

5. INSTITUTIONAL REQUIREMENTS OF DEMOCRACY

Democracy needs certain institutions for expressing itself freely and effectively. The most important institutional requirements of democracy are the following :

1. A Good Written Constitution

A good written constitution is an essential institutional requirement. All organs of government in a democratic state should exercise power in accordance with the provisions of a written constitution, and there should be no scope for the exercise of arbitrary power by any individual or group of individuals. All authorities in the state will have to function within the four corners of the constitution. (Even though England does not have a written constitution, democracy works successfully, because the British people have wholesome respect for constitutional traditions, usages, conventions and customs. Side by side, the written parts of the British constitution in the form of statues uphold sound democratic principles.)

Democracy will succeed, if the constitution clearly spells out democratic principles and ensures that sovereignty is vested in the people. E. B. Schulz gives the requirements of a democratic type of government: (1) popular control of key officials; (2) a liberal suffrage; (3) willingness to adhere to the rules of the democratic process; (4) freedom of speech, of assembly, of association and safeguards against arbitrary imprisonment; and (5) adequate sources of information. (See *Essentials of Government*—1961, p.218.)

2. A Legislature with Elected Members

Another institutional requirement is a legislature with members directly elected by the people on the basis of adult franchise. The elected representatives will hold deliberations and discussions in the legislature and will safeguard the interests of the people. The legislature will reflect the opinion of the people and will make laws for the good of the people. The legislature is a basic democratic institution making a success of a democratic form of government.

3. An Accountable Executive

An executive which is accountable directly to the legislature and indirectly to the people is also necessary for the smooth functioning of democratic government. The executive should not have scope to exercise arbitrary power. There should be constitutional provision to control the executive. In Britain the executive is responsible to the legislature particularly to the House of Commons, the lower house. In the USA the President is not responsible to the legislature. He is indirectly elected by the people through an electoral college for a term of four years. The Senate, the upper house, having very wide powers exercises a real check on the President. Appointments made by the President are subject to the approval of the Senate and treaties have to the ratified by it. The Presidential executive is subjected to close scrutiny by the legislature. The legislature will not co-operate with him, if the misuses power and turns hostile to it.

4. An Independent Judiciary

A learned, impartial, fearless and independent judiciary is another institutional requirement of democracy. All cases should be settled and justice meted out impartially according to the law. The judiciary should uphold the rule of law as against arbritrary law. It should uphold the principles of liberty and equality, and give full protection to the basic rights of the individual. An unfettered judiciary is an important institutional requirement for the smooth working of democracy.

5. Political Parties

Political parties which are well organised and dedicated to democracy form another essential institutional requirement of democracy. A democratic constitution (as of India or Britain) is silent about political parties. They grow spontaneously but in an extra-constitutional manner. No democracy can function without political parties. They render numerous services and make it possible for democratic institutions to work smoothly provided they are organised and led properly along the right lines. They keep the electorate well informed, help candidates to participate in election and serve as powerful instruments of democracy.

6. An Effective Opposition

Another institutional requirement is an effective opposition party. A party, which is in power, is likely to develop dictatorial tendencies unless it is effectively opposed in the legislature. True democracy is not possible without an opposition organised by democratic leader. A strong opposition can emerge when there is a good two-party system, as an Britain. If the ruling party misses power, tyrannises over the people and acts contrary to democratic principles, the opposition party should curb it or overthrow it and forms its own government in a democratic manner. The ruling party should have the wholesome fear of the opposition. The two political parties, however, should strictly follow the rules of the political game bearing in mind national interests and democratic principles.

7. Local Self-Governing Bodies

Local self-governing bodies are of tremendous importances for developing democracy at the grass roots level. These bodies give maximum scope to the people to express themselves on democratic lines. All individuals cannot aspire to find seats in the national parliament, but many of them can aspire to find places in local self-governing bodies and serve the cause of democracy. Local bodies come into direct contact with the people at the lowest level. In fact they take democracy to the very doors of the people.

8. Free and Fearless Press

A free, fearless and unfettered press, which can vigilantly guard democracy is an important institutional requirement. The press places before the people facts and its own opinions, and when government errs, it strongly criticizes it. It informs, enlightens and educates people and enables them to understand the problems of democracy and discharge their duties and responsibility. People anxiously watch how the press reacts to government policies from time to time and those in power see that they do not come in for criticism. How a democratic government functions can be known from the press. A great democracy has a really great press, which is objective and independent.

All those institutional requirements are found in the highly advanced democracies of the West, and, therefore, democracy has a proud record in them. In several countries having democratic government, all these institutional requirements are not present; and even if they have been provided, they do not function satisfactorily.

6. MERITS OF DEMOCRACY

Superiority of Democracy

Among the various forms of government, with all its defects, democracy has been regarded as the best. Democracy upholds certain values, which put it on a plane superior to that of other forms of government. H. B. Mayo mentions the specific values of democratic systems: (1) The peaceful voluntary adjustment of disputes; (2) ensuring peaceful change in a changing society; (3) orderly succession of rulers; (4) minimum of correction (5) diversity; (6) attainment of justice; (7) promotion of science; (8) freedom etc. (*See An Introduction to Democratic Theory*—1960, pp. 218-41.)

Case for Democracy

A classical case for democracy has been prepared on certain grounds.

(1) *Precautionary.* Democracy takes into consideration the wishes and grievances of the people.

(2) *psychological.* Democracy seeks the co-operation of life in solving problems; it lays greater emphasis on co-operation than efficiency.

(3) *Educational.* Democracy provides training to the people in citizenship and government.

(4) *Moral.* Democracy is justified on moral grounds; as it relies on the individuals's initiative and development of personality.

(5) *Practical.* Democracy is practical use, as it develops the spirit of patriotism and eliminates the risk of revolution.

It is conceded that from the efficiency point of view, one can cavil at it seriously. Moreover, democracy requires several conditions for the fulfillment of its aims. It most of the requisite conditions are satisfied, democracy can have several merits.

Merits

The following are the merits of democracy.

1. *Protects Interests of All.* Democracy protects the interests of the people. A monarchy or an aristocracy may not know the grievances of the people but a democratic government which is bound to know them, will try to redress them. This is because those in power are the representatives of the people, who can know where the shoe pinches. "...the end of democratic government is to minister to the common life of society, to remove the disharmonies that trouble it . . . it (common life) can only be known by those who live it...It is their shoes that pinch and they only who can tell where they pinch. No doubt the ordinary voters has the vaguest ideas as to what legislative or administrative reform will stop the pinching of the shoes." (See . A. D. Lindsay, *The Modern Democratic State*—1951, p. 270.) Democracy is not expected to serve interests of a particular individual or a class, but to serve the interests of all.

2. *Upholds Human Dignity.* Democracy respects the dignity of the human personality. Every individual, however insignificant he may be, is given the importance due to him. Every adult is a voter, that is, one who chooses hid leaders in government. The importance of his personality is fully recognised, and he is allowed to express himself freely and act freely. The common man has a voice in the government; he can speak against the government, and can suggest ways to improve the administration.

In forms of government, which are the rivals of democracy, the individual of either ignored or his personality is suppressed. For instance, in a totalitarian dictatorship, the individual is treated as a tool of the state and the dignity of his personality is trampled under foot. E. B. Schulz says on page 222 in *Essentials of Government* (1961): "An asserted view of democracy is that each individual is regarded as an end in himself and not merely as a pawn to be manipulated for the benefit of a privileged few. The dignity of the individuals is enhanced, a high value is attached to his personal freedom, and every person knowing that he and his fellow citizens wield ultimate control over government normally develops a state of mind that is dominated by hope rather than despair concerning present and future opportunities for development."

Democracy fully protects the individual, and no violence can be done to his person against the law of the country. The individual is ensured freedom of though and expression, and freedom from arbitrary arrest. He is guaranteed certain minimum rights, which are quite essential for the development of his personality.

3. *Upholds Liberty and Equality*. Democracy upholds liberty and equality. Every individual is free to think, speak and act, and develop his own personality in the way in which he deems fit. He has freedom to live in his own way, speak the language he likes, read the books of his choice, express his opinion as the pleases, have his own culture, choose the vocation he likes and hold his own religious beliefs. The individual cannot be coerced to do any thing against his will. He can enjoy certain rights, which are regarded as inviolable.

Moreover, no discrimination can be practised against any particular individual or class. All are equal before the law, and the same punishment is meted out to all, when the law is broken. All those who value liberty and equality above anything else regard democracy as the best form of government. A. D. Lindsay makes a significant observation on democracy on page 266 in *The Modern Democratic State* (1959): "Democracy is a revolutionary form of government. For its aim is to find a place for continual change within government. Its law exists to foster freedom. Its force exists to protect law. It is an organisation to preserve, leave room for these precious things of the spirit, which in their nature cannot be organized."

4. *A responsible Government*. A democratic government is responsible to the people, It shall not act arbitrarily or the ride rough shod over their wishes. While in an absolute monarchy or a dictatorship, government may regard itself as above reproach, a democratic government has to be responsive and responsible to the people. A democratic government, whether parliamentary or presidential, shall respect the wishes of the people. If rulers

in a democratic state misbehave and act contrary to the wishes and interests of the people, they will be pulled up by the people, and the various agencies of public opinion will express themselves against them. If rulers wish to continue to remain in power, they shall act as the servants of the people and serve in public interest.

5. *Trains People.* Another great merit of democracy is that it encourages people to come forward in governing themselves, and thus trains them in the art of government. In a democracy the people can participate in political and other activities, and have scope to learn how to run their own institutions. A democratic government functions in the open, and sovereignty is vested in the people. It is not like aristocracy, monarchy or dictatorship aloof from the people. J. W. Garner says that "the greatest glory of democracy in the opinion of its votaries does not flow so much from its own inherent excellence as a form of government, as from its influence in elevating the masses of people, developing their faculties, stimulating interest among them in public affairs, and strengthening their patriotism by allowing them a share in its administration." (See *Political Science and Government*—1955, p. 358.)

6. *Promotion of Social Welfare.* Democracy has its economic aspect of promoting social welfare. Democratic governments in modern times are guided by the principle of the welfare state. Much can be done by a democratic government, if democracy enters the economic field. There was a time, when democracy worked in the political field only and other fields were neglected. Now the concept of democracy is understood differently. Democracy to be meaningful should do economic justice to the people and should undertake social welfare schemes. Governments in Britain, the USA and other countries have done much to promote people's welfare. No monarchy or aristocracy has done so much in the interests of the people as some democracies have done in recent years. While it is true that even authoritarian governments have taken steps to promote the people's welfare it must be emphasized that only a democracy can serve the people's welfare without annihilating the dignity of the human personality. India as a democracy is wedded to the principle of establishing a welfare state, as given in the Preamble and the Directive Principles of State Policy in the Constitution.

7. Faith in Human Capacity. Democracy puts faith in human capacity to think and act. It does not believe that only a few persons are competent to take part in political activities to the complete exclusion of others. In a democracy, a few individuals are leaders and others are followers; but if the people are intelligent, they do not follow their leaders blindly. Men may disagree with one another. But they do not settle questions through violence. They have the capacity to understand each other and settle, their problems peacefully. A true democrat has faith in the conflict of ideas and ideologies, but he is against violent conflicts and bloodshed. E. B. Schulz observes on page 211 in *Essential of Government* (1961): "Democracy is also favored on the ground that it is the only system that permits the people to bring about a change in government in a peaceful and orderly manner is soon as, or at least shortly after dissatisfactory policies are put into effect." Democracies function with the help of the ballot and not the ballot. In legislatures, members argue with one another, exchange their views, make use of their sweet reasonableness and arrive at conclusions.

7. DEFECTS OF DEMOCRACY

Hollowness Exposed

The claims of democracy as the best form of government proved to be false, and their hollowness was fully exposed in the difficult years of the present century. Much was expected of democracy in the first two decades of the twentieth century; in fact before 1914 it was taken for granted that some form of democracy was the only possible government for a civilized country. But during the inter-war period (1919-39) democracies in Europe let down people badly. As democracies suffering from several infirmities were limping, dictatorships were progressively and dynamically galloping in Europe. It was then that all the drawbacks of a real democracy (as against an ideal one as pictured in books) revealed themselves. Some have criticised democracy most vehemently and unjustly and their words need not be taken seriously at their face value. J. W. Garner says that "we need not consider seriously the equally uncritical and sweeping generalisations of men like Talleyrand, who defined democracy as 'an aristocracy of blackguards', of Carlyle who sneeringly referred to 'the people as a certain number of millions, mostly fools', of H. G Wells, who asserts that there is no case for elective democratic government of modern states that cannot be knocked to pieces in five minutes." (See *Political Science and Government*—1955, p. 356.)

Democracy has been severely criticised by Sir Henry Maine Lecky, De Tocqueville, Bluntschi, Treitschke, Giddings and others. In ancient Athens, Alcibiades said: "As for democracy, why should we discuss acknowledged madness?" Lecky regarded it as "the government of the poorest, the most ignorant, the most incapable, who are necessarily the most numerous."

Drawbacks Listed by Bryce

James Bryce mentions the following serious defects of democracy.

(1) "the power of money of pervert administration;

(2) the tendency to make politics a gainful profession;

(3) extravagance in administration;

(4) the abuse of the doctrine of equality and failure to appreciate the value of administrative skill;

(5) the undue power of party organisation;

(6) the tendency of legislators and political officials to play for votes in the passing of laws and in tolerating breaches of order."

Money talks loudly all over the world, and every government, democratic or non-democratic, is plagued by bribery and corruption. It is wrong to say that democratic governments only open their doors to brides and gifts. It is also true that everywhere in a democracy or an autocracy, interested parties desire to make politics a source of rich dividends. Thus democracy alone is not exposed to this evil.

However, there is much substance in the point that democracies are extravagant. But here it must be noted that extravagance can be seen in other forms of governments too. For example, the Bourbon monarchy of France was notorious for its extravagance. The poor were taxed heavily, and public money was squandered on wars and luxuries.

As regards the misuse of the principle of equality, the evil can be remedied. The principle of equality is not to be abolished because it has defects. Equality as a complement of liberty is quite essential for democracy.

Regarding the evil of party politics, it has to be conceded that in this imperfect world democracy can function only on a party basis. It is too early to speak of a partyless democracy. Even though political parties are evils, they are quite necessary.

The malpractices about which Bryce speaks in connection with law-making are real in several democracies. Though Brye himself admits that all forms of government suffer from the first three-evils, there is no reason why they should not be criticised in a democracy. If democracy is to be superior to other forms of government, it should not have in it evils found in other forms. As Bryce monitions, the last three evils are particularly associated with democracy.

Great Disadvantages of Democracy

The following great disadvantages of democracy have to be mentioned:

(1) Inefficiency

Democracy is criticised as an inefficient form of government in which inexperienced and ignorant men wield power to the detriment of the larger interests of the state. Several democratic governments bear the stamp of gross inefficiency, and they are totally incapable of achieving anything that a worthwhile to the people. As notoriously inefficient men in government commit one blunder after another; taxpayers feel that democracy is the worst type of government. Men of calibre, competence and integrity and hardly rewarded, and inefficient and dishonest men need not fear dismissal from their government posts.

Democracy is based on the party system, which provides scope for inefficient and corrupt men to capture power. Competent and honest men, who desire to keep away from the rough and tumble of politics, remain in the backwaters. Incompetent, ignorant and dishonest friends of powerful men may enjoy lucrative posts.

(2) Corruption

Another charge levelled against democracy is of bribery and corruption. Democratic institutions have to follow many laws, and rules of procedure, which inevitably promote corruption. The party system is to a great extent responsible for increasing corruption on a large scale. Political parties collect large sums of money from business houses, which have to be favoured. Candidates contesting elections spend money like water, and when they are successful they do not leave any stone unturned to reimburse themselves and wipe out the losses. In almost every democracy power goes to the wealthy patrons of political parties. To many rich men, politics forms a very fruitful source of profit, and those who succeed in seizing power use it as an instrument of self-aggrandisement. Corrupt democratic governments shield corrupt men and befoul the atmosphere in public life.

(3) Slow and Sluggish

Democracies are proverbially slow and sluggish in their movement, and they take much time to execute their plants. As democracy is government by consultation and criticism, decisions are taken after prolonged discussions. In a monarchy or dictatorship prompt decisions can be taken; but red-tapism in democracy entails much loss of time and money. Even intelligent and able men in high seats of power cannot act with energetic promptitude, as procedural delays are inevitable. Many a time procedures kill the spirit of good government making real progress extremely difficult. In the inter-war period (1919-39), tardiness, sluggishness and reluctance to take quick decisions brought European democracies into disrepute and ultimately dug their grave.

(4) High Cost of Administration

Democracy is an expensive type of government. In many of the democracies, which are really aristocracies or oligarchies, no effort may be made to practise economy, and public money may be thrown down the drain. New departments may be opened, the number of posts may be multiplied and sinecure jobs may be created to oblige party men, relatives and friends of those in power. The paraphernalia of democracy has proved to be very costly in several countries. Compared to a monarchy or dictatorship, democracy is expensive, because governmental machinery is complex and complicated. There are legislatures, consultative and advisory bodies, committees and commissions, which all mean a heavy burden on the public treasury.

(5) Tyranny of the Majority

In a parliamentary democracy, government may fall into the hands of the majority party, which can afford to tyrannise over the people. This is particularly true in parliamentary democracies like Britain and India. The party commanding vast resources is able to seize power and use the government as its tool. Though technically speaking, it runs a democratic government in actual practice it may violate the true spirit of democracy by misusing power. F. W. Coker says on page 309 in *Recent Political Though* (1957): "What standard of judgement can make us believe the opinion of any 55% of the people to be wiser or fairer than that of the other 45%? What quality has majority in greater amount of higher value, except the one quality of superior force?" The government of the brute majority may lead to be oppression of the minorities. The political, social and cultural interests of the minorities may be completely neglected or trampled under foot. It is not uncommon to see men in government making use of public money and property to further their own interests and those of the party. To those in power, the party may be everything. This is pa...cularly true at the time of election.

A democratic country may have to tolerate all kinds of evils, as practically nothing can be done against the steamroller majority party in power. Laws may be passed not in the interests of the people, but in the selfish interests of the majority party. Bad laws may be passed for oppressing the people and for favoring party men. Sometimes highly controversial laws, which are difficult to be enforced, may be passed most thoughtlessly.

(6) People's Power a Myth

It is a myth that power resides in the hands of the people. Generally, the people are controlled and blindly led by a few people, who rise to the top by means fair or foul. In various ways people may be deceived and flattered to make them feel that power is located in their hands. Real despotism may be practised under the cloak of democratic principles. F. W. Coker says on page 331 in *Recent Political Thought* (1957): "All the institutional and ideological paraphernalia of modern democracy facilitate rather than obstruct the operation of despotic rule..... Unorganised masses are always controlled by some alert, resolute, organised minority—military despots, big business, men, party mangers or social reformers—who are skilful in adjusting popular ideas and emotions to the limited interests or beliefs of some small groups." The very fact that the masses of people have to obey unjust, oppressive and ridiculous laws helplessly and suffer silently proves beyond a shadow of doubt that popular sovereignty is a myth.

(7) Gap between Precept and Practice

There is a wide gap between democracy in theory and democracy in actual practice. Most of the democratic governments do not act strictly according to democratic principles. There is eloquent talk of popular sovereignty, the welfare of the people and the principle of consent and criticism. But what is spoken is violated in practice. Many democratic governments violate in letter and spirit the true principles of democracy. C. D. Burns says on page 341 in *Democracy* (1935) that democracy "rests upon certain pretences, not to say frauds. Political parties are supposed to be free associations.... But in fact most of the members of the party belong to it because of their parents' politics as because of some irrelevant connection between the party any some locality or economic interest or religion." Critics of democracy say that there is wide gap between precept and practice, because according to them true democracy cannot be realised. "The democratic idea has also been attacked as impracticable, because, it asks for qualities which the ordinary man cannot possibly be expected to possess. Consequently, to try to realise it would produce a parody of democracy at best." (See Benn and Peters, *Social Principles and the Democratic State*—1951, p. 341.) The British historian Lecky strongly criticises democracy for its failure to safeguard liberty and provide good government. "Democracy insures neither better government nor greater liberty; indeed some of the strongest tendencies are adverse to liberty. On the contrary, strong arguments may be adduced both from history and from the nature of things to show that democracy may often prove the direct opposite of liberty."

(8) Incompetence and Indifference of People

Even though the advocates of democracy lay emphasis on

the sovereignty of the people. Ordinary people, it is argued, are not fit to exercise sovereignty or supreme power. The complicated science and art of government is far beyond their comprehension. Generally, ordinary citizens have neither the time and energy nor inclination to take an active part in politics. Most of the citizens in democracies are indifferent to what happens around them in the political fields. Even during elections they are lethargic and unwilling to cast their votes. They have to be flattered, or persuaded or pressurised to go to the polling booth. Only a chosen few with their vast knowledge and wisdom are competent to lead and exercise power on behalf of the people. The critics of democracy uphold the doctrine of the *elite*. There is much substance in their argument that the elite alone are fit to rule. Here we may refer to India as democracy and ask the question: how many people in the whole sub-continent of India are competent to govern themselves or even to understand the problems of a democratic government? If we go deep into the fitness of people in India in general to have democracy, we may be compelled to conclude that the vast masses of Indians have not yet become mature for democracy.

8. DEMOCRACY IN INDIA

A Sovereign Democratic Republic

India won her independence on August 15, 1947, and the Constitution of India came into force on January 26, 1950. Under the Constitution, India is a Sovereign Democratic Republic. The Constitution upholds the principles of liberty and equality and Fundamental Rights are guaranteed. India has adopted the parliamentary system of democracy. India (which is called Union of States in the Constitution) is federation with a strong centre.

Difference between Britain and India as Democracies

India, like England, is a democracy; but there is a much difference between the two countries.

(1) *Little Experience*. India cannot challenge comparison with Britain as far as her actual experience in running parliamentary institutions is concerned, as Britain has a long and impressive background of parliamentary history.

(2) *Adult Franchise at One Stroke*. India introduced adult

franchise in 1950 at one stroke of the pen, though many critics regarded this as a risky step. In Britain till 1918 women had no franchise. In that year women aged over 30 won the right to vote and in 1928 all women were put on a par with men and enfranchised.

(3) *Difference between Peoples.* There is a vast difference between the people of India and the people of Britain from the political and constitutional points of view. While the Indians lack the necessary experience to run a democratic form of government, the British people are well experience. The British enjoyed for a long time liberty and equality, which Indians did not have before the introduction of their own constitution. English people have cultivated a high level of political consciousness and civic sense, which Indians lack.

(4) *Difference in Standards of Living.* The standard of living in Britain is high, while it is still very low in India. In the case of Britain, the Industrial Revolution preceded the introduction of full democracy, but in the case of India the Industrial Revolution in the true sense of the term began only after independence. India's poverty, which has been proverbial is the mother of several evils, which are great obstacles to democracy. For Britain, there is almost cent per cent literacy, but in India illiteracy and ignorance are rampant.

Relative Success of India as a Democracy

Despite the disadvantages from which India suffers, while carrying on with her democratic experiment on a large scale, she has been doing much better than most of the countries, which won independence in recent years.

The following factors explain the relative success of India:

1. Experience

Indians have more experience in the political and constitutional fields than people in most of the other developing countries.

2. Good Leadership

Indians have been fortunate in having eminent leaders, whose keen intellect, commonsense, sobriety, patience and tolerance could stand the test of the most trying years on the eve of independence and also in the post-partition days. The country had the advantage of the wealth of wisdom and experience of dynamic leaders like Mahatma Gandhi, Pandit Jawaharlal Nehru, Sardar Vallabhabai Patel, C. Rajagopalachari, Dr. Rajendra Prasad and several others. N. Weiner says: "India, however, has been fortunate in that its nationalist leaders have served throughout the constitution-making, the initial task of integration, the first and perhaps most crucial phase of national economic planning, and more recently a period in which regional agitation has increased." [See Park and Tinker (Ed.), *Leadership and Political Institution in India*—1951, p. 28.]

(3) Co-operaction of People

With all their weaknesses, the masses of people co-operated with their leaders, and showed much tolerance and patience. On several occasions, they showed great alertness and sense of awakening. When China committed aggression in 1962, and Pakistan attacked India in 1965 and 1971, people rallied round their country's banner, and considered no sacrifice too great for the sake of their motherland. In 1971, since the Bangla Desh refugees poured into India and Pakistan declared war, the people as a nation expressed their full support to their democratic government and led it to victory over Pakistan.

(4) Support of Foreign Countries

Several advanced nations were friendly towards India, and took genuine interest in the progress of India's democratic institutions. Particularly, the USA was very generous to India and extended her helping hand, whenever India needed it. America's food aid in times of famine and her military support when China invaded India in 1962 came as a great solace to India. The Soviet Union also became friendly with India. This was particularly favorable to India, when the USA became friendly with China and Pakistan. The USA helped Pakistan to arm herself with the most sophisticated weapons with the result Pakistan was tempted to attack India in 1965 and 1971. It appeared that China and

Pakistan might form an axis of jointly attacking India. At this juncture, the Soviet Union signed with India the historic 20-year treaty of peace, friendship and co-operation.

(5) Self-Government in Small Doses

India did not gets independence from Britain at one stroke. It took a very long time for India to win her independence. Britain gave self-government to India in very small doses as evident from the Parliamentary Acts of 1861, 1892, 1909, 1919 and 1935. Though the transfer of power was an extremely tardy process, in a way, it was a blessing in disguise. In fairness to Britain, it may be said that the she did not leave India in the way in which Belgium left the Congo in Africa in 1960.

(6) Democratic Spirit

By and large, the people of India have shown a democratic spirit. But for this, the Constitution of India would have remained a dead letter. Though the vast majority of people are illiterate and ignorant, they have shown that they are not unworthy of adult franchise and democratic institutions. India has held so far seven General Elections in 1952, 1957, 1962, 1967, 1971 (Mid-Term Lok Sabha Election), 1977 and 1980. The unexpected result of the Fourth General Election in 1967 in which many Congress leaders were defeated revealed the sound commonsense of the people in electing their representatives. While the people voted in favour of the Congress led by Smt. Indira Gandhi in the Mid-Term Lok Sabha Election in 1971, they voted the Janata Party to power in 1977 and swept aside the Congress for the first time since the commencement of the Constitution. In 1980 Smt. Indira Gandhi was voted to power again since the electorate was disillusioned with two-and-a-half-year rule of the Janata Party.

Obstacles to Democracy in India

India's democracy is facing several obstacles. K. M. Munshi mentions the factors responsible for the setback of parliamentary democracy in India:

(1) Nehru, a gifted man is far above his contemporaries.

(2) Democratic values are immature.

(3) There are fissiparous tendencies.

(4) Political-minded leaders lack fearless independence.

(5) People have an apathy towards the future of democracy in India.

The following are the obstacles on the path of India's democracy:

1. Illiteracy, Ignorance and Immaturity

Widespread illiteracy and ignorance constitute the most serious obstacle to democracy in India. Since independence (1947) the government has taken steps to spread literacy, and with the spread of eduction the path of democracy will be gradually smoothened. When people are uneducated and backward, there cannot be political maturity P. J. Shroff aptly observes: "When people resort to *satyagraha*, hunger strike, *morchas*, and marches on frivolous pretexts, they make an exhibition of their political immaturity." [See *Democracy in India (A Symposium)*—1960, p. 27.]

2. Prejudices

People suffer much from linguistic, regional, caste, communal and religious prejudices. Among these caste has the strongest pull. It is well said: "....the very fact that a caste is capable of functioning as an effective pressure group, and that its members cannot leave it an join another group at will, places it into a position of political power, which cannot be ignored by the political parties depending for their mandates on the good will of the voters." [See C. H. Phillips (Ed.), *Politics and Society in India*—1963. p. 54] A person with strong caste prejudice cannot understand the value of liberty and equality, and he is unfit to be democratic minded. Prejudices work most vulgarly at the time of elections. M. Weiner says: "The fact is that India's leadership has a set of ideals far in advance of existing practices, and the problem for India's leaders is not only to narrow the gap between ideals and practices, but to inculcate in the masses of the country a respect for a new set of ideals, which are in many ways the antithesis of the old." [Park and Tinker (Ed.), *Leadership and Political Institution in India*—1959, p. 30]. The outbreak of large-scale riots, arson and looting when the States' Reorganisation Commission (SRC) Report (1955) was released showed how dangerous linguistic lunacy could become. The report was like the proverbial Pandora's box. Even 37 years after independence, casteism, linguism and regionalism have not been diluted; in fact these fissiparous tendencies have become stronger. To many, caste comes first, the community in general afterwards; to many the region and the regional language count more than the nation and the national language. Narrow-mindedness and parochial prejudices are working have on national solidarity.

3. Emphasis On Personalities

In India personalities are given greater importance than principles; and people have yet to develop the spirit of self-reliance. People are reluctant to critics their leaders even if they are wrong and act contrary to democratic principles. Whatever the leaders say is regarded as gospel truth. This has done great harm to the cause of democracy. As the people are unable to judge the various issues before them and arrive at the right decisions owing to their backward condition, they leave the issues to be decided by their leaders whom they blindly follow. Many a time, the various parties and groups take a certain stand, not on the merits of issues before them but on the basis of the opinions expressed by their leaders.

4. Poverty

Poverty is the greatest hurdle on the path of democracy. J. B. Kriplani says: "The greatest danger to democracy in India is to my mind the poverty of the masses and their large scale unemployment. A starving man's vote can be nullified by his poverty, which also means ignorance of his duties and rights as a citizen and his low vitality." (*The Illustrated Weekly of India*—August 20, 1961, p. 8.) The vast masses of people who suffer from grinding poverty are engaged in the endless struggle for securing dry bread, and they have neither the time nor the capacity to work for the cause of democracy.

5. Absence of a Strong Opposition Party

India as a parliamentary democracy failed to evolve a strong and viable opposition party. Both at the Centre and in the States, the opposition parties are extremely weak and they are nowhere in the presence of the ruling Congress Party. In Britain, the Opposition, which is strong and ever vigilant, capable of providing an alternative leadership, when the ruling party is defeated in the House of Commons. For nearly two decades since August 1947, the Indian National Congress dominated the political and constitutional scene and all other parties were in the shade. It was able to brush aside any criticism of the pale and lifeless opposition groups in Parliament and State Legislatures. Pandit Jawaharlal Nehru's charismatic leadership, the proud record of the Congress Party in the national movement and other factors put it in a highly advantageous position. But gradually the misuse of power by Congress leaders shattered the image of the party.

In the Fourth General Election (February 1967) to the great surprise of all, many stalwarts of the Congress Party including the Congress President Kumaraswamy Kamaraj, S. K. Patil, and Atulya Ghosh were defeated at the polls. In the Lok Sabha, the Congress lost 80 seats and its majority became paper thin. In Madras (now Tamil Nadu) and Kerala, the Congress was routed. In the former state, the Dravida Munnetra Kazhagam (DMK) formed the government and in the latter the United Front of Leftists came to power. In Orissa, the Swatantra Party and the Janta Congress together formed a coalition government. In Rajasthan, riots broke out when the Governor, Dr. Sampurnanand, asked the leader of the Congress Party, Mohanlal Sukhadia, to form government. Even though the opposition groups, which united were stronger than the Congress, the Governor did not invite the opposition to form government. The favoritism and partiality of the Governor were deeply resented by the opposition and the people, and violence broke out. Then President's rule was imposed and the Legislative Assembly was suspended. After some time, Mohanlal Sukhadia was able to form a ministry. In West Bengal, a United Front of 14 parties and groups was formed by the Bangla Congress leader Ajoy Mukherjee.

The election results clearly revealed the unpopularity of the Congress in many parts of India and the rising fortunes of the Jana Sangh and the Swatantra Pary. The monopoly of the Congress to rule India completely ignoring the opposition groups and the people was broken by the Fourth General Election and the hope of the emergence of a strong opposition was raised. Though no single party by itself could offer an effective opposition, two or more parties could form a united opposition.

In August 1969 the Congress monolith was broken into two groups, and it seemed that the Congress might become very weak. But the Congress (R) under Smt. Indira Gandhi's leadership swept the polls in the March 1971 mid-term Lok Sabha election. The Congress (O) was almost wiped out, and several opposition groups were routed at the polls.

On June 25, 1975, Prime Minister Smt. Gandhi recommended to the President Fakhruddin Ali Ahmed to impose Internal Emergency after she was unseated by the judgement of the Allahabad High Court. She refused to step down, and to save herself this extraordinary, unprecedented, and unconstitutional step was taken. The Constitution was amended, and new laws were passed by a captive Parliament to enable Smt. Gandhi to remain in power. For 19 months the country was governed in a dictatorial style, thousands of people including big leaders of the opposition parties were thrown in prison without trial and thousands were torture in police custody. In March 1977 immediately after the Emergency was ended, Lok Sabha elections were held. The Congress led by Smt. Gandhi was swept aside in all the States in the Hindi-belt north of the Vindhyas. This enabled the Janata Party to form a government at the Centre with Shri Morarji Desai as Prime Minister. But the people, who had given power to the Janata in a golden platter, were disgusted and disappointed, as Janata Ministers openly quarrelled and indulged in reckless mutual recrimination. While in March 1977 after the elections people thought that the sun of Smt. Gandhi's power had set, in the later days the Janata Party leaders cut a sorry figure before the country and people developed the feeling that they were not worthy of remaining in power. In two and a half years, the Janata Government fell, and in 1980 Smt. Gandhi's party was voted to power again. All these events and developments clearly showed that the voters who had sound common sense could not be taken for granted either by the Congress or the Janata.

In January 1983 in the Assembly Elections the Congress (I) was defeated in Karnataka (where Shri Ramakrishna Hegde formed the first Janata Government) and in Andhra Pradesh (where the leader Shri N. T. Ramo Rao formed the first Telugu Deshan Government). For the first time the monopoly of the

Congress rule was broken in these two southern states which were the strongholds of the Congress (I).

6. Corruption

Corruption has become widespread and is eating into the vitals of the country. From top to bottom at all levels the administration has been gangrened by corruption. Lakhs of rupees are spent by candidates during elections, and if they are successful, they try to reimburse themselves and their political patrons. They try to reimburse themselves and their political patrons. They do not hesitate to make as much money as possible in the shortest possible time by the most questionably methods. Honest political leaders and administrators have become very rare. Every member of the legislature in certain states has a price tag, and defections are freely encouraged. Efforts are made to corrupt even the most honest members.

7. Press

The press in India, which is in the hands of industrial barons, is not in a position to play as effective a role as in the Western countries. A few press barons directly or indirectly control chains of newspapers. Small newspapers and journals of independent views find even their very survival difficult. Several newspapers side with the ruling party, whose patronage they are always eager to secure even at the cost of their independence. Some newspapers falsely report and mislead the public. Investigative journalism is very rare.

9. DEMOCRACY AND SOCIAL BACKGROUND OF INDIAN POLITICS

If political affairs of India are to be understood in the correct perspective, it is necessary to know something about the social background. The following factors enable us to understand the social background of Indian politics and the impact of this background on India as a democracy:

1. Caste System

The caste system pervades throughout the length and breadth of India making its influence felt at all levels in the democratic structure of the country. At some levels, the caste system works overtly and in a more pronounced manner, while at others it works covertly. Caste influence is undoubtedly one of the worst evils in India today. While it is true that caste did serve certain good ends in the past and preserved India's culture and civilization through the ages, it is an unmixed evil in India as a democracy. Caste makes Indian society undemocratic, and people having caste prejudices cannot take kindly to liberty and equality, the basic principles of democracy. Caste has built a rigid hierarchy, which is diametrically opposed to liberal ideas. Caste is obscurantist and utterly anti-democratic.

2. Language

Language is another dangerous factor coming in the way of democracy. Western countries like the USA and Britain do not have this type of linguistic problem. The Linguistic Survey of India recorded 179 languages and 544 dialects. Leaders, advocating the cause of certain languages and dialects, have created much bitterness and fissiparous tendencies, which are a real menace to democracy and national solidarity.

Language as a divisive force in Indian politics raised its ugly head, particularly after the States Reorganization Commission Report (1955) was released. To satisfy certain groups States were recognized on a unilingual basis. Passion for language provoked widespread riots and unprecedented violence. Language has created ugly fanaticism and a measure of intolerance and hatred, which will destroy democracy, if not effectively curved.

India has been unable to have a national language, which is acceptable to the vast majority in all states. Hindi, whose cause had been strongly espoused by national leaders like Mahatma Gandhi, is no more acceptable to people in many areas, particularly in the Southern States.

3. Regionalism

The federal pattern (for which it seems Indians are not mature) has unconsciously but surely encouraged regionalism, contrary to the expectations of the founding fathers of the Constitution.

Regional prejudices have become dangerously strong, and these are unwilling to reconcile themselves with democratic principles and practices. Whether it is a question of establishing an oil refinery of steel plant, regional interests are trying to assert them selves violently, undermining the cause of democracy.

4. Communalism

Communalism is another deadly enemy of democracy in India. Indians blamed the British for sowing the dragon's teeth of communal electorate and for mischievously playing one communal group against another. But now it is obvious that Indian leaders themselves encourage and fan communal interests for the purpose of winning political support and votes during elections. Some parties themselves are rabidly communal. Several political parties are guilty of hobnobbing with such communal parties and making electoral alliances with them. Several examples can be given to show how short-sighted leaders kindled communal passions for the realisation of petty and selfish ends.

5. Narrow Loyalties

The cumulative effect of casteism, linguistic chauvinism, regionalism and communalism is the manifestation of dangerously narrow loyalties. Many people, who are struck by narrow loyalties, are incapable of thinking in terms of India as a democratic nation state. To small and narrow minds, democracy as a form of government and a way of life is meaning less as caste and communal feelings rule their minds.

6. Deficient Leadership

In the peculiar, social background of Indian politics, it has been possible for a large number of petty leaders to fish in the communal, regional, casteist and linguistic waters. National leadership is decidedly on the decline, particularly after the death of great men like Mahatma Gandhi, Pandit Jawaharlal Nehru, Sardar Vallabhbhai Patel, Dr. Rajendra Prasad, Dr. Shyama Prasad Mukherji, Shri Lal Bahadur Shastri, Dr. K. M. Munshi, Shri C. Rajagopalachari Loknayak Jayaprakash Narayan and Acharya J. B. Kripalani. The old generation of truly great leaders who with their great integrity and high standards had actiyity participated in the freedom struggle and sacrificed much for the sake of their country is dead. Its place is taken now by second and third rate leaders, who lack foresight, breadth of vision, great ideals and moral values. It is truly pitiful to see the nation being misled by political adventures. Who work for immediate gain and know nothing beyond the worship of Mammon, P. D. Sharma observes on page 434 in *Studies in Indian Democracy*—1965 (edited by Aiyar and Srinviasan): "The basic challenge of free India is to survive as a democratic nation and to develop herself economically through democratic methods. However, the aggressive stances of linguism and regionalism subvert the democratic process of various levels of popular voting, party operations, democratic leadership and the crucial areas of decision-making.

7. Indiscipline at all Levels

Indiscipline has assumed dangerous proportions in institutions of public life at all levels, with the result national indiscipline is posing itself as major danger to the country as a democracy. At the highest level of political life, leaders who should set good examples to the people themselves openly indulge in acts of gross indiscipline. They do not cherish great values, do not follow noble ideas, do not have high standards of probity and do not care much for the future of the nation. Lawlessness and crime are on the increase as moral values steadily decline. With political patronage dacoity and brigandage are waxing. Strikes and lockouts have led to serious fall in production. Colleges and universities are no more true temples of learning but centres congenial for low intrigues and power politics.

State of Internal Emergency Declared

President of India Fakhruddin Ali Ahmed declared a state of Internal Emergency at 7.00 A.M. on Thursday, June 26, 1975, on account of threat to the "security of the country due to internal disturbances." The Presidents's proclamation followed an early swoop in which the government arrested and jailed without trial Loknayak Jayaprakash Narayan, Shri Morarji Desai, Shri Charan Singh, Shri Raj Narain, Shri Samar Guha, Shri Piloo Mody, Shri Chandra Shekhar (then a member of the Congress Working Committee), Shri Ram Dhan (Secretary of the Congress Parliament Party), Shri L.K. Advani, Shri A. B. Vajpayee and many other leaders. Thousands of ordinary people, who were leaders in their respective localities, were also thrown into prison. India came under a double Emergency, as Emergency declared in 1971 to face the threat of external aggression from Pakistan was still in force. In and unscheduled broadcast to the nation at 8.00 A.M. On June 26, 1975, Prime Minister Smt. Indira Gandhi referred to a "widespread conspiracy" and attempts "to destroy democracy in the name of saving it" and to "incite" the police and armed forces. The general condition all over the country following the proclamation of Internal Emergency and arrests of thousands of people was peaceful. It seemed that people who were fed up with frequent *bandhs,* violent outbursts and destruction of property, never-ending industrial strikes and lockouts, students boycott of classes and strikes, teachers, strikes and all kinds of anti-national activities welcomed the proclamation of Emergency. But before long the people's attitude changed, as police terror was let loose and thousands of people were arrested daily and tortured at police stations. People lost their Fundamental Rights and a captive Parliament passed undemocratic laws and recklessly amended the Constitution. It was then realised that the Internal Emergency, which was supposed to be a remedy for the malady of national indiscipline, proved itself to be worse than the disease.

10. CONTROLLED DEMOCRACY IN PAKISTAN

Dissolution of Constituent Assembly and Framing of New Constitution

For 10 years (1958-March 1969) Pakistan was under the military dictatorship of Ayub Khan, who claimed that Pakistan also had democracy. But this was a special type of democracy, which he called Controlled Democracy. This label, however, proved to be misleading, as it was nothing but a camouflage for unabashed dictatorship.

On October 24, 1954, the Governor-General of Pakistan declared a state of Emergency on the ground that the constitutional machinery had broken down. The Constituent Assembly, which tried to grapple with the constitutional problem for seven years since the establishment of Pakistan (August 1947) was dissolved. Ayub Khan appointed a Constitution Commission with Justice Md. Sahabuddin of the Supreme Court as Chairman. The recommendations of this Commission modified and finally shaped by Ayub Khan gave rise to the New Constitution of Pakistan. The Commission, it was claimed, worked on the basis of the earlier parliamentary government of Pakistan.

Controlled Democracy and Basic Democrats

Dictators like Ayub Khan exercise power to realise their own selfish ends under the cloak of Controlled Democracy. Ayub Khan, who captured power in 1958, became that first Pakistan President under the Constitution framed at his instance. In January 1965 Ayub Khan and Miss Fatima Jinnah contested the Persidentship; the former secured 61% votes as against 39% polled by the latter. This enabled the dictator to secure a new "constitutional" lease of life. President Ayub Khan had no faith in free and fair elections conducted by democratic countries. He said that the election results do not necessarily register the true views of the people, and therefore, a government formed on the basis of election results may not truly represent the people. So, Ayub Khan wanted to consult the people *indirectly* instead of giving them the right to elect their own representatives. Eighty thousand electoral units were to be formed and each of them was to elect one elector; thus there were 80,000 electors or basic *democrats* (40,000 from each of the two Provinces—East Pakistan and West Pakistan), who formed the electoral college to elect the President and the members of the National and Provincial Assemblies.

Presidential Form

Under the New Constitution based on *Controlled* democracy. Pakistan has a presidential form of government. The President in whom executive authority is vested appoints his Council of Ministers, who are responsible to him. All laws passed by the National Assembly are to secure the assent of the President. The President can exercise his veto, which can be overridden by the National Assembly by passing it again by two-thirds majority. Controversial issues may be decided by the President on the basis of a referendum. Here, it should be noted that the referendum is to be held among the electors (*i.e.* 80,000) and not among the people.

Two Provincial Assemblies

The constitution makes provision for two Provincial Assemblies: one for West Pakistan and the other for East Pakistan. It does not make provision for federal government; only a legislative devolution with the courtesy of the Central Government has been provided.

Limited Rights of People

Unlike people in India, people in Pakistan do not enjoy rights, which are guaranteed by the constitution. Rights are provided, but they are not enforced by courts. People can have liberties like civil liberty only with the approval of the President and the National Assembly.

Impeachment of the President

The President enjoys very wide powers subject only to the powers of the National Assembly which is empowered to impeach him; but here too this power is subject to great limitations and it may not be real. The constitution provides for three-fourths majority of the National Assembly for impeachment. If the impeachment proposal does not get the support of at least half the number of the members of the National Assembly, the proposes of impeachment will be penalised by the forfeiture of their membership of the Assembly.

Unlimited Powers of President

The President of Pakistan enjoys extraordinary powers, which are almos dictatorial. While the amendment of the constitution requires two-thirds majority, the impeachment of the President requires three-fourths. Thus Ayub Khan managed to make himself superior to the constitution.

Criticism of Controlled Democracy

President Ayub Khan chose not to have a parliamentary form, as the he was afraid that a parliament might call upon him to explain his policies and defend them on its floor. No dictator would like to reduce himself to a position in which he will be held responsible to parliament. Controlled democracy, which is not democracy in the real sense of the term, can be criticised as follows:

(1) The President enjoys very wide powers. Impeaching him is more difficult than amending the constitution.

(2) Sovereignty is really speaking not vested in the people, because the voters are to elect 80,000 persons who form an electoral college to elect the President and members of the National and Provincial Assemblies. In democratic

countries members of the legislature are elected directly by the people; but in Pakistan they are elected indirectly.

(3) People do not have basic or fundamental rights, which are justiciable or guaranteed by the constitution. They cannot be enforced with the help of the judiciary. The rights, which are enumerated in the constitution, depend upon the President and the National Assembly, who have to permit them. Thus civil rights have hardly any meaning.

(4) President Ayub Khan cleverly mixed the features of the British, French and American constitutions for his controlled democracy to suit his own selfish ends.

In March, 1969, Ayub Khan was overthrown by the army chief Yahya Khan. East Pakistan openly rebelled against the Pakistan Government. In December 1971 Pakistan attacked India without any provocation; but the Pakistan army was routed and the whole of it was captured by India in East Pakistan, which became independent Bangla Desh. The rout and disgrace compelled Yahya Khan to resign and Zulfiquar Ali Bhutto became President and Chief martial Law Administrator. Bhutto, who got himself elected President of the Pakistan National Assembly in Islamabad on April 14, 1972, declared that martial law would be lifted on April 21, provided the Assembly approved the interim constitution. He secured the approval and Pakistan returned to civilian rule on the promised day under the interim constitution. In this constitution Bhutto, secured the powers of "the Governor-General of India, the Viceroy of India, the American President and everything else". The constitution "combined the worst features of the Ayub constitution of 1962, the Independence Act of 1947 and the Government of India Act of 1935." On October 20, 1972, Bhutto yielded to the opposition and agreed to have a parliamentary form of government.

Bhutto overestimated his own strength and underestimated the power of his enemies. In the fierce struggle for power Bhutto lost. He committed the mistake of rigging elections and enabled Zia-ul-Haq to capture power by a military coup on July 5, 1977. Zia managed to get Bhutto arrested and convicted for murder. Ultimately Bhutto was hanged on April 4, 1979, at Rawalpindi though all the great leaders of various countries appealed to Zia for clemency.

Since Zia grabbed power, Pakistan is under military rule, and he has been postponing the holding of elections on some pretext or the other. He broke the promise of reviving the 1973 'Constitution, which envisaged the establishment of parliamentary democracy. He introduced a series of measures for establishing an Islamic system from December 2, 1978. He set up Shariat Benches at the High Court level and one such Bench at the Supreme Court level. On March 23, 1979 that about 12 days before the execution of Bhutto Zia declared that he would hold elections on November 17; but on October 16 he broke the pledge and imposed stringent measures to strengthen his dictatorship. Political parties were dissolved, all political activities were banned, and many important political leaders were flung into prison. On March 24, 1981, a provisional order was issued for setting aside the democratic Constitution of 1973.

On August 12, 1983, Zia announced that he would introduce a new political system for Pakistan, which would envisage the revival of the 1973 Constitution with certain amendments. No body should hope that Zia would hold force and fair elections according to the provisions of a democratic constitution, because the avowed purpose of his latest constitutional proposal is to make Pakistan a truly Islamic state by giving the Constitution of 1973 "real Islamic" substance. (According to the 1973 Constitution Pakistan was to have a parliamentary system in which the President had to exercise power on the Prime Minister's advice.)

Zia's August 12 proposals envisage the establishment of the presidential system. The President appoints the Prime Minister and shares power with him. The other features of the proposed system are : (1) separate electorates, (2) nomination of persons to represent special interests like labour, peasants, technocrats and religious scholars; (3) election of a strong President by an electoral college.

The people of Pakistan, who have lost faith in the amusements of Zia, have sharply reacted against his policies. After the new proposals were announced, there were widespread riots in Sind. The Movement for the Restoration of Democracy (MRD) had announced that there would be national agitation from the Independency Day in August 1983. Zia arrested large number of persons all over the country, though serious disturbances were mostly confined to Sind.

11. GUIDED DEMOCRACY IN INDONESIA

Birth of Republic

On August 17, 1945, two days after the surrender of Japan, Sukarno and Hatta proclaimed the establishment of Republic of Indonesia. Sukarno became President and Hatta Vice-President. In 1949 the Dutch agreed to transfer power completely to Indonesia and on December 27, 1949, the Federal Republic of the United States of Indonesia was set up. Sukarno became President and Hatta Prime Minister. [See G. M. Kahin (Ed.), *Government and Politics of South East Asia*—1962, p. 172.]

No Stability

Owing to various factors, the Indonesian Republic did not have smooth sailing. From 1950 power fell into the hands of the leaders of the Republic of 1945 *viz*. Sukarno and Hatta. The government was not stable, as no party could get a comfortable majority. The Masjumi and the P. N. N. (Indonesian Nationalist Party) where the main parties; besides there were several small parties.

1955 Elections and Protracted Crisis

In 1955 elections were held for a Parliament and a Constituent Assemble. The new House of Representatives of 250 members had four important parties and several small parties. Therefore, it was difficult to form a stable government according to the principles of the constitution. "Since December 1956, Indonesia has been in the grip of protracted crisis. Dissatisfaction with the course of the country's politics erupted in that month in a series of bloodless coups which put the reins of government of Central, North and South Sumatra in the hands of the army regional councils." (*Ibid*,. p. 178.) Indonesia became proverbial for its lack of political stability. "No less than seven cabinets have held office since December 1949, none for longer than two years. In general, cabinets have been weak and unable to take resolute action on contentious issues except at the risk of being overthrown." (*Ibid*, p. 179.) The fight between Djakarta and the regions became more, and more serious. Leaders in the rebel areas made the position of the government untenable. In 1957, efforts were made to bridge the gulf between Djakarta and the rebel areas. A new proclamation of martial law was made, and a ground was prepared for negotiations with the military leaders of troublesome areas.

Guided Democracy

Arriving at a settlement was difficult, but all the time President Sukarno was in a leading position. He sought to end the crisis by establishing "guided democracy" or democracy with leadership. When the situation was critical and confused, a cabinet headed by the non-party leader Djuanda was formed in April 1957; its members belonged to several parties. Several important cabinet ministers were responsible to Sukarno rather than to Djuanda. "This council was created in May 1957 as a part of the implementation of the President's conception of Guided Democracy of Democracy with leadership which would supersede liberal parliamentary democracy." (*Ibid.*, p. 205) Sukarno said that the Indonesian Parliament (1956) was "to work on the basis of real *Indonesian democracy* and not on the basis of 50% plus one always right. . . . In the West people's thinking was individualistic, and thus a 50% plus one majority system was necessary. But Indonesian society was not individualistic. Rather it was a family-like society, a society of brotherhood . . . or mutual help." (See H. Feith, *The Decline of Constitutional Democracy in Indonesia*—1962, p. 515).

Confusion and Civil War

In Indonesia a National Council (later known as the Supreme Advisory Council) under the chairman ship of Sukarno and a cabinet of all parties, even communists, were formed. The inclusion of communists angered their rivals. In the 1957 provincial elections, the communists registered increased strength, and this was taken with alarm by anti-communists. In November 1957, efforts were made to assassinate President Sukarno. Confusion continued and in 1958 civil war broke out. Fortunately for Indonesia, civil war did not assume dangerous proportions as to invite intervention by big powers and to a great extent substantial unity was restored.

Attitude of the Elite

In Indonesia, the elite are in favor of democratic values. H. Feith says on page 38 in *The Decline of Constitutional Democracy in Indonesia*—1951: "In the constitutions and platforms of the fourteen parties . . . the word 'democracy' is used frequently and almost always with unqualified approval."

Sukarno's Five Principle. In 1945 President Sukarno had proclaimed the five Principles of State: (1) Faith in God, (2) Nationality, (3) Humanity, (4) People's Sovereignty or Democracy, and (5) Social Justice.

Sukarno and others favored "a distinctively Indonesian form of democracy, a form which gives expression to *musjawarah*, the traditional Indonesian method of coming to agreement not through majority decisions." (*Ibid*, p. 192.)

Constitutions of 1945, and 1950

In August 1945, when Indonesia became independent, a hurriedly prepared Constitution was adopted. In December 1949, with the establishment of the Federal Republic of the United States of Indonesia, a new Constitution was formed.

The second Constitution made way for a third one in August 1950, and a unitary form of government was introduced.

In 1957, a Constitutional Convention consisting of 25 members was elected to prepare a basic law for the country, and for the time being the Constitution of 1950 was followed. Though the Constitution made the President a mere titular head, in actual practice owing to the towering personality of President Sukarno, very wide powers were exercised by him.

Sukarno's National Council and Guided Democracy

In 1957 Sukarno introduced a novel institution, that is, the National Council for having a peculiar type of democracy, that is, Guided Democracy. It may be noted that Sukarno was not responsible to Parliament or people. The Indonesian Parliament functioned according to the Constitution of 1950. Indonesia followed the Western type of parliamentary procedure with modification to suit the wishes of President Sukarno, who could wield dictatorial power in the name of Guided Democracy. The cabinet and parliament were weak and important discussions took place not at cabinet or parliamentary meetings, but at conference of military officers and in the National Council. The political set-up was such that political parties were of little significance; however, the communist party was moving from strength to strength.

Drawbacks

The following are the drawbacks of democracy in Indonesia.

1. Dictatorship with Cloak of Democracy

Indonesia's democracy under Sukarno's leadership was a farce. Naked dictatorship was palmed off as Guided Democracy. The instability of Indonesian politics and frequent changes in government necessitated abandonment of democracy as understood in Western countries. President Sukarno was able to exercise power, which a President of parliamentary democracy like India may never have, "as parties and parliament had lost their legitimacy, and as the claim of regionalist leaders to political authority had been destroyed through military defeat. Furthermore the President succeeded in maintaining himself as the nation's chief seeker for and discerner of ideological truth." (*Ibid*., p. 591.)

2. Helplessness of Parliamentary Institutions

The flambuoyant President Sukarno held Indonesia under his spell for nearly two decades. Under his charismatic leadership, his word was law, and parliamentary institutions were treated with scant respect. Sukarno could introduce new institutions, and modify or abolish existing institutions as he liked. In a speech in August 1959 President Sukarno spelt out the principles of his political manifesto: the 1945 Constitution, Indonesian Socialism, Guided Democracy, Guided Economy and Indonesian Personality of Identity."

The Parliament elected in 1955 became powerless, as much of its authority was taken away by the formation of the National Council (which was later changed into the Supreme Advisory Council), the National Planning Council and the Interim People's Consultative Council. (See *Ibid*, p. 592.)

The Constitution of 1945 was revived by Presidential decree after the dissolution of the elected Constituent Assembly of 1959.

A few months after the dissolution of the elected Parliament in March 1960, a new *mutual help* Parliament was appointed by a decree.

3. *Control over Political Parties.*

In Sukarno's Guided Democracy political parties were at the mercy of Government. They could not function freely, as their activities were subject to several restrictions and army controls.

4. No Civil Liberties and Freedom of the Press

People lost their civil liberties with the frequent and arbitrary arrests of the people. The freedom of the press vanished. Journalists were arrested, and their papers were banned, if their columns were unpalatable to the government.

Fall of Sukarno

Over-reached Himself

Sukarno over-reached himself in his national and international dealings. Internally the dictated as he liked and suppressed all opposition against him. Internationally too, he tried to show off and for some time it seemed that Indonesia had become a great force, which could easily administer rebuffs even to a Super Power like the USSR.

Tricked by Chinese

Sukarno hobnobbed with the Chinese communist leaders like Mao Tse-tung and Chou En-lai and supported China against Soviet Russia in the ideological conflict. It may be mentioned here that Soviet Russia had given considerable material help to Indonesia. Unwittingly, Sukarno walked into the Chinese trap and it was soon evident that Indonesia had become the tool of Red China.

Abortive Communist Coup

In September 1965 there was an abortive *coup d'etat* in Indonesia. Sukarno's palace guard under Lt. Col. Untung aided by PKI (the Communist party of Indonesia) attempted to get rid of the topmost military leaders. Yani and other general were murdered and their bodies were flung into a well. Since the *coup* a lakh or two peoples were killed.

Condonation of Sukarno and Subandrio

Sukarno's neutrality between rebels and loyalists was deeply suspected by the people. Particularly, the Indonesian students openly declared that President Sukarno and Foreign Minister

Subandrio who were responsible for selling the country to communists should be tried. Subandrio was actually tried and death sentence was imposed on him

Sukarno Disgraced and Overthrown

In March 1966 Sukarno surrendered authority to his right-wing Army Commander Lt. Col. Suharto. In January 1967 the Indonesian army asked Sukarno to step down or face civil war. In March 1667 Indonesia's Congress announced the end of Sukarno's stormy rule of 21 years. Since his fall from power, he was under house arrest totally isolated from his people and friends. On June, 21, 1970, he died. The editorial comment in *The Times of India* of June 23, 1970, said: "Despite his charisma, he could neither organize a mass party with a pragmatic programme nor build a democratic political structure. The so-called guided democracy which he evolved was no more than a cover for erratic personal rule.".

12. FUTURE OF DEMOCRACY

Dangers of War and Internal Dissensions

International conditions and internal conditions have much to do with the future of democracy. Wars and infighting in various countries are the two great dangers to democracy. E. B. Schulz says on page 227 in *Essentials of Government* (1961): "Two menaces to democracy are international warfare and bitter internal dissensions concerning the proper way of dealing with the deep-seated social maladjustments. A frequent consequence of the latter is the breeding of irreconcilable attitudes which are likely to result in the settlement of controversial questions by bullets rather than by ballots. . . . A continuation of international crises involving war or serious threats of war will have adverse effect on the future of democracy."

Conditions for Bright Future

Certain conditions are essential for a bright future of democracy. It does not require a prophet to say that democracy has a good future only if the people in a country want it and cherish it as a form of government and a way of life. Countries having good democratic traditions, a passion for liberty and equality and a democratic temperament will make necessary sacrifices to keep alive the flame of democracy. They will not forget the principle that democracy is government of the people and good government is no substitute for self-government. In countries like Britain and the USA the democratic spirit is ingrained in the people. Democracy will be safe, provided governments keep the man in the street satisfied and free from the worries of poverty and unemployment. "Democracy stands a good chance of survival in any country in which it has proved reasonably satisfactory and its successful functioning at one or more places may lead to imitation in others. On the other hand, failure of the democracies to solve their various social and economic problems may retard the spread of democratic government and even may lead to its disappearance." (*Ibid.*, p. 225.)

Dangers of Communism and totalitarianism

Communism and totalitarianism are other real dangers to democracy. Communism has been able to register spectacular progress in the twentieth century, and about one-third of the world has gone red. (See Chapter 31 on Communism.) Communism covertly or overtly tries to enter every country. If democrats are able to solve the problems of the people, it will not be easy for communists to spread their tentacles;

Future of Democracy in Developing Countries

The future of democracy in the underdeveloped countries of Asia and Africa (euphemistically called developing countries) cannot be bright, when one looks at the developments that took place in them since they won their independent. Rupert Emerson says in his essay *The Erosion of Democracy* in the new states: "The story which has repeated itself over and over again is that people have set out on the democratic path with revolutionary enthusiasm, but before long they have lost their way and settled back into authoritarian or dictatorial regimes. [See Eckstein and Apter (Ed.), *Comparative Politics*—1963, p. 635]. A survey of countries where democracy was established in recent years makes depressing reading. Besides Pakistan and Indonesia, the unfortunate examples of other countries can be given. In Burma and Sudan as in Pakistan, power fell into the hands of army leaders, who sidetracked constitutional methods. In Iraq, a general seized power and in Lebanon the army chief became President.

President Kwame Nkrumah of Ghans ruled his country in an authoritarian way. But he himself was overthrown in 1976. Guinea, after winning her independence, chose the one party system under the leadership of Sekou Toure.

Africa in which many independent states emerged since the end of World War II is a continent of *coups*. Several *coups* engineered by army leaders were staged in Africa. It is significant to note that foreign powers have directly or indirectly tried to interfere in the internal affairs of these countries to change the course of politics in their favour.

13. RIVALS OF DEMOCRACY

Any form of government in which power is exercised without the consent of the people and which the people have no state is a rival of democracy.

Absolute Monarchy

Absolute monarchy is a rival of democracy. (See Chapter 40 for details.)

Aristocracy or Plutocracy. An aristocracy or plutocracy too is a rival of democracy. (See Chapter 40 for details.

Dictatorship

Dictatorship of any type (viz. Nazi, Fascist and Communist) is also a rival of democracy (Details of dictatorship are dealt with in the next chapter.)

14. N. DEMOCRACY AND SOCIAL JUSTICE

Social Justice a Main Objective

One of the main objectives of a democratic government is to give social justice; in fact in modern times the greatest emphasis is laid on social justice. Every individual in a truly democratic country is done justice; besides he feels that justice is done to him. He feels that he is completely free as others are and enjoys all kinds of rights as others do. He is not denied rights which are given to others.

Justice according to Law

When the individual goes to a court of law in a democratic country, he is given justice according to the law. He carries with him a feeling that justice is done to him, and is not denied any rights or privileges, which are accessible to others.

No Exploitation

In a true democracy, no favour is shown to any class, and no class is allowed to exploit other classes, as the principle of social justice is followed.

Welfare

A democracy aims at the welfare of all, and not at the welfare of any particular individual or a group of individuals only.

Social Justice and Social Welfare in India

As given in the Preamble and the Directive Principle of State Policy in the Constitution of India, the Union and State Governments should exert themselves for promoting social welfare. The Preamble speaks of social, economic and political justice, and Directive Principles provide the guidelines for the realisation of social welfare.

In the USA, Britain and other democracies, ambitious and comprehensive social welfare schemes have been implemented without throwing overboard the principles of liberty and equality.

In Soviet Russia and several other states having forms of government which are the rivals of democracy, steps have been taken to promote social welfare, but the individual is brought under totalitarian control, which means denial or rights.

REFERENCES

Adams, H., *The Degradation of Democratic Dogma.*

Aiyar and Srinivasan (ED.), *Studies in Indian Democracy*, 1965.

Allen, C. K., *Democracy and the Individual.*

Asirvatham, Eddy, *Political Theory*, 1968, Upper India Publishing House, Lucknow,

Benn and Peters, *Social Principles and the Democratic State*, 1951.

Burns, C. D., *Democracy*, 1935.

Burns, C. D., *The Challenge to Democracy.*

Burns, E. M., *Ideas in Conflict*, 1960.

Coker, F. W., *Recent Political Thought*, 1947, The World Press, Calcutta.

Cummngs, M. C., and Wise, David, *Democracy Under Pressure.*

Dahl, Robert A., *Modern Political Analysis,* 1963.

Dahl, Robert A., *Pluralist Democracy in the United States,* 1967, Scientific Books Agency, Calcutta.

Faguet, E., *The Cult of Incompetence.*

Feith, H., *The Decline of Constitutional Democracy in Indonesia,* 1962.

Finer, H., *The Theory and Practice of Modern Government,* 1960, Asia Publishing House, Bombay.

Garner, J. W., *political Science and Government,* 1955, The World Press, Calcutta.

Hearnshaw, F. J. C., *Democracy at the Crossways.*

Labin, Suzanne, *The Secret of Democracy,* 1958, Comet Books, Collins, London.

Lindsay, A. D., *Essentials of Democracy.*

Lindsay A. D., *The Modern Democratic State.*

MacPherson, C.B., *The Real World of Democracy.*

Maine, H., *Popular Government*

Mill, J. S., *Representative Government,* 1890.

Maxey, C. C., *Political Philosophies,* 1959.

Mayo, H. B., *An Introduction to Democratic Theory,* 1960.

Palmer, N. D., *The Indian Political System,* 1961.

Panikkar, K. M., *The Afro-Asian States and Their Problems,* 1946.

Park and Tinker, *Leadership and Political Institutions in India,* 1951.

Rockefeller Panel Report on American Democracy, *The Power of the Democratic Idea,* 1967, Popular Prakashan, Bombay.

Roucek, J. S. and others, *Introduction to Political Science,* 1954.

Sait, E.M., *Democracy,* 1929.

Sartori, Giovanni, *Democratic Theory,* 1962.

Schulz, E. B., *essentials of Government,* 1961.

Simon, Y. R., *Philosophy of Democratic Government,* 1951.

Wells, H. G., *Democracy under Revision.*

Willoughby, W. F., *The Government of Modern States,* 1936.

6

Dictatorship

DEFINITION AND MEANING OF DICTATORSHIP

Unrestrained Power

The term *dictator* has been borrowed from ancient Rome. Dictatorship is a form of government, which is a rival of democracy, and its principles are quite opposite to those of democracy. While democracy upholds liberty, dictatorship suppresses liberty, and stands for unbridled power. F. Neumann says: "By dictatorship we understand the rule of a person or a group of persons who arrogate to themselves and monopolies power in the state, exercising it without restraint." (See *The Democratic and Authoritarian State*—1957, p. 291.)

One Man's Arbitrary Government

Dictatorship has also been defined by R. H. Soltau as "the government of one man who has not primarily obtained his position by inheritance but either by force or by consent. Usually by a combination of both. He must possess absolute sovereignty, exercising it arbitrarily by decree rather than by law." (*An Introduction to Politics*—1959, p. 211.)

Not Responsible

In a democracy, government is responsible to the people, directly or indirectly. On the other hand, a dictatorial form of government, as found in Fascist Italy, Nazi Germany. Soviet Russia and communist China follows policies and exercises power without the least regard for the people's opinion or criticism. A dictator is not responsible to anyone. Dictatorship upholds the principle of non-accountability of government.

Base on Force. A dictator dictates, that is, the orders and rules by decrees as he pleases; his government passes laws to strength them his own hands and to keep the people within his tight grip. The people shall obey and follow him blindly. There are no restraints on his authority, and if any individual or a group of individuals. Tries to question his authority, he responds violently, and ruthlessly suppresses them or even liquidates them.

Supreme Leader as Law unto Himself. Democracy is based on consent, whereas dictatorship is based on force. "Dictatorships have, as a rule, been governed by individual control. The Hitler type of dictator is the supreme leader and is law unto himself, responsible to no one. Mystical adulation is heaped upon him by his subordinates and loyal followers. Contrasted somewhat with this concept is dictatorship based on a royal family, a church, an arn y or a political party." (See J.S. Roucek and Others, *Introduction to Political Science*—1954, p. 230)

2. KINDS OF DICTATORSHIP

Dictatorships can be classified in a threefold manner: (1) Old and New, (2) Rightist and Leftist, and (3) Fascist, Communist and Military.

(1) Old and New

Old Dictatorship

The old type of dictatorship can be traced to ancient Rome. In the Republican Constitution of ancient Rome, there was provision for temporary dictatorship but only during times of emergency according to certain principles. While in normal times the highest executive authority was exercised by the Consuls, during emergency a dictator superseded the Consuls. For instance, when Hannibal invaded Rome, Consular authority yielded place to the power of the dictator. But the dictator in Rome was to step down as soon as normal conditions wee restored. The normal constitution was suspended for a short time, but it was not scrapped.

Old dictators had a very simple governmental machinery at their disposal according to traditional values and principles. On the other hand, modern dictators, who are generally the products of an industrialized society, have unlimited scientific and technological devices at their disposal, and precise political principles and ideologies to follow. They organise government in a thorough manner to suit their own principles and ideas and those of their party, and proceed scientifically and ruthlessly to enslave the body and mind of the citizen. Their governmental machinery is highly complex and streamlined.

Modern Dictators

Modern Dictators, who wield extra-constitutional authority, aim at world domination, and the sky alone is the frontier of their ambitions. Ancient dictators pale into insignificance, when compared to their modern counterparts. Once they capture power, they try to remain in power indefinitely. Only widespread public revolt or superior military power or death can remove them from power.

Crude and Caesaristic Dictatorships

Old dictatorships are of two-types: Crude and Caesaristic. The crude dictaror merely relies on force. But the Caesaristic dictator has extraordinary qualities.

Permanence in Modern Dictatorship

Modern dictatorship which is extra-constitutional is not transient and temporary. It tries to strike deep roots in the soil and strongly entrench itself in power. Soviet totalitarian dictatorship not only survived since its establishment in 1917, but became immensely strong. The same is the case with Chinese Red dictatorship. Both these dictatorships spread their tentacles all over the world, and have moved from strength to strength. Unlike the dictators in ancient Rome, modern dictators rise to power by sheer brute force taking advantage of the defects of the constitution and the general conditions in the country.

Constitutional Cloaks

Some of the modern dictators manage to have constitutional cloaks to cover their exercise of authoritariansim. The term 'president', for instance, becomes a misleading expression, when used in connection with dictators like Ayub Khan, Yahya Khan, and Zia-ul-haq of Pakistan, Sukarno of Indonesia, and Liu Shao-chi and Lin Piao of Communist China.

(2) Rightist and Leftist

Modern dictatorships are of two kinds: Rightist and Leftist. Righ ist dictators stand for or tolerate capitalism, while the Leftist dictators stand for socialism, Nazi Germany, Fascist Italy, Turkey, Greece, Spain, Portugal and other countries have Rightist dictatorship, while Soviet Russia and China have Leftist.

(3) Fascist, Communist and Military

Modern dictatorship can be classified in another way: (1) Fascist *e.g.* Italy and Germany; (2) Communist *e.g.* Soviet Russia and China; (3) Military *e.g.* Indonesia, Pakistan and Egypt.

3. Rise of Modern Dictatorship

The twentieth century has a bumper crop of dictators. In the inter-war period (1919-39), dictatorship rose in several countries. Spain under Primo di Rivero in 1923, Poland under Pilsudski in 1929, Yugoslavia under King Alexander, Rumania under King Carol in 1931, and Greece under John Metaxes in August 1939 came to have dictatorial governments. But Germany, Italy and Russia became good examples of dictatorship which were followed by other countries. After the end of World War II (1939-45), dictatorship rose in China, Indonesia, Pakistan, Burma, Sudan, Egypt, Iraq and other countries. The 1930s came to be called the Age of Great Dictators.

Reaction Against Democracy

Modern dictatorships shot up as a strong reaction against democracy, which had its brief golden period in the fist two decades of the twentieth century. During the inter-war period (1919-39), democracy failed miserably and became a casualty in several European countries; and even the old democracies were rudely shaken to their very foundations. States which were carved out on the principle of self-determination immediately after World War I had democratic constitutions, which unfortunately could not bear the strain of the challenging times. In the new democracies, which were feeble, progress was painfully slow, and all the drawbacks of democracy had an upper hand in them.

Causes

Modern doctorship emerged owing to the following causes:

(1) Arrogance of Victorious Powers

Victorious powers like Britain and France were arrogant, and were not fair in their dealings with small powers in the international field. While they waxed eloquently on high-sounding principles like self-determination on the one hand, they arrogantly followed capitalist and imperialist polices on the other. The defeated powers like Germany which were treated unduly harshly and with contempt bore a grudge against the victorious powers, which paid only lip sympathy to democracy. The principle of self-determination was denied to several subject countries like India. Double standards were followed, and efforts were made by self-righteous leaders of the world to keep down peoples in the various parts of the world on the some pretext or the other.

(2) Failure of Democracies

In the inter-war period, democracies, which were weak and hollow, stood thoroughly exposed, and this led to the spread of dictatorship like an epidemic in several countries. Grand democratic constitutions were made for countries in which the necessary conditions for the smooth and efficient working of democracy were totally lacking. The genius of people in them did not match the letter and spirit of their democratic constitutions. Though President Woodrow Wilson of the USA had triumphantly declared that the world was made safe for democracy, conditions were highly unfavorable in several countries for democracy to strike roots. On the contrary, the climate was congenial for the emergence of the opposite type of government, that is, dictatorship. They glory of democracy, particularly Anglo-American democracy, faded, as it offered no immediate and satisfactory solutions to serious and urgent problems of the people. Moreover, people who secured democratic constitutions did not have the requisite training and experience to make them successful.

In Germany, for instance, the democratic Weimar Constitution was unable to face the challenge of the times. Germany's great distress after World War I (1914-18) beggared description. People lost faith in democracy, as inflation, unemployment and demoralisation were mounting day by day. The constitution was meaningless to the miserable Germans. Hitler then rose to power, and held out a rosy future for Germany. He offered immediate solution to every German problem.

In Italy (the disgruntled victor of World War I) too, the people were deeply frustrated, and Benito Mussolini was able to dictator in the guise of saviour.

In other countries like Spain, Poland, Yugoslavia, Rumania, Bulgaria, Austria, Hungary, Greece, Portugal, Turkey and Japan, democratic institutions broke down one by one in rapid succession. There was a cavalcade of fading or falling democracies. In some Latin American states, instability and revolution gave rise to dictatorship. In Spain, Primo di Revera became dictator; then there was civil war after which Franco became dictator.

In Russia, the Czarist regime was overthrown in 1917, and communists got themselves entrenched in power. Lenin exercised dictatorial power in the name of the proletariat, and after him Stalin established his ruthless dictatorship. Stalin was succeed by Malenkov, who was followed by Bulganin. In 1958 Bulganin was ousted by Nikita Knrushchev, who remained in saddle till 1964, when he was overthrown by Kosygin. Dictatorship became permanent in Soviet Russia.

In China, which became a republic in 1911, conditions were favorable for the rise of a communist dictatorship as the republican leaders failed to solve the problems of the people. In 1949, the Kuomintang Government of Chiang Kai-Shek was overthrown and Mao Tse-tung became China's dictator. The President, the Prime Minister and all other officers were hardly better than the tools of Mao Tse-tung. In China also dictatorship became permanent.

Japan-witnessed the rise of the dictatorship of Tojo. Japanese dictatorship was partly responsible for World War II.

(3) Rise of Men of Extraordinary Ability

In several countries, dynamic men of extraordinary capacity rose to lead people from despair to hope and become saviours. They captured the imagination of the people, instilled public confidence and used the army to seize power. They disliked the long and meandering tracks of democracy, and had the short-cut of dictatorship. The masses of people were shepherded and made to obey them without much opposition. Perhaps people in their dejection and frustration felt that democracy was not worth much for being saved.

(4) No Saviour for Democracy

Democracy had no saviour in many countries. It had no practical use for disgruntled people. People disowned democracy, and welcomed dictatorship, as it was purposeful and meaningful to them. In countries in which national pride was hurt, the people were thrilled to hear the inspiring speeches of prospective dictators.

The Germans were humiliated and placed in dust by the Treaty of Versailles (1919), but Hitler was able to save them and bring them back to national honour.

In backward countries like Turkey, people were led by force after being roused to fever pitch. Here too leaders like Mustapha Kamal emphasised patriotism and nationalism.

In Russia, where totalitarian dictatorship was permanent after the Revolution, people were terrorized and coerced into utter submission.

The indifferent attitude of the masses of people or their lack of enthusiasm for democracy was a highly favourable factor for the emergence and growth dictatorship.

(5) Helplessness of League of Nations

The League of Nations began to look ridiculous, as it could do nothing to save democracy. It was toothless and spineless, and it, did hardly anything effective for safeguarding peace and democracy, when Hitler's Germany went on committing a series of aggressive acts, when Mussolini's Italy, annexed Ethiopia, when Soviet Russia attacked East European countries, and when Japan seized Manchuria from China. Leaders in the League of Nations, who condemned aggression looked, foolish in the eyes of dictators.

4. FEATURES OF MODERN DICTATORSHIP

The following are the salient features of modern dictatorship:

(1) Authoritarianism of One Man or of Minority Group

Modern dictatorship is thoroughly authoritarian. E. B. Schulz observes on page 205 in *Essentials of Government* (1961) : "An authoritarian government is characterised by the possession of supreme authority either by one persons or by a minority group in no way accountable to the people over whom control is exercised." There are two forms of authoritarianism *viz.* the Fascist in Italy, Germany, Portugal and Spain; and the Communist in Soviet Russia, Communist China and other countries. It its based on brute force, and not consent. A party or a minority group wields authoritarian control. In Russia, all are not communists; but the party controls the entire country. The same was the case with Nazi Germany and Fascist Italy.

(2) Totalitarian Supervision and Control

Dictatorship in some states in totalitarian. Italy under Mussolini, Germany under Hitler, Soviet Russia under Stalin, Khrushehev and Kosygin, and China under Mao Tse-tung became totalitarian states. In these states the individual's personality is suppressed and all aspects of his life are regimented and brought under state control. E. B. Schulz says: "A totalitarian policy is characterised by the exercise of strict supervision and control over human thought and action for the purpose of establishing and all-embracing and exclusive way of life or social order that is asserted to be ideal." (*Ibid.*, p. 203.) As Roucek and Others observe in *An Introduction to Political Science* (1954) on page 232, the state "extends its influence over the whole of public and private life and exacts the full submission of everyone to its dictators." In schools and other educational institutions, students are taught to worship the dictator. People are made to understand that no aspect of their life should be left uncontrolled by the state, if there should be progress.

F. Neumann mentions five essential factors of a totalitarian state; (1) transition from the rule of law to a police state; (2) transition from the diffusion of power to the concentration of power; (3) existence of a monopolistic state party; (4) transition from pluralist to totalitarian social controls; and (5) reliance upon terror. (See *The Democratic and the Authoriatrian State*—1957, p. 244.)

(3) Ruthless One-party Rule

In a dictatorship, the party to which the dictator belongs exercises ruthless control in the state from top to bottom, allowing no individual or party to rise against it. Even though there may be a written constitution outlining the formation of various institutions in which the people can work, one single party dominates over all institution. Brutal methods are used to keep out anti-party people and to weed out the enemies of the government and the party. There is no difference between the party and the government. The Nazi party in Hitler's Germany, the Fascist party in Mussolini's Italy, and the Communist party in Soviet Russia exercised complete dictatorial control.

(4) No Rights

Rights, which people enjoy in democratic states, are totally denied to people under a dictatorship. People do not have political and civil rights. They are regarded as tools or instruments of the state. They are not allowed to express their opinion or criticise, and those who venture to do so are sent to concentration camps or slave labour camps or liquidated. All agencies of public opinion and means of communication are controlled and censored by the state. Only "rights" which are allowed by the dictator can be enjoyed by the people. People have to remain silent, and suffer totalitarian control and humiliation with stoic patience. Dictators manage to control both the body and the soul of the individual. The Fascist oath said: "In the name of God and Italy, I swear to execute without discussion the orders to the Duce and to serve with all my strength and if necessary with my blood the cause of the Fascist revolution." Mussolini asked the youngsters in Italy to follow the motto: "To believe, to obey, to fight."

(5) Cruel Suppression at Home and Aggression Abroad

All modern dictatorships use brute force to realise their goal. In numerous ways, fear is struck into the minds of the people who are forced to be submissive and toe the dictator's line. Secret police are employed to deal with "enemies" of the state. *Confessions* are extracted. And *justice* is meted out. Undersirable elements are killed or hounded out of the state so that others are terror-struck and made timid and submissive. The atmosphere is charged with fear and suspicion, and there is all-round ruthless suppression. In the external sphere, a policy of naked aggression is followed. The dictatorships of Hitler, Mussolini and Stalin were based on brute force, egoistic and militant nationalism, aggressive imperialism and war. Stalin and Mao developed the communist brand of imperialism.

(6) Worship of the Irrational

It is strange but true that fascist dictatorships worshipped the irrational. They created an impression that only the irrational (and not rational as Hegel said) was real. It was only after much suffering when World War II (1939-45) ended, that Europe realised that it was emerging from what was irrational.

(7) Wide Gulf between Dictator and People

The dictator distrusts people and deliberately keeps himself isolated. Therefore, there is a wide gulf between the dictator and the people. The distinction between state and government is eliminated. Like the absolute monarch Louis XIV of France, the dictator regards himself as the state. As power is based on coercion and not on consent, the dictator suspects all and takes steps to protect himself from any plots and conspiracies against his life. He takes no risk and moves about under full protection and rides in bullet-proof cars.

5. MERITS AND DEFECTS OF MODERN DICTATORSHIP

Merits

Let us briefly discuss the basic merits of dictatorship.

(1) Simplicity and Singleness of Purpose

The governmental machinery is simple, and the wheels of government can revolve quickly, as all power is concentrated in the hands of one man and his intimate friends. Dictators show a singleness of purpose, which one rarely finds in leaders in a democratic country. The dictator knows his targets and follows clear-cut methods to reach them. People know the simple structure of government. They have no share in the exercise of power. The are freed of all responsibilities. Their only responsibility is to obey the orders of the dictator.

(2) Low Cost of Administration

The low administrative expenditure is another advantage. While the cost of administration in a democratic state is heavy, the cost is relatively low in a dictatorship. The paraphernalia of a democratic government is complex and costly; but in one man's rule one does not find the costly luxuries of sinecure and superfluous posts, parliamentary committees, sub-committees and commissions. Much public money is saved in this respect.

(3) Efficiency and Progress

Even the worst critics of dictatorship admit that dictators move smoothly, swiftly and with energetic promptitude. If a dictator is dynamic, has government functions most speedily and effectively. A democracy is nowhere near a dictatorship in efficiency and vigour. While a democratic government takes a long time to discuss and introduce new measures, and improve conditions, a dictatorship can do much in a short time. A dictator appoints the right type of people to get things done swiftly and efficiently, and he can dismiss them if the are inefficient or disobedient. This is difficult in a democracy, in which many in time worthy person cannot be appointed, and unworthy and incompetent government employees cannot be easily sacked. Regarding the functions of the Spanish dictatorship, Jackson gave fulsome praise in his book *Europe Since The War*: "For the first time in their history the Spanish trains ran punctually. New railways were laid down, and a system of fine motor roads took the place of traditional mule tracks of Spain. . . . The commerce and industry flourished under the dictator.

Defects

The drawbacks of dictatorship more than counter balance the advantages. The following are the main defects of dictatorship.

(1) Brutal Suppression

Brutal suppression is the basic feature of dictatorship. Dictators have no compassion or consideration for any one and do not care for the feelings of the people. Love, understanding and sympathy are alien to a dictator. Dictatorship is based on brute force and fear, and seeks to annihilate everything coming across its path. It attaches no value to the dignity of the human being. People have no rights, and they are treated as the tools of the state. The personality of the individual is suppressed and his moral and intellectual growth is stunted.

(2) Egoistic and Selfish

Dictators are highly egoistic and selfish. They use all their energy and coerce all people to follow their path in order to realise their own selfish aims or those of their party. The real interests of the people do not count. People are thrown to the tender mercies of power-drunk, egoistic and selfish leaders. People become aware that it is dangerous to hurt the ego of the dictator.

(3) Imperialism, War and Destruction

Dictators are imperialistic and are committed to a policy of aggression and aggrandisement. They lead their countries to war, and bring destruction to all including themselves. Hitler, Mussolini and Tojo ruined their respective states, and also brought destruction and sorrow to other countries. In the long run, dictators face a miserable end. Dictators who are against international peace and good will are totally committed to war and destruction. Sacrificing the lives and blood of thousands is necessary to remain in power.

(4) State an End

Under a dictatorship state is made the end and not the means to an end. The individual is made a helpless tool to realise the end of the state. The fact that the individual is governed well is a poor consolation for the loss of freedom.

(5) No Continuity

A dictatorship may come to an end after the death of the dictator. His son or successor may not have his outstanding qualities and strength, and a struggle for power endangering the stability of the state may inevitably break out. Democracies make provision for an orderly succession or change in government. The transition is smooth and peaceful; but conditions are different in a dictatorship.

(6) Against Accepted Values

Dictators throw overboard all the generally accepted values of society, if they come in the way of their power. Spiritual, moral and religious values are brushed aside for the sake of remaining in saddle.

REFERENCES

Asirvatham, Eddy, *Political Theory*, 1968, Upper India Publishing House, Lucknow.

Cobban, Alfred, *Dictatorship.*

Ford, G. S., *Dictatorship in the Modern World.*

Friendrich, C. I. and Brezezinski, Z.K., *Totalitarian Dictatorship and Autocracy*, 1969, Harvard University Press.

Hoover, C. B., *Doctorship and Democracies.*

Neumann, F., *The Democratic and the Authoritarian State*, 1957.

Parkinson, N. C., *The Evolution of Political Thought.*

Prasad, Beni, *The Democratic Process.*

Roucek, J. S. and Others, *Introduction to Political Science*, 1959.

Schulz, E. B., *Essentials of Government*, 1961.

Soltau, R. H., *An Introduction to Polities*, 1959.

7

Division of Powers: Unitary Government

1. TERRITORIAL AND FUNCTIONAL DIVISIONS OF POWERS

Two-Fold Division of Powers

It is necessary to make a division of powers in a state for the sake of convenience, and for the smooth and efficient working of the governmental machinery.

The division is made in two ways: (1) territorial, and (2) functional. F. W. Willoughby says on page 165 in *The Government of Modern States* (1936): "These two are not alternative methods. Both are employed in the organization of all modern governments. In their employment a wide divergence of policy is, however, possible. . . . According as one principle or another is followed in distributing powers territorially, there is brought into existence a type of government known as Unitary Government or one to which the designation of Multiple Government may be given, though the term more usually employed is that of Federal Government." States like England and France have unitary government, while the USA, the USSR, Canada and Australia have federal. British India had unitary government; but according to the present Constitution (1950), India is a Union of States, a unique type of federation with a strong centre.

Territorial Division

In the case of territorial division, the territory of the state is divided and subdivided; each of the divisions or subdivisions is charged with the duty of performing particular functions and the necessary powers are conferred on it for the purpose.

Functional Division

In the case of functional division, functions and the necessary powers to look after them are assigned to specific organs or authorities. In British India, which as stated above, was unitary, territory was divided into Presidencies or Provinces; each of them was divided into districts, and each district was divided into *Talukas*.

Greater Efficiency at Lower Cost

Territorial and functional division; or powers enables a government to function smoothly, by taking off the load of functions from one centre of authority and giving it to the authorities in the geographical division or subdivision, and by assigning functions to different authorities according to the principle of functional division. Another advantage in the division of powers is that work can be conveniently done by the different divisions and subdivisions and the various authorities, as it mostly pertains to the interests of a particular area or locality. It must also be noted that division of powers enhances the efficiency of government and reduces the cost of administration.

2. DEFINITION, MEANING AND FEATURES OF UNITARY GOVERNMENT

Definition

A unitary government is one in which the highest executive, legislative and judicial authority is located in the central government at the capital of the state. This government conducts the administration of the whole state with the aid of the provincial governments, which function under it in a subordinate capacity.

In the unitary system, a single integrated system of government exercises all powers, and the legal sovereign gives all powers into the hands of a *single central government*.

Relations between Centre and Provinces or Units

The relations between the central government at the capital and the governments in the provinces or units will show whether the government is unitary. If the central government wields supreme power and is competent to order the government in the units or provinces, the form of government is clearly unitary. In a unitary system, provincial governments do not have an independent constitutional status.

We may briefly refer to the following salient features of the unitary form of government:

(1) Supreme Single Central Government

As the name itself suggests, in a unitary system, there is one set of government, to which all authorities are subordinate. There is one central government armed with full authority. C. F. Strong says in *Modern Political Constitutions* (1958: 61): "A unitary state is one organized under a single central government; that is to say, whatever powers are possessed by the various districts within the area administered as a whole by the central government, are held at the discretion of that government, and the central power is supreme over the whole without any restrictions imposed by any law granting special powers to its parts." A unitary form of government is one in which all governmental powers are exercised from one centre consisting of one supreme legislature, one supreme executive and one supreme judiciary for all the territory in the state. The central government does not treat the provinces as its equals or share any power with them; on the contrary, it treats them as its subordinates and issues orders to them. J. W. Garner defines unitary government as "that form in which the supreme governing authority of a state is concentrated in a single organ or set of organs established at and operating from a common centre." (*Political Science and Government*, 1955: p. 377.)

In countries like India (under the Act of 1919), Britain, France, Denmark, Belgium, Holland, Spain, Norway, Sweden, Italy, Turkey, Japan, Iran, Afghanistan and New Zealand, which have a unitary form, the central or national government exercises undivided power.

(2) Provincial and Local Bodies under Central Control

In a unitary form of government, there may be several provincial and local bodies and corporations, but all of them function in a subordinate capacity at the discretion of the central government. All provincial and local governments are the creatures of the centre, and they shall exercise only those powers conferred on them by the centre. All legislative bodies in the unitary system are under the control of the central legislature, which is the only supreme law-making body. Though powers are given to the various geographical subdivisions, they are to be exercised strictly according to the will of the centre.

As regards the position of the central legislature, an important point has to be clarified, and that is, the central legislature is not superior to the constitution. This can be said particularly with reference to states like the Irish Republic. The central legislature is bound by the provisions of the constitution. Thus, in this respect there is a similarity between a unitary state with a written constitution and a federal state. In England, a unitary state, it is the Parliament and not the constitution that is supreme.

At the same time, it must be noted that while legislative supremacy is the feature of the unitary state, the supremacy of the constitution is the feature of the federal state. Legislative supremacy in a unitary state means the inferior status of the various law-making bodies and the superior status of the central legislature.

(3) Centre Creator and Units Creatures in an Integrate System

Unlike in a federal system in a unitary system, the political divisions and subdivisions are the integral part of the government at the centre. (See Chapter 7 on Federal Government). There is no constitutional distribution of powers between the central government on one hand and the provinces or divisions on the other. J. W. Garner says: "..... Local government derive whatever authority or autonomy they possess and indeed their very existence from the centre." (*Ibid.*, p. 317.) E. B. Schulz also points out: "Ordinarily the central government may determine the number and nature of self-governing political subdivisions and may to away with them at pleasure. That being the case local bodies politics are clearly the offspring of this government." (*Essentials of Government*, 1961: p. 178.)

The central government is the creator of the divisions and subdivisions and so it can increase or decrease their number, if it deems fit. As the divisions and subdivisions are the creatures of the central government, they have to obey the order of the centre. Local units in a unitary state receive authority as gift from the government and not as a right. The centre can contract or enlarge the powers of the subordinate governments, according to its own discretion. It is free to withdraw fully or partially any authority given to the divisions.

Thus unlike in a federal system, in unitary system, the divisions do not have a co-ordinate status, but a subordinate status.

(4) Supremacy of Central Legislature

The supremacy of the central legislature is another important feature of the unitary system. All legislative bodies in a unitary state are subservient to the central legislature. Negatively speaking, the non-existence of subordinate *sovereign* bodies is a conspicuous feature of a unitary state. While in a unitary state like England a Country is created by the Parliament, in a federal state like the U.S.A., the federal units or states have their own subsidiary sovereign bodies, which are not the creatures of the fede al legislature, but the products of the constitution. S. Leacock says on page 115 in *The Elements of Political Science* (1933): "In a unitary government the organs of local authority (provincial and country bodies, etc.) exist by virtue of an express creation, or by tacit recognition from the central government. The latter has power, legally, to terminate their existence or alter their form."

In England divisions like Counties have powers not because any constitution has conferred on them, but because Parliament created the division by its Acts. These divisions shall obey the orders of the central government.

Similarly, France, a unitary state, is divided into administrative units called Departments, which are subdivided into cantons, *aggrandizements* and communes. These divisions are merely the agents of the central government. It may be noted here that while in England local divisions enjoy a good deal of autonomy, in France there is excessive centralisation, and it is said that it is misleading to talk of local autonomy.

3. MERITS AND DEFECTS OF THE UNITARY SYSTEM

Whether a unitary or federal system is suitable for a particular country depends upon its size, the genius of the people and other factors.

Merits

The following are the merits of the unitary system:

(1) Good for Small States

The unitary system is particularly good for small countries like England, Belgium and Italy. The whole country can be conveniently and effectively governed from one centre. A federal form of government with its two sets of government and a complex and complicated governmental machinery involving great expenditure will not be suitable for a small state. England has wisely selected the unitary system.

(2) Strength and Stability

The unitary form is highly favorable to the maintenance of stability, unity and national solidarity in a country. Government can be very strong and stable. Relatively speaking, fissiparous tendencies cannot easily rise in a unitary state, as the loyalty of the citizen is not divided between two sets of government. Policies at home or abroad can be followed with great vigour and promptitude.

As all power emanates from a single centre, and policies are made at one centre, the unity in a country can be easily built and maintained. The question of the centre consulting the divisions every now and them in the formulation of policies does not arise, and this saves much time and money, not to speak of the maintenance of efficiency. As the divisions are the creatures of the centre, generally there is no occasion for them to get into controversies with the centre. We do not find in the unitary system overlapping or conflict of jurisdiction.

In a federal system, the units can find occasion to challenge the authority of the centre, if they have reason to feel that the centre is not acting fairly.

In formulating foreign policy and in looking after defence, the unitary system is more advantageous than the federal.

(3) Flexibility

A unitary government commands great flexibility. The centre can change its policies and methods to suit the changing times and improve the administrative system. Its hands are not tied, and it can make the necessary modifications and adjustments. As times change, the required socio-economic changes can be introduced by easily amending the constitution. But this is not possible in a federation. Such flexibility is absent in the federal system. E.B. Schulz observes in *Essentials of Government* (1961: 179): "The principal advantage of a unitary system is its flexibility in the matter of distributing and redistributing powers on a territorial basis. Since the central government, which is in full command of the local government problem, may allocate powers though the ordinary law-making process, the transfer of authority from one level of government to another is easily accomplished." A federal system is comparatively very rigid, and it cannot easily adjust to meet the sudden requirements at any time.

(4) Simplicity and Uniformity

The unitary system is simple, whereas the federal system is complex. It is easier to run a unitary government than a federal one. An ordinary man finds it easy to understand the unitary system. The federal structure and the interstate relations are difficult for the lay man to understand. Side by side with simplicity there is uniformity of law and administration, as there is only one supreme legislative authority. All the provinces under a unitary system (unlike the units in the federal system) have the same law, and therefore there is no conflict and confusion.

(5) Low Cost of Administration

The expenses on administration in a unitary government are decidedly lower than those in a federal government. The former has to maintain only one set of government, while the latter has to maintain two. In a unitary government we do not have a multiplicity of administrative and legislative authorities. This saves much money besides avoiding confusion. Therefore states with limited resources should choose the unitary system.

Defects

The unitary system suffers from the following defects:

(1) Central Despotism

The unitary system may be misused by those who have craze for power, as it provides ample scope for the despotism of the centre. F. B. Schulz says: "The primary objection to the unitary system is its lack of formal safeguards against undue centralization of government functions. If the central agencies so desire they may either monopolize the exercise of controls and the condition of services of confer only insignificant discretionary powers on political divisions." (*Ibid.*, p. 181.) Political and administrative leaders at the centre may behave in an arrogant and dictatorial manner towards those in the provinces. Harold Laski says on page 101 in his *A Grammar of Politics* that "the formidable centralisation of the modern state is so great an enemy to an ideal system of rights. For only where power is distributed widely is there an effective restraint upon those who wield it."

(2) Top Heavy Centre

As administration has to be conducted from one centre, the centre may become top heavy, and this may lead to inefficiency and fall in the administrative standards.

(3) Side-tracking Distant Areas

Several factors may make the centre side-track the distant areas. The requirements of the people in the distant regions may not be met by the centre, and their interests may go unprotected. The hopes and aspirations of the people in the provinces do not have much scope in a unitary pattern. Rulers at the centre may have neither the time nor inclination to study and settle the problems of distant areas.

(4) Local Initiative Discourage

The unitary system throws a wet blanket on the enthusiasm of the people in the different areas to come forward and associate themselves with the work of the government. J. W. Garner says on page 381 in *Political Science and Government* (1955): "Of unitary government wherever found it may be said in criticism that it tends to repress local initiative, discourages rather than stimulates interest in public affairs, impairs the vitality of the local government, and facilitates the development of a centralised bureaucracy. "While on one side the unitary system may nourish all the evils of a centralised bureaucracy, it may utterly overlook local talent and initiative on the other. In the ultimate analysis the right to local self-government may be denied to the people.

(5) Vulnerability of Centre

In times of danger, a unitary government is more vulnerable than the federal. Internal rebels or external enemies can easily seize the national government which is the nerve centre of the whole country.

REFERENCES

Garner, J. W., *Political Science and Government*, 1955.

Leacocok, S., *Elements of Political Science*, 1933.

Ogg, F. A., *English Government and Politics*.

Schulz, E. B., *Essentials of Government*, 1961.

Strong, C. F., *Modern Political Constitutions*, 1958.

Willoughby, F. W., *The Government of Modern States*, 1936.

8

Division of Powers: Federal Government

A. DEFINITION AND MEANING OF FEDERATION

Foedus or Agreement

The term *federation* is derived from the Latin word *foedus*, which means treaty or agreement, which is made by the different states intending to federate. They all agree by the written treaty or instrument, to form the dual polity of co-ordinate authorities, neither subservient to the other, and each having a clear constitutional field of its own.

Association of States, Common Aims and Large Measure of Original Independence

A federation is an association of states formed by a written constitution. Several states having common aims and objectives may form an association on constitutional, legal and permanent basis. In this association having two sets of authorities, the states surrender their sovereignty for the common good, but at the same time, maintain a large measure of their original independence as far as the regional matters are concerned.

Like several other terms in political science, the term 'federation' is often used loosely and carelessly, K. C. Where says in *Federal Government* (1946: 1) that "most of those who use it agree in this, that they have in mind an association of states, which has been formed for certain common purposes but in which the member states retain a large measure of their original independence".

In a federation we discuss:

(1) two sets of government constitutionally co-ordinate;

(2) division of powers between centre and units according to a fairly rigid written constitution;

(3) a federal court as a guardian of the constitution; and

(4) supremacy of the constitution, which is rigid.

Important Definitions

Here we may take note of certain important definitions. K. C. Wheare, a great authority on federalism, says in *Modern Constitutions* (1958: 27):

> "In a federal constitution the powers of government are divided between a government for the whole country and governments for parts of the country in such a way that each government is legally independent within its own sphere."

J. W. Garner says in *Political Science and Government* (1955: 318):

> "Federal government as distinguished from unitary government is a system is which the totality of governmental power is divided and distributed by the national constitution or the organic act of parliament creating it, between a central government and the governments of the individual states or other territorial subdivisions of which the federation is composed."

M. *Stewart in his Modern Forms of Government* (1950:145) defines a federation as

> "a permanent union of communities so distinct that they might have been sovereign states linked by common interest that they have surrendered absolute sovereignty, but so conscious of their distinctness that they have made the surrender in a form which protects those separate rights short of sovereignty itself, which they most cherish."

Montsequieu says that federation is a "convention by which several petty states agree to become members of a large one which they intend to establish."

Herman Finer says in the *Theory and Practice of Modern Government*:

"A federal state is one in which part of the authority and power is vested in the local areas while another part is vested in a central institution deliberately constituted by an association of the local areas."

Two Sets of Government Constitutionally Knit together

In a federal government, two sets of government are constitutionally and legally knit together. The status, functions and powers of each set of government are clearly and unambiguously spelt out in a written constitution so that each acts strictly within its own sphere assigned to it.

The two sets of government are:

(1) Federal, National or Central Government to deal with subjects of general or national importance;

(2) Regional Government, which may be called States (as in the USA and India), Cantons (in Switzerland) or Provinces (in Canada) to deal with subjects of regional importance.

E. B. Schulz observes in *Essentials of Government* (1961: 181):

"The principal earmark of a federal system is the guarantee, by *adequate constitutional arrangements*, of some degree of autonomy for major local units.... A division of governmental authority along territorial lines is embodied in the constitution and both the central government and the major local units may exercise their constitutionally prescribed powers as they please."

The division of powers is made in such a way that national interests and the distinctness of the communities or units coming together into the union of states are reconciled. The individuality of the federating partners is clearly retained, while their absolute sovereignty is surrendered.

Allocation of Subjects

In any state, there are firstly subjects of national importance like defence, foreign policy and currency and coinage and secondly, subjects of regional or local importance like public order, police and local government. In a unitary state, both the types of subjects are dealt with by one integrated system of government, and all powers are exercised and functions discharged by the central government and its agents. But in a federation subjects of general of national importance are given to the federal or central government, and those of regional importance are given to the units.

The allocation of subjects is made by a written constitution. Considerable care is taken while dividing the subjects between the centre and the units so that, as Bryce points out, a proper balance is maintained between the jurisdiction of two sets of governments. The maximum scope is provided to units to function freely and enjoy local autonomy. Subjects of common importance and of the national level are left in the hands of the federal government. The federal government moves only within the framework provided to it by the written constitution, and each one of the units, understanding its rights and limitations also functions strictly within the circle drawn by the constitution.

Thus, a federal government unlike a unitary government is dual. Subjects of national importance like defence, foreign affairs, currency, foreign trade and maritime shipping are under the control of the Central Government, and those of local or regional importance like police, peace and order, education, civil rights, hospitals and property are under the Regional Governments.

The allocation of powers may be made in three ways:

(1) to enumerate the subjects to be dealt with by the central government and the units;

(2) to enumerate only the subjects of the centre and to give the rest to the units; and

(3) to enumerate the subjects of the units and give the rest to the centre by a general grant.

Each federation has its own way of distributing powers according to historical conditions, the needs of the state and the genius of the people.

In some federations, the balance of powers is distinctly in favor of the federal government, whereas in others it is in favour of the units. In the first case the centre becomes strong, and the units enjoy relatively less autonomy. But in the second case the centre remains weak, and the units enjoy good deal of autonomy. The USA is a good example of a relatively strong centre.

In the USA, Switzerland, Australia and the USSR, the powers of the centre are written down, and residuary powers are given to the units.

In the case of Canada, the powers of the units (provinces) are enumerated and the residuary powers are with the centre.

There are three types of powers under any method of distribution:

(1) powers exclusively assigned to the centre;

(2) powers given exclusively to units; and

(3) concurrent powers, that is, powers belonging both to the centre and the units.

A federal court is set up to interpret the constitution, to settle disputes, concerning jurisdiction and maintain the proper balance of jurisdiction according to the constitutional provisions.

The USA, Switzerland, Canada, Australia, the USSR, Argentia and Brazil have federal constitutions.

The Union of S. Africa has features of both unitary and federal states.

India has a federal pattern, which has a strong centre.

Constitutional States of Units

In a federation, the units have a *constitutional* status. They are not to be treated as the mere creatures of the centre, and the centre cannot order them as it likes. The units owe their existence not to the centre, but to the written constitution.

Supremacy of Constitution

In a federation, the constitution is supreme. Neither the centre nor the units can claim supremacy. Each set of government functions according to the provisions of the constitution. The constitution clearly defines the powers of the centre and the units, and none of them shall transgress the boundaries of constitutional law. All laws, whether made by the central legislature or by the legislatures of the units shall be strictly within the framework of the constitution, and any law violating the provisions of the constitution is liable to be declared *ultra vires* by the federal court.

Federal Court

A federal court is indispensable to a federation. It is the guardian of the constitution, and settles disputes between the federal government and the units, or between two or more units. Like the centre and the units, the federal court is created by the constitution, and judges have to function according to the provisions of the constitution.

Origin of Federation

Though the federal system, as we know it now, is clearly an American invention, even in ancient times people had some dim ideas about it. Sobei Mogi says on page 21 in *Problem of Federalism* (1931): "The first glimpse of the federal principle was about the third century B.C. (218-146) in Greece. There is, however, no sufficiently clear description of federalism in Greek political thought even though the first confederacy in history was the Achaen League." In the middle ages, the principle of federalism was known to some of the Italian cities.

All federations are not exactly like one another. According to the conditions prevailing in a state, federalism is modified. The USA, a pioneer in federalism on a large scale, drew up a federal constitution, according to the needs and genius of the American people. Other countries, which chose to have the federal pattern did not fully copy the American model, but modified federalism in the light of their peculiar conditions and problems. Therefore, Canada, India and Australia do not follow identical principles.

B. UNITARY GOVERNMENT AND FEDERAL GOVERNMENT

We have already studied the salient features of the unitary and federal systems.

The following table summarises the difference between a unitary government and a federal government.

Unitary Government	Federal Government
1. One integrated set of government. This is the central government in which power is concentrated.	1. Two sets of government. Powers are divided between the two sets. These are the Centre and the Units.
2. Political divisions or provinces are integral part of government.	2. Federated units have complete autonomy regarding subjects under them.

Unitary Government	Federal Government
3. Central government is the creator of the political divisions, and the provinces are its creatures.	3. Central government is not the creator of the federated units. Both the central government and the units owe their existence to a written constitution.
4. Central government can issue orders to the provinces as it pleases, as they are subordinate to it; it can increase or reduce their powers; and can even abolish any of the provinces or create new provinces.	4. Federal or Central Government can deal with the federated units only in accordance with *the provisions of the* constitution; it cannot order them as it pleases and cannot reduce their power. Units have a constitutional status, which the centre cannot undermine.
5. At the centre, there are the *supreme* executive, the *supreme* legislature and the *supreme* judiciary.	5. *All* power is not vested in the centre, according to the provisions of a written constitution; each unit in the federation has its own executive, legislative and judicial organs. The centre has its own separate organs.
6. Government is highly centralised, as all decisions are taken by the centre.	6. There is much decentralisation, and the units enjoy much autonomy within the constitutional framework. Decisions regarding subjects of national importance are taken by the central government; but decisions of regional importance are taken by the units. But all these are subject to the clearly written provisions of the constitution.
7. There is unity.	7. There is union; and a compromise between unity and diversity is struck.
8. Generally suitable for small countries like *Britain, France* and Belgium.	8. Generally suitable for big countries like the USA, Russia and India.
9. Cost of administration not so high as in a federation, as there is only one set of government.	9. Cost of running government is relatively high, as there are two sets of government.
10. There can be no disputes between the centre and the provinces, as the former is superior to the latter.	10. Disputes between the centre and the units, and between two or more units are settled by the supreme or federal court, which is indispensable.

Unitary Government	Federal Government
11. Governmental machinery is simple and flexible.	11. Governmental machinery is complex and rigid.
12. Good for maintaining stability and national solidarity.	12. Stability and national solidarity are comparatively difficult to be achieved.
13. Centre may become top heavy, and the various regions may be neglected.	13. The question of topheaviness at the centre does not rise, as there is a good deal of decentralisation.
14. Discourages local or regional talent, initiative and enthusiasm, and suppresses hopes and aspirations of local or regional people.	14. Encourages local talent, initiative and enthusiasm, by giving vast scope for autonomy.
15. There is possibility of despotism at the centre, and power-crazy leaders may misuse a unitary government to increase their own power. Examples: Britain, France, Italy and China.	15. As the centre and the units are bound by the principles of the constitution, there cannot be despotism. The centre cannot go beyond the line marked out by the constitution, and similarly, the units cannot over-reach themselves and encroach on the field of the centre. Examples: USA, Switzerland, Australia and India.

C. FEDERATION AND CONFEDERATION

The terms *Federation* and *Confederation* do not mean the same thing, though both have the same root. It is necessary to know the difference between them.

A federation is a permanent union or association of states or units in which both the sets of government come under a common sovereignty; but a confederation is an association of sovereign states formed temporarily for realising a *specific purpose.*

In a federation, the centre and the federated units are bound by the provisions of a written constitution; the centre deals with subjects of national importance, and the units deal with subjects of local importance. The division of subjects is made according to the constitution. But in the case of a confederation, there is no constitution binding the various member states each of which is completely sovereign, and can have the type of government it chooses.

The American Confederation (1781-89), the German Confederation (1815-66), and the League of Nations (1920-39) are examples of confederations; and the USA, Switzerland, Canada, Australia and USSR are examples of federations.

The units of a federation (except the federation of the USSR) do not have the legal right of secession, but the states of a confederation have the right.

The following table summarises the difference between a federation and a confederation:

Federation	Confedertion
1. An association of states or units formed according to a written constitution.	1. An association of *sovereign* states formed by a treaty or agreement.
2. Permanent.	2. Temporary.
3. Formed for the sake of a compromise between unity and diversity.	3. Formed for realising a specific aim or objective.
4. The centre and the federated units have a common sovereignty. Units surrender their sovereignty, and the constitution is supreme.	4. Each member of the confederation is completely sovereign. There is absolutely no surrender of sovereignty to the confederation.
5. A federation, that is, its centre and its units has full control over all citizens. Citizens in a federation have to obey the laws of two governments *viz.* federal and regional.	5. A confederation has no control over citizens of the member states. Citizens of a member state are under the control of that particular state, and the confederation has no sovereign control over them.
6. A federation is the result of the union of people in the various states, which make a permanent constitutional agreement surrendering their sovereignty.	6. A confederation is the product of the temporary union of states, which do not surrender their sovereignty.
7. A federation is a new state and nation.	7. A confederation is not a new state; it is a loose association of states, and each state continues to retain its separate identity and sovereignty.
8. A federated unit cannot secede or legally withdraw from the federation.	8. Member states may withdraw, if they so choose, at any time from the confederation.
9. If war breaks out between units, it is a civil war.	9. If member states resort to war, it becomes an international war.
10. Examples: USA, Switzerland, Australia and India.	10. Examples: American Confederation (1781-89) and German Confederation (1815-66).

D. FORMATION OF FEDERATION AND ESSENTIAL REQUISITES

Two ways of Forming Federations

W. F. Willoughby thinks that federations were formed by historical reasons and not by judging the relative merits of the unitary and federal systems. (*See the Government of Modern States*—1936, p. 980.)

A federation may be formed in two ways:

1. *By Integration by Centripetal Forces.* A number of states, at first separate and sovereign, may come together and form a federation by accepting common sovereignty. Favorable centripetal forces may aid the formation of federation. The federations of the USA, Switzerland and Australia were formed in this manner. Here the process is of integration.
2. *By Disintegration by Centrifugal Forces.* A state, which was formerly unitary, may be transformed into a federation as a result of centrifugal forces. Canada which was originally unitary was converted into a federation. Similarly, India, a unitary state under British rule, was broken up and reorganized into autonomous units to form a Union of States, a federal structure with a strong centre. The federal constitution for India, was drafted by the Constituent Assembly (1946-49). Here the process is of disintegration.

Essential Requisites of Federation

Federal government "requires the co-existence of several characteristics which are not often found together in the world, and which should be perceived more distinctly than they often are."

Broadly speaking: we may say that certain conditions are essential for the formation of a federation.

1. Desire for Union

A strong desire for union (as distinguished from units) is the most essential requisite for the formation of a federation. In the words of K. C. Where states or communities " must desire to be between unity and diversity. United, but not to be unitary". (Federal Government, p. 36). People in areas, which want to federate, must show a conspicuous and genuine desire to come together in the interest of union. Small states, which are separate and independent, but locally adjacent may develop a strong felling that for defence, rapid economic development and other reasons, they should federate. When the desire for federating becomes so keen as to develop into a passion, it becomes easy to form and make a success of a federation.

2. Threat of Big States.

People in certain areas may be under the shadow of the military threat of big and powerful states. The keen desire for survival in the light of the continuous threat of an aggressive neighbor may goad small states to come together. K. C. Where says on page 45 in *Federal Government* (1946): "Thus hostility to or fear of a common enemy and the need for common defence produces the desire to unite. It also provides cohesive forces which compel the communities concerned to stand together and accustom them to work together. They develop common external antagonisms which override internal antagonisms." Mostly threat from big states serves as an essential requisite.

3. Desire for Local Autonomy.

The various federating units must however be anxious to retain their local autonomy. If they do not retain their autonomy, what they intend to form will not be a federation, but another unitary state. In other words, they should hanker for union and not unity, and try to bring about a reconciliation between union and local autonomy. The desire for union must be strong and spontaneous for the successful working of a federation. The desire may be genuine, and it should be naturally born within and not imposed from outside. While the people in the various federating units should have certain common aims and objectives, to come together, they should not surrender their local or regional interests. They should desire to preserve their own language, culture, their mode of living and the peculiar regional institutions whether political, social, religious or economic. A federation can be formed only when people desire for a union and are prepared to work earnestly for a reconciliation between unity and diversity.

4. Reasonable Degree of Homogeneity

A reasonable degree of homogeneity is another essential requisite of a federation. Similarity to some extent at least among the people is necessary. People who are totally different from one another cannot desire for a federation. Racial, linguistic, cultural and other types of strong heterogeneity will prevent the formation of a federation. People who are similar by nature, habits, culture, language, religion, race and political objectives can easily come together for building up a federation. Factors of similarity among people should be immensely stronger than factors of dissimilarity. Homogeneity should be more conspicuous than heterogeneity among people. The various groups in areas which desire to federate may differ from one another in certain ways: but they must have a certain degree of homogeneity, which is indispensable for the formation of a federation. The groups must be prepared to overlook differences among themselves, and develop common sympathies, aspirations and objectives. Racial, linguistic and religious sympathies may bring together people spread over a large area and a strong desire to federate may manifest itself. However, even if there are religious, linguistic and other differences, it is still possible to form a federation provided there are other strong factors to counterbalance the difference. For instance, the threat of a strong and aggressive neighboring state may compel people to sink their racial and linguistic differences and try to discover areas of common interests and sympathies. A similarity in social and political institutions works as a very favourable factor. K. C. Wheare says that... the desire for union has practically never been aroused unless similarity of political institutions was present either actually or potentially among those who envisaged the union." (*ibid.*, p. 46.) J. S. Mill emphasizes the importance of mutual sympathies for having homogeneity. He says: "The sympathies available for the purpose are those of race, language, religion, and above all, of political institution as conducive most to a feeling of identity of political interest. (*Representative Government*, p.36.) Ignorant, illiterate and politically backward people not knowing anything about federalism cannot form a federation with people who are educated, enlightened, dynamic and eager to have much freedom and local autonomy.

5. Good Leadership

Another essential requisite is wise and far-sighted leadership. A federation can be formed if people desirous of having a federation have leaders of great foresight, courage, breadth of vision, deep sympathy and understanding. They should be able to awaken in the minds of the people of the various areas the feeling to come together without submerging their individuality. Much depends on the calibre of leaders behind the movement for federalism. Bad leadership may spoil even the good chances of federalism. There have been instances to show that leaders with sincerity, purpose, stoic patience, integrity of character, wide knowledge, statesmanship and power of eloquence were able to pave the way for the formation of federations. In America, the people were fortunate to have the wise leadership of George Washington, Alexander Hamilton, Benjamin Franklin, James Wilson and others. In Canada, James Macdonald, Alexander Galt, George Etienne and other leaders were responsible for mobilising the forces of union for the formation of federation.

6. Good Calibre of People

Good calibre and genius of the people constitute another essential requisite of a federation. Leaders will not be successful in establishing and in working out a federation, unless people themselves are educated, enlightened, public spirited, competent and worthy of a federation. People must be prepared to make the necessary sacrifice for the sake of union and show a spirit of accommodation and tolerance. They should study the problems confronting them intelligently, and prepare the ground for a federation. If the calibre of the people matches good and wise leadership, the formation of a federation becomes easy.

A federation is not meant for a people, who are ignorant and illiterate, and devoid of qualities so very essential for its success. Even if a federation is formed owing to the initiative and enthusiasm of a few great leaders, it will be torn to pieces before long, if the people are found wanting.

7. Love of Democracy

Love of democracy is another essential requisite. People must have faith in democracy as a form of government and a way of life. They must have experiences in running their own political institutions, and there should not be much difference between the political institutions of one area and those of the others. If any region is in favour of a dictatorial form of government, it will be harmful to the interests of others, who wish to have democracy. It is taken for granted in a federation that there is equality of status among the states. Dictatorship, in any of the regions, is bound to spell disaster on the remaining areas of a federal state. It obvious that democracy and dictatorship cannot coexist. In this connection, a reference may be made to the Government of India Act, 1935, which envisaged the establishment of a federation of two types of units : (1) Autocratic Princely States, and (2) Autonomous British Indian Provinces. Fortunately, such a strange type of federation did not see the light of the day. Even if it had been formed it would have been wrecked before long owing to the world of difference between Princely States and Autonomous British Indian Provinces. However, it is wrong to think that democracy and federalism are inseparable. E. B. Schulz says on page 191 in *Essentials of Government* (1961): "The fact of the matter is that there is no necessary relationship between democracy on one hand and unitary or federal system on the other. Various countries with a unitary or federal system have democratic political institutions *e.g.* Great Britain, France and Norway; others have authoritarian governments. Federalism and democracy exist side by side in the United States, Switzerland, Canada and Australia, but in Germany of 1871-1918 the federal system was combined with aristocratic government both nationally and in the major political divisions." The USSR is a dictatorship, though the constitution is federal. K. C. Wheare thinks differently, and says that "dictatorship with its one-party government and its denial of free election is incompatible with the working of the federal principle. Federalism demands forms of government which have the characteristics usually associated with democracy or free government." (See *Federal Government*, 1946: 48.)

8. Geographical Contiguity

Geographical contiguity is another essential requisite. People, who desire to form a federation, should not be scattered over areas, which are separated from one another by water or by foreign states. There should be geographical contiguity, as it is essential, for political, economic and military reasons. There is geographical contiguity in the federations of the USA, Canada, Switzerland, Australia and India.

9. Equality among Federating Units

Equality among units is another requisite. If a federation should work successfully, there should be equality of status among the federating units. Equality does not mean absolute equality, but the absence of wide disparity between one unit and another. If a unit in a federation is a better placed than the rest in size, population and economic resources, there is bound to be imbalance, which is likely to violate the principle of equal partnership among the federating units. The smaller units are likely to look at the bigger and more powerful units with jealousy, distrust; and suspicion. The atmosphere in a federation will be vitiated owing to imbalance, mutual hatred and unfriendliness. J. S. Mill says on page 367 in *Representative Government*: "There should not be any one state so much more powerful than the rest as to be capable of vying in strength with many of them combined. If there is such a one, and only one, it will insist on being master of the joint deliberations; if there be two, they will be irresistible when they agree and whenever they differ everything will be decided by a struggle for ascendancy between the rivals."

One of the essential conditions for the success of a federation is co-operation, which will disappear when the component parts dislike one another, owing to wide disparity. In the federation of the German Empire formed in 1871, the predominance of Prussia violated the federal principle.

In federations, in which some units are small, the imbalance may be rectified in two ways:

(1) by giving equal representation to all units, big or small, in the second chamber as is done in the USA, Australia, Switzerland and the USSR and

(2) by seeing that amendments to the constitution are valid, when they are ratified not only by the majority of the people, but also by a majority of the units.

10. Adequate Economic Resources

A federation needs ample economic resources. As already

observed earlier, a federal type of government is definitely more expensive than the unitary type. Two sets of government have to be maintained. Each federating unit has its own governmental machinery to deal with subjects under its control. All this means that adequate economic resources should be available. If a federated unit has to depend permanently on the centre for the balancing of its budget, the federation can never work smoothly. This is because the unit may feel that financially justice is not being done to it, while the centre may feel that it is doing far above the federal principle. The paucity of economic resources in a couple of units is bound to go against the principle of equality of status. Countries, which cannot afford the heavy governmental expenditure, should not choose a federal type of government; to them a federation will be a very expensive luxury.

When federal constitutions are being framed, the constitution makes should carefully examine the problems confronting a federation and ensure that the constitution provides as little scope as possible for people to enter into controversies.

A federal government can function smoothly only when:

(1) a fair and realistic division of powers between the centre and the units is made;

(2) justice is done to all areas;

(3) healthy relations are maintained between the centre and the units, and between one unit and another;

(4) small units feel as secure as the relatively big ones; and

(5) the method of amending the constitution is reasonable.

E. EXAMPLES OF FEDERATION

We have noted earlier that the USA, Switzerland, Canada, Australia and the USSR are examples of federation. India has to be treated separately, as it combines the features of the unitary system with those of the federal.

1. The united States of America

Confederation

Till 1776, the thirteen American colonies were separately linked with Britain, and were under her control. 'A Continental

Congress in 1777 drew up the articles for an American Confederation, which lasted from 1781 to 1789. The colonies, which rebelled against England, made the Declaration of their Independence according to which they were to be independent of Britain, and also independent of one another. The common enmity towards England and the desire to win the war of independence against England promoted the colonies to form a Confederation (1783) known as the United States.

Great Weakness of Confederation. By the Treaty of Paris (1783) the colonies became independent. But there was the danger of fissiparous tendencies, as the confederation consisted of dissatisfied member states. N. C. Roy says on page 18 in *The Federal System of The USA* (1940): "The confederation thus established conformed as a writer puts it to the idea of co-operative system of sovereignties. The sense of separate independence among the colonies was too keen and their mutual suspicion too strong for any union with a sovereignty of its own to be formed at this time." In such a pattern, it was not possible to build a strong and well-knit nation.

The American Confederation had certain weaknesses.

(1) According to the articles of the Confederation, the Congress was weak, and it could not deal effectively with recalcitrant members.

(2) The Congress was "a body of delegates which had no power to compel the states to its will and no power to command or to tax the individual citizens of the thirteen states."

(3) The Congress 'was to look after foreign relations, declare and conduct war, build and equip a navy, and issue requisitions upon the states for soldiers and for funds."

(4) The Congress was woefully weak, as it could only pass resolutions without the requisite authority to make law and enforce it in the states.

Abolition of Confederation and Establishment of Federation. Seeing the weakness of the Confederation, several far-sighted leaders felt that there was an urgent need to stabilise their independence, consolidate gains, follow a uniform commercial policy, and take steps to bring the general uplift of all states. This could be done by abolishing the confederation and establishing a new federation.

On May 14, 1787 the delegates at the Convention of Philadelphia decided to draft a new constitution, which brought about a reconciliation between the powers of the central government and the powers of the states; and also eliminated the dependence of the central government on the state governments. The central government was armed with adequate powers to deal with and make laws on subjects given to its jurisdiction. The powers and functions of the central government were clearly defined and the remaining powers (that is, residuary) were to being to the states.

By the end of 1787, three states ratified the constitution; the other states agreed to have the new constitution after some time.

On June 21, 1788 the constitution was adopted, and it came into effect on March 4, 1789.

Residuary Powers with States

A very important feature of the American federation is the relative wakens of the centre and a large measure of autonomy enjoyed by the states. The constitution enumerates the powers of the central government, and the residuary powers are with the states. Within their own spheres, the central government and the states are to be supreme.

The states in the USA enjoy far more powers than their counter-parts in India and Canada. While these two federations have a strong centre, the USA has a comparatively weak centre.

USA as Pioneer in a Federation

The establishment of the federal constitution of the United States of America is a great landmark in the field of constitution-making. The USA became a model to other peoples having problems similar to those of the Americans. Mexico, Brazil and Argentina followed the example of the USA. The Americans, with their dynamic and far-sighted leaders, a sober and pragmatic approach, and with determination to make a success of the federal system became pioneers in federalism on a large scale. K. C. Wheare significantly points out on page 1 in *Federal Government* (1946): "The modern idea of what federal government is has been determined by the United States of America..... Indeed the words *federal* or *Federation* occur nowhere in the American Constitution. Nonetheless it has always been called the 'Federal Constitution'.... Any definition of federal government which failed to include the United States would be thereby condemned as unreal.' The Americans gave the first large scale example of a written constitution with a federal pattern.

2. Switzerland

Switzerland was the first country to follow the American federal example.

Danger of Secession

The federal constitution of the USA was a source of inspiration to the people of Switzerland. Like the American confederation, which was vulnerable, the Swiss confederation also faced a great challenge in 1847, when seven Catholic cantons made efforts to secede. The Protestant majority crushed the secessionist movement of the Catholics, and paved the way for national unity.

Swiss Confederation with Strong Centre

The Swiss then had a new constitution called the Swiss Confederation after the American model. The constitutionalists spoke in terms of the Swiss Confederation, though it was a real federation. Thus in the official title the term *confederation* is misleading.

The centre in Switzerland is stronger than the centre in the USA. The Swiss centre can militarily intervene to a greater extent than the centre in the USA. War, industrialisation, social services and economic depression were the main factors which put more and more powers into the hands of the central or federal government.

Residuary Powers with Cantons

In Switzerland and in the USA, the residuary powers are given to the units.

Unlike in the USA, in which the federal government directly administers its own laws through the federal officials, in Switzerland federal subjects are administered by the officials of the cantons. Thus, there is administrative decentralization in Switzerland.

Federal Tribunal

While in the USA the Supreme Court can declare a federal law unconstitutional, the Federal Tribunal in Switzerland is not competent to do so; it can only declare cantonial law unconstitutional. Thus the court is not the guardian of the constitution, as its power of judicial review is only concerning cantonial legislatures.

In the USA in the category of the Supreme Court there are ten federal Circuit Courts of Appeal and eighty-five subordinate Federal District Courts; but in Switzerland there are no courts belonging to the category of the Federal Tribunal, and so it has no subordinate courts.

Referendum for Constitutional Amendments

Unlike in the USA, in Switzerland constitutional amendment cannot be valid, unless it is adopted in a referendum by a majority of voters any by a majority of the cantons.

No Right to Secede. As in the USA, in Switzerland also, the units have no right to secede.

3. Canada

Canada also has federal government. She was the second country to follow the American federal example.

Canada's position was weak and precarious, as the British and the French nationalities were dead against each other. Racial, economic and military problems made it appear that a unitary government was not suitable for Canada. Particularly racial conflict between the British and the French, whom the Durham Report regarded as "two nations warring within the bosom of a single state' strengthened the movement for federalism.

In 1867, the British Parliament passed the North America Act, and the Dominion of Canada was born.

Strong Centre with Residuary Powers

Seeing the USA's national unity in serious jeopardy during the Civil War (1861-65), Canada did not follow the American example regarding the distribution of powers.

In the Canadian Constitution, there is a list of enumerated

subjects assigned to the exclusive jurisdiction of Provinces (Federated units); over the remaining subjects the Dominion Government is to exercise control. Thus the residuary powers in Canada are with the centre, and not with the states as provided in the American. Constitution.

For the sake of clarity, the subjects under the control of the Dominion are enumerated, though it is quite clear that all residuary powers are vested in the Dominion Government. The centre in Canada is very strong, while the centre in the USA is relatively weak. Federalism has been slightly diluted in Canada.

In making the Union Government strong in India, the founding fathers of the Constitution of India (1950) followed the Canadian example.

4. Australia

Australia also became a federation on January 1, 1901.

Threat of Big Power. Defence and other problems made the six Australian colonies give up their rivalries regarding tariffs, railways and other matters, and form the Commonwealth with a federal system. Particularly the real threat of a big imperialist power brought about a great urge among the states in Australia for union in 1900.

Favourable Racial and Linguistic Factors

Certain factors were favourable to the formation of a federation. Michael Stewart says on page 143 in *Modern Forms of Government* (1959): "In Australia almost the whole people were of one stock and language, nor did the forms of government differ greatly between one colony and another. Yet each by virtue of its geographical position, had its own economic interests and they were separated from each other by vast unpopulated stretch of land."

Residuary Powers with States

According to the Constitution, the centre is given very wide powers, and the residuary powers are with the units.

No right to Secede

The units have no right to secede.

5. The Union of Soviet Socialist Republics

Among totalitarian states, the USSR has a federal government.

Residuary Powers with Constituent Republics

To bring about a union of various nationalities and tribes, a federal government was established in Soviet Russia in 1936. According to the 1936 Constitution, the powers of the Union Government are specified, and the residuary powers are with the constituent republics.

Right to Secede

It must be noted here that the republics have the right to secede, technically speaking.

Theory and Practice

There is however a vast difference between theory and practice in Russia; for ". . . if one examines the actual operation of the system, it becomes apparent that federalism as known in the United States and Canada is not to be found in the USSR. Proof. Wheare, an authority on the general topic of federalism, regards the constitution of 1936 as 'quasi-federal' but he does not consider the USSR a working example of federal government." (See Ogg and Zink, *Modern Foreign Government*—1957, p. 850)

India is a unique example of a federation.

Combination of Unitary and Federal Features

India is an example of a state, which combines the features of a unitary state with those of a federal state. The Union (Central) Government in India is stronger than the centre of any other federation. In the Constitution itself, there is provision to convert the federal state into a unitary state in times of emergency. Michael Stewart in his *Modern Forms of Government* (1959) describes on page 62 the Indian Union as "a hybrid between a federal and a unitary state." K. C. Wheare says that the Constitution of India established "a system of government which is at the most quasi-federal almost devolutionary in character; a unitary state with subsidiary federal features rather than a federal state with unitary features.

According to the Constitution of India, which came into force on "January 26, 1950, India is a Union of States. The word federation' has not been used in the Constitution. India as a federation cannot be put in the category of the USA and Switzerland.

Strong Unitary Bias

The following features of the Indian Constitution show its strong unitary bias:

1. *Three Lists with Residuary Powers with Centre*

There are three lists of subjects: the Union List, the State List and the Concurrent List.

Unlike in the USA, residuary powers are with the Centre.

The distribution of subjects in the three lists is in favour of the Union Government. Ninety-seven subjects are in the Union List, while only sixty-six subjects are in the State List. In the Concurrent List, there are forty-seven subjects on which both the Union and the State Legislatures can pass laws. The most important subjects with wide powers have been given to the Centre, and the relatively unimportant ones have been given to the States.

In case there is a conflict between a Union law and a State law, the former supersedes the latter.

The Union Government can make law on any subject, even on the one in the State List, if it is declared by the Rajya Sabha (Upper House) that it has assumed national importance. Such a law remains in force for not more than a year, but the period can be extended.

States have to obey the directions given by the Union Government.

2. *Wide Powers of the President*

The President of India enjoys the following wide powers.

(1) He appoints the Governors of States.

(2) When the President declares an emergency in a State, owing to the breakdown of its constitutional machinery, the Governor becomes the agent of the centre.

(3) A bill passed by a State legislature may be reserved by the State Governor for the consideration of the President.

(4) In times of national Emergency, the President can assume extraordinary powers, and Parliament can make laws even on a subject which is in the State List.

All these powers of the President make the Centre very strong.

3. One Citizenship

Unlike in the USA and Switzerland, in India there is only one citizenship.

4. One Judicial System

In India, there is only one unified judicial system; but in the USA federal courts cannot interfere in the affairs of the state courts, and federal courts and the state courts work in parallel lines. In India, the Supreme Court (which is the federal court) and the High Courts belong to the same integrated judicial system.

5. No Right to Secede

States in India are not given the right to secede. The right to secede is found in the constitution of the USSR. But even here it is practically not possible for a state to secede.

F. ESSENTIAL FEATURES OF A FEDERATION

True Test of a Federation

Some scholars are of the opinion that a constitution can be regarded as really federal, only if the powers of the federal government are enumerated, and the residuary powers are assigned to the units. According to this principle, the USA, Switzerland and Australia are federations. K.C. Wheare, a great authority on federalism who does not agree with this view, says that this principle is relatively superficial. The basic feature of a federation is the constitutional division of powers between the centre and units. This means that neither the national nor the regional government is subordinate to the other. Neither is supreme, and it is the constitution that is supreme. Wheare says on page 13 in *Federal Government* (1946): "It is true that the question where the residue of power is to rest is an important question in framing a federal government. It may effect the whole balance of power in a federation. It is likely also that when previously sovereign states federate, they will not sign a blank cheque. But these are not essential to the principle. They may be usual characteristics of government, which are federal, but they themselves do not make government federal."

The most important difference between a unitary government and a federal government is that in the former the units are subordinate to the centre, while in the latter regional governments are not subordinate, as they owe their very existence and powers to a constitution.

We may now refer to the most essential features of a federation. A written constitution, a federal court and rigidity of constitution are the most essential features of a federation. A bicameral legislature is desirable, though not quite essential.

1. Dual Polity and a Written Constitution

To a federation, a dual polity a clearly written constitution are absolutely essential. The units in a federation, which has a dual polity (Centre and Units) must feel, that their autonomy is constitutionally safe, and that the central government is not allowed to encroach on their field. Hence, it is essential to put in black and white the powers of the centre and those of the units. It is only when there is a written constitution that the centre and the units clearly know their respective powers and limitations to their powers. There will be never-ending controversies and disputes between the centre and the units, if the powers of both are not put in a definite written form. Regarding the need of having a written constitution, A. V. Dicey says on page 142 in his *Law of the Constitution*: "To base an arrangement of this kind upon understandings or conventions would be certain to generate misunderstandings and disagreements."

A clear and carefully worded federal constitution, free from any type of ambiguity, ensures the position and status of the centre and of the units.

2. A Federal Court

Even when the authors of a federal constitutions try to make everything precise, it is likely, that on occasions, differences of opinion between the centre and the units may arise. Sometimes controversies may arise regarding the interpretation of the constitution. Therefore, an authority to interpret the provisions of the constitution and to settle disputes between the centre and the units, or between two or more units, becomes essential. J. S. Mill says on page 370 in *Representative Government*: "It is evidently necessary not only that the constitutional limits of authority of each (central and regional governments alike) should be precisely and clearly defined, but the power to decide between them in any case of dispute should not reside in either of the governments, or in any functionary subject to it, but in an umpire independent of both. There must be a supreme court of justice, and a system of co-ordinate courts in every State of the Union before whom such questions shall be carried, and whose judgement on them in the last stage or appeal, shall be final."

A federal court owes its existence to the constitution, and it is in no way under the control or influence either of the centre or of the units. The court is empowered to give its verdict impartially, without fear or favour, and act as the watchdog of the constitution. The appointment and service conditions of the judges are in accordance with the articles of the constitution, and they ensure the independence of the judiciary.

In the USA and Australia, courts settle the disputes between the centre and the units; but in Switzerland and the USSR, the judiciary has no power to pronounce a federal law as unconstitutional. In Switzerland, constitutional laws are subject to the referendum and the initiative. In India, the Supreme Court functions independently as a federal court, and acts as the custodian of the constitution.

3. Rigidity of Constitution

Rigidity of constitution, which is supreme, is another essential feature of federalism. While explaining the meaning of supremacy of the constitution, K. C. Wheare says on page 55 in *Federal Government* that "the terms of the agreement which establishes the general and regional governments and which distributes power between them must be binding upon the general and regional governments. This is a logical necessity from the definition of federal government itself." The principle of supremacy of the constitution goes hand in hand with the principle of its rigidity. A federal constitution has to be rigid, and constitutional law has to be placed above ordinary law. A special procedure for amending the constitution has to be provided. Amending the constitution is made difficult, and several meaningful hurdles are created to prevent the constitution from being made into a toy in the hands of scheming politicians. A. V. Dicey says: "The law of the constitution must either be immutable, or else capable of being changed only by some authority above and beyond the ordinary legislative bodies, whether federal or state legislatures, existing under the constitution." (*Law of Constitution,* p. 142.)

It is likely that certain interested parties at the centre or in the units may find certain provisions in the constitution unpalatable and irksome, and they may try to remove these "offending" provisions to suit their convenience. To prevent meddling or tinkering with the constitution, the authors of a federal constitution make it rigid.

The power to amend the constitution should not be vested exclusively in the centre or in the units. E. B. Schulz observes on page 182 in *Essentials of Government* (1961) : "A sharing of amending authority is necessary unless the constituent power be vested in some natural agency. Otherwise, either the central authorities or the political subdivisions could establish a monopoly of governmental power." The method of amendment should be such that full justice is done to the centre and to the regions.

Amendment in the USA

The constitution of the USA is rigid. Article V of the constitutions says: "The Congress, whenever two-thirds of both Houses shall deem it necessary, shall propose amendments to this constitution, or on the application of the Legislatures of two-thirds of the several States, shall call a convention for proposing amendments, which, in either case, shall be valid to all intents and purposes as part of this constitution, when ratified by the Legislatures of three-fourths of the several States, or by conventions in three-fourths thereof, as the one or the other mode of ratification may be proposed by the Congress."

Amendment in India

The Constitution of India is a mixture of rigidity and flexibility.

The procedure for amendment is given in Article 368. It says:

(1) A bill for amendment has to originate on one of the two Houses of Parliament.

(2) It has to be passed by (a) the total majority of the membership of the House; and (b) a majority of not less than two-thirds of the members present and voting.

(3) A bill for amendment cannot be introduced in any State Legislature.

(4) A bill for amendment is to be passed in the same way as an ordinary bill.

(5) Any provision of the Constitution can be amended. Even Articles regarding Fundamental Rights can be amended.

Amendments

An amendment means "an addition or change within the lines of the original instrument as will effect an improvement or better carry out the purpose for which it was formed." Amendments are as follows:

(1) Amendments, which can be passed by a bare majority as that which is adequate for the passing of ordinary law. These are regarding Article 2 (concerning the admission and formation of new States) and Article 3 (relating to the formation of new States and alteration of areas, boundaries and names of existing States). In fact "no such law (*i.e.* the one pertaining to the formation of new States etc.) as aforesaid shall be deemed to be an amendment of this Constitution for the purpose of Article 368." (Article 368 lays down a two-thirds majority.)

(2) Amendments, which cannot be passed without ratification or approval of the legislatures of not less than half of the States.

Desirability of Bicameral Legislature

A bicameral legislature is highly desirable for a federation. In the USA, the Senate, the second chamber, gives equal status to all the units by having an equal number of members from each irrespective of its size and population. The Senate has 100 members two from each of the 50 States. The second chamber guards the interests of the units against any amendment, which might weaken them. However, it must be noted that a second chamber is not essential, though it is of great significance.

In India, the States do not have equal representation in the Rajya Sabha at the Centre as in the USA. The number of members from a state depends upon the population. The U.S. Senators are directly elected, while members of the Rajya Sabha are indirectly elected.

G. EVALUATION OF FEDERAL GOVERNMENT

We shall now discuss the merits and defects of the federal form of government

Merits

The federal system has the following merits:

1. For Union of Small States

A federation provides scope for small states to come together for solving their political, economic and military questions. The modern times have witnessed the rise of large territorial states, and in their midst the existence of small states is precarious. Small states can find a solution to their difficulties in a federation without losing their autonomy.

2. Scope for Autonomy

Another merit is that a federation provides vast scope for local autonomy. In large countries in which there are various types of groups, the different regions can come together in a federation without losing their identity. They will have the double advantage of building a strong nation and of retaining their local autonomy. E. B. Schulz says on page 188 in *Essentials of Government* (1961): "The principal argument in favour of federalism is that a constitutional guarantee of local autonomy serves as a reasonably effective barrier to over centralisation." It was for this reason that the USA, the USSR, Switzerland, Canada, Australia and India became federations.

3. Prevents Rise of Despotism

Federalism is an antidote to central despotism. A federation brings about wide decentralisation of power and does not allow power to fall exclusively in the hands of the centre. While a unitary government facilitates the despotic power of the centre federal government prevents it.

4. Unity with Diversity

A federal government blends unity with diversity. In large countries, in which there is diversity in race, language, religion and culture, federalism is an dissolution. Each small cultural group in a region is anxious to retain its complexion; it does not wish to merge with others, as it fears that its identity may be lost. At the same time, it cannot have state of its own, and even if it has, its existence may become precarious. History bears witness to large states preying on small states, and therefore having a separate existence may not always be advisable. The only alternative open to them is to join a federation, which brings about a reconciliation between unity and diversity.

5. Scope for Training

A federation provides ample scope for training in the political filed. A federal state is a large laboratory in which there is a scope for experimentation. Each unit of a federation has full autonomy in its own sphere to do what ever it likes without waiting for the courtesy or the pleasure of the centre. It can conduct political experiments and try to put on a permanent basis what is good from the long range point of view. Generally, in federations democratic principles are upheld. People can take full advantage of the democratic institutions, and in a free atmosphere can live and let live, and learn from one another.

6. State not Vulnerable

Unlike a unitary government, a federal government is not vulnerable, particularly in times of emergency. A unitary government may be destroyed, when internal rebels or foreign aggressors attack the central government, the nerve centre of the entire country. But, in the case of a federal government, there are different nerve centres, and government cannot be overthrown easily.

7. Economically Profitable

A federation can be economically profitable to all the states which form it for availability of raw material, sale of manufactured goods, freedom from tariff walls and inter-state industry and trade.

R.G. Gettel summarises on page 238 the merits on the federal system in his *Political Science* (1956): "The federal from of government stimulates interest in political activity, enable small areas to try experiments that might be dangerous if applied to the entire country, diminishes the dangers that threaten a state composed of diverse nationalities or interests, and relieves the central government of many burdensome functions."

Defects

Now we shall briefly deal with the drawbacks of the federal system. They are as follows:

1. Expensive

A federal from is more expensive than a unitary one, as two sets of government are required. Only countries commanding adequate resources can have the federal form. Finer says on page 184 in *The Theory and Practice of Modern Government* (1961): "It is financially expensive, since there is much duplication of administrative machinery and procedure. It is wasteful of time and angary, in that it depends on much negotiation, political and administrative, to secure uniformity of law and proper administrative fulfillment thereof."

2. Complex Structure

The governmental machinery is complex. An ordinary man, not having at least some knowledge of political science in general and of federalism in particular, is not able to understand the complex governmental pattern, multi-licity of authorities and jurisdiction, and the relationship between the two sets of government. How many people in a country like India have adequate knowledge of the federal structure? Simplicity, an important feature of a unitary government, is conspicuous by its absence in a federal form.

3. Controversies and Disputes

There may not be co-operation and co-ordination between the centre and states in a federation. E. B. Schulz says on page 192 in *Essentials of Government* (1962) that "... may result in lack of co-ordination between the policies of the central government and those of the major political subdivisions. But..... if there be unwillingness co-operate there is no simple way of rectifying the situation." In spite of the precaution taken by the makers of a federal controversies and conflicts between the centre and units are bound to rise. As times change, it may become necessary for the centre to pass certain laws to meet the requirements of people in a changed context: but any attempt by the centre to pass legislation will be resented and opposed. It is also possible that some units may maintain low standards of administration, but no effective remedial measures are possible.

4. Difficulty in Foreign Policy

Particularly in the field of foreign relations, the weakness of the federal system may be exposed. The agreement made by the centre with a foreign state may not be acceptable to a federated unit. The centre, for instance, in the USA may promise a state in Asia or Africa that it will not countenance racial discrimination, but all the states may not uphold this. The centre becomes helpless, the states may have the authority to act as they please in the case concerned. This not only leads to a rift between the centre and the states, but also brings about ill-feeling between the USA and a foreign state.

5. Divided Loyalty of People

A state having a federal government may not be able to command as much loyalty of the people as a state with a unitary government, because in the former the loyalty of the citizen in divided between the centre and the units, but the loyalty of the citizens in the latter is undivided. Not only, the loyalty of citizens, but the loyalty of a union also may not be firm. The possibility of a unit trying to secede from a federation cannot be ruled out. In the constitution of the USSR, secession is allowed. In the USA unity was threatened by the attitude of the southern States, and they were forced to remain in the federation, by an actual civil war, in which they were defeated. However, experience shows that the fear of secession is rather a theoretical weakness than an actual one.

6. Not so Efficient as Unitary System

A federal system is not so efficient as the unitary system. In uniformity, in national solidarity, in efficiency of services, in prompt and energetic action, and in several other matters, a federal government lags behind a unitary government. In India, a federal state, it is said that the food problem would not have been so acute, as it is today, had there been a unitary system. So also, fissiparous tendencies in India would not have been so strong and ugly in a unitary pattern. As a rule, a federal government is weaker than a unitary government.

H. PROBLEMS OF FEDERALISM WITH SPECIAL REFERENCE TO INDIA

A federal government has to face several problems. As we have observed earlier, it is a complicated system with a dual polity demanding difficult pre-requisites, which if not present the federal government may break down under heavy strain.

The following problems of a federal government can be mentioned:

(1) Problem of Power Equilibrium

The problem of equilibrium or balance of powers between the Centre and the Units in a federation is a difficult one. Even though a carefully written constitution distributes powers between the two sets of government on mutually agreed fair principles, in course of time, the equilibrium may be distributed by the new needs and challenges of a dynamic society. The centre may try to exercise more and more power to enlarge the social services; but the states may resent the attitude of the centre, however right it may be. As times change, a new balance of powers between the centre and the units may have to be struck, but it the two sets of government do not reconcile their differences regarding distribution of powers, the federal system may become unworkable, and may not serve the original purpose for which it was formed.

(2) Disputes

Federalism gives great scope for controversies and disputes. In a dual policy, both the authorities (the centre and the units) have to work with a truly federal spirit. While each set of government is right in sticking to the articles of the written constitution, it should not try to sacrifice the federal spirit by making a fetish of the constitutional provisions. As times change, the spirit of the federalism changes. For instance, there was a time in the USA, when maintaining slaves was considered as a right and the Supreme Court in 1857 held the law against slavery as invalid. In the time of Abraham Lincoln, the Southern States in the USA threatened even to secede on the question of slavery. The US federal structure came under heavy strain, and the country was on the verge of disintegration. In was only victory to the Northern States in the Civil War (1861-65) that saved the American Federation. As the Americans failed to solve their question of slavery peacefully at the conference table, they had to go to the battlefield, where the verdict of victory to the North clinched the issue.

However, it has to be conceded that after the Civil War, owing to the far-sighted statesmanship of American leader and the genius of the American people, the wounds of the War were healed, and the USA emerged stronger than what she was before the Civil War.

(3) Attitude of the Judiciary

Sometimes the judiciary may not function in a federation as it should. A judiciary in a federal state has to exercise its jurisdiction with utmost wisdom, tact, impartiality and independence while upholding the supremacy of the constitution. But at the same item, it has to exercise imagination in interpreting the provisions of the constitution. A rigid, wooden and unsympathetic attitude of the judges who cannot move with the times may spell as much harm as their partisan attitude. An unimaginative an self-righteous judiciary may itself create a great problem with its misguided overenthusiasm.

In the USA, the Supreme Court came in the way of President F. D. Roosevelt's *New Deal*. E. S. Graffiths observes on page 171 in *The American System of Government* (1966): "Because several of the cardinal economic measures of the *New Deal* were thrown out by the Supreme Court, in 1937 President Roosevelt made its proposal which came to be known as the *court-packing* bill. Under this measure, he would have been empowered to appoint an additional judge for each sitting judge who had passed the age of seventy. The motive was so obvious and the sense of propriety so outraged that the measure never passed. However, the move seemed to have an effect, for certain judges voluntarily retired and others were apparently more receptive to the extensive economic controls subsequently instituted."

(4) Problem of Leadership

A federal state may have to face the great problem of leadership. Selfish, narrow-minded, ignorant and power-hungry leaders, who cannot understand the implications of federalism may wreck a federal system. The leaders at the federal level and the leaders at the level of the federated units should be rational, parotitic and tolerant, and capable of understanding a true federal spirit, which stands for national solidarity and regional autonomy and which strikes a sensible and sound balance between the centripetal and the centrifugal forces. Good leadership is capable of making a success even of an imperfect federal constitution, while incompetent, self-aggrandizing, short-sighted and fanatical leadership will spell the doom even of a well-worded federal constitution

(5) Problems Posed by People

No federation can functions smoothly, if the bulk of the people are not equal to the great task of implementing a federal constitution. What should the people do? The people scattered in the different units of the federation should support the right leadership, expose bad leaders and withdraw their support from such leaders. Who should show the spirit of co-operation, and be ready for the statement of disputes in a peaceful and constitutional manner.

People who unjustly trouble or lead rebellions against the centre on petty problems and tariffs strike at the root of federalism; so too, people of one unit, who hate people of other units on emotional, religious, linguistic or racial grounds seek to undermine federalism.

As stated earlier, people of the Southern States in the USA reached the point of no return in connection with the problem of slavery, and refused to have any type of reconciliation with the people of the North.

In the Swiss Federation (technically called Confederation),

Catholics hated Protestants, and the Catholics Cantons tried to secede. However, the Protestant majority could crush the secessionist move of the Catholic minority.

(6) Problem of Finance

One of the greatest problems facing a federation is of distribution of finance between the centre and the units. All units in a federation may not be equally affluent. The principle on which financial distribution takes place must be realistic, but at the same time fair. No unit should feel that it has been left in the lurch. Financially, justice has to be done, and care has to be taken to ensure that no unit nurses a grudge on the ground that it has been left financially high and try.

(7) Emotional Problem

Sometimes a federation may have to face an emotional problem. While solving the various problems in a federation, the feelings of the vast multitudes of people should be gauged, and efforts should be made to conciliate people, who rightly or wrongly feel hurt. Sometimes, people misunderstand central leadership or leadership in other units, and nourish imaginary grievances. However unjustified these may be, they should not be ignored, but should be met with patience, sympathy, sagacity, and imagination.

A federation in not an end in itself, but only an instrument for meeting the requirements of a state, in which two co-ordinate authorities are expected to function strictly according to the constitution. It is left to the human beings to use the constitution intelligently and wisely and work it out satisfactorily.

Problems of India as a Federation

We have noted that India is a unique type of federation.

India became a Union of States on January 26, 1950. The federation (or quasi-federation as some would like to call it) commenced working with great hopes as well as fears. India has now reached a stage of great stress and strain, when people have started asking the question, whether federalism is suitable for India, and whether it would have been better, if the Constituent Assembly (1946-49) had hammered out a unitary system.

In other words, India as a federation seems to be at the crossroads, when highly tangled problems have cropped up, subjecting the federal mechanism to an unusually heavy strain. Whether the Union of States will survive the strain, time alone can say.

What are the problems confronting India as a federation? A little thought will provoke us to list the following problems:

(1) problem of Lack of Will

One of the greatest problems facing India as a federation is lack of will. The will to work out the federal system sincerely and smoothly is woefully lacking in India, particularly among leaders. The masses of people in India can be easily led or misled by leaders. Who can exercise great pull at the seats of power both at the Centre and in the States. The majority of people in India do not know what federalism is. Selfish leaders, betraying very narrow prejudices and loyalties, have done much to weaken Indian federalism. They seem to forget that unless there is the spirit of compromise, the desire to make reasonable adjustments, and the decency to play the game of politics according to rules, federalism will be shattered to pieces.

(2) Problem of Ignorance

Coupled with the problem of want of will to adjust and compromise amicably is the problem of shocking ignorance. The poverty sticken, illiterate and ignorant masses of people do not know the ABC of federalism, and they cannot judge correctly whether their leaders are right or wrong. Even in big cities, the seemingly informed and enlightened people do not know the deep implications of federalism. The leaders are found wanting for various reason, and they too display a lamentable lack of understanding of the principle and spirit of federalism. How can a nation work out federalism, if leaders as well as the led are found wanting?

(3) Problem of Emotions

Emotionally, people and their leaders in India are deficient to conduct the federal experiment. The emotional urge for union (as against unity) and for regional autonomy is weak, and hence, emotions are expressed through wrong channels. The accent on regionalism at the west level at the expense of the Centre of the other States has strengthened the ugly fissiparous forces, and the requisite harmony is jeopardised. Unless people in all the States of India are emotionally prepared to survive as a nation following federal principles, India will have to face worse days in the future than at present.

(4) Unhealthy Trends in Political Parties

The trends in almost all the political parties that count in India are deleterious to the cause of federalism. Until recently, the undivided Indian National Congress had done much for the cause of federalism and parliamentary democracy. But in August 1969, when the party split into two factions, nicknamed Indicate or Cong (I) and Syndicate or Cong (O), the political game became ugly. The posture and stance of each one of the factions at the Centre and in the States were contrary to the spirit of the federal Constitution. Fortunately, under the leadership of Mrs. Indira Gandhi the Congress (R) emerged very strong and the Congress (O) was almost wiped out.

In the South, the Dravida Munnetra Kazhagam had nursed a move to secede in the name of Dravidastan, and the Constitution was amended to counter this move. The Tamil Nadu (originally called Madras) Government, run by the DMK, since the party captured power after the Fourth General Election (1967), did not seem to have healthy respect for federal principles. It had been openly preaching in terms of expanding the regional autonomy which is a euphemism for a furtive secessionist move. On March 8, 1970 the Tamil Nadu Chief Minister, Mr. Karunanidhi, said at Madras that if parliamentary means fail to achieve the DMK's objective of a provincial autonomy and a loose federation at the Centre, the DMK would launch an agitation. (*The Times of India*, March 9, 1970). The Karunanidhi Government set up a committee consisting of three eminent men of the State, Dr. Lakshmanaswamy Mudaliar, former Vice-Chancellor of Madras University, Dr. Rajamannar, former Chief Justice of the Madras High Court, and another former Cheif Justice of the Madras High Court, Dr. Chandra Reddy and former Governor of Tamil Nadu, to formulate proposals for enlarging the powers of the State. (*Himmat*, March 6, 1970) Prime Minister Mrs. Indira Gandhi had to pacify the DMK Government by giving certain concessions, which were denied to other. On 31st January, 1976, the DMK Ministry headed by Mr. M. Karunandihi, was dismissed, President's rule was imposed.

In various degrees, the other political parties also have damaged the principle of federalism.

Change of party loyalties, party defections for the sake of seizing power, favoritism shown by the Centre to certain States, stepmotherly treatment to certain States, partial attitude of Governors, and efforts to topple State Ministries have done incalculable harm to federalism.

(5) Gordian Knots in Inter-State Relations and Centre-State Relations

The spirit of co-operation, which is indispensable in a federation, is conspicuous by its absence in several States. A State may not be prepared to co-operate with its neighbors, and may also be unwilling to be on good terms with the Centre. River water disputes, boundary disputes, disputes over cities like Chandigarh and Belgaum, disputes over locating steel plants and other large under-takings, disputes over national language and medium of regional instruction and other disputes have vitiated the atmosphere endangering the federal body politic. It seems some of the problems have no solution at all.

Given the will, most of the disputes can be solved; but linguistic chauvinisms, narrow-mindedness, regional patriotism, false prestige, and stubbornness have converted these disputes into veritable Gordian knots.

With reference to Chandigrah, the Sikhs in the Punjab held out a massive threat, and finally the problem was solved in favour of Punjab leaving Haryana to sulk helplessly. In the dispute between Mysore (now known as Karnataka) and Maharashtra, the former warned the Centre of dire consequences, if it did injustice to it, while the latter was not prepared to budge an inch. Here again, much avoidable fear, suspicion and misunderstanding have been created by the vacillation and unsympathetic leadership at the Centre. The policies of local parties and the narrow mindedness of local leaders added fuel to fire.

Sikhs in Punjab came under the leadership of extremists, who demanded in 1983 Khalistan, a separate home-land for the Akalis.

The Centre could neither put down lawlessness and murder in Punjab nor win over the Sikhs by offering a reasonable solution. The Sikh problems is posing as a great danger to the body politic of India.

For more than two years Assam has been a great problem. Anarchy has been spreading, and the Centre has not been able to tackle the issue of foreigners. This is another great danger to the integrity of India as a federation.

The failure to set up a proper machinery to solve various kinds of disputes, even though many precious lives were lost and property worth crores of rupees was destroyed, shows how leaders, have badly let down the true spirit of the federal constitution. The leaders owe it to the Constitution and to the people of India to follow the provisions of the Constitution both in letter and spirit. The vacillation of leaders, their unwillingness to judge issues on merits, the want to moral courage to act rightly, the reluctance to face any difficult problem and the inclination to placate the aggressive sections of the population have embittered Centre-State relations.

(6) Efforts to Belittle the Judiciary

The enemies of federalism have not spared even the judiciary, which undoubtedly has functioned satisfactorily in interpreting and upholding the provisions of the Constitution. Any effort to denigrate the Supreme Court, or the High Courts, which alone can act as the watch-dogs of the Constitution, will further endanger the cause of federalism.

The Centre, desirous of neutralising the verdict of the Supreme Court in the Golaknath Case in 1967, wished to pass Nath Pai's bill, empowering Parliament to amend any part of the Constitution, including the part dealing with Fundamental Rights. The bill could not be passed during the life-time of Nath Pal; but after his death, the Congress (R) succeeded in getting the 24th Constitution Amendment Bill passed in Parliament in 1971 after the mid-term Lok Sabha poll. This bill too had the same objective as that of Nath Pai.

(7) Problem of Finance

The problem of finance has caused much heart-burning in certain States, which openly say that the Centre treated them in a cavalier fashion. States, which complain that the Planning Commission and the Union Cabinet meted out step-motherly treatment to them, do not miss any opportunity to weaken the bonds between the Centre and the States, and erode the spirit of federalism. The leaders in some States would have done better by not issuing provocative statements.

(8) Linguistic Reorganisation of States

The linguistic Reorganisation of States is the greatest single factor that brought have on the federal fabric. What seemed to be a remedy to some of the problems of India, proved to be worse than the disease itself. The vulgar exhibition of linguistic chauvinism and the outbreak of violence on a large scale, provoke those who are anxious about the future of federalism and parliamentary democracy in India to say that the creation of linguistic States was a calamitous blunder. Some people even speak of the need to abolish linguistic States and reorganise India into zones.

Wrong Presumptions of the Constituent Assembly

India federalism under duress and the serious pitfalls revealed by *it in the actual implementation of the various provisions of the* Constitution make us say that the Constituent Assembly (1946-49) laboured under wrong and misleading presumptions. Several leaders must have thought that India was not wanting in calibre to experiment on federalism. In the Constituent Assembly, it seems, enthusiasm stole a march over reason, and therefore even though the essential prerequisites of a federal system were absent, the Constitution makers incorrectly felt that federalism or quasi-federalism could be easily introduced in India.

The British established a highly centralised system of government. Experienced British administrators had cautioned themselves against, the introduction of provincial autonomy at one stroke. Here, it may be pointed out that the British introduced partial Provincial Autonomy (that is, the much maligned Provincial Dirarchy) by the Act of 1919, and full Provincial Autonomy (subject to Governor's powers) in 1937 in accordance with the Government of India Act of 1935.

Thirty-three year-after the commencement of our federal

Constitution we can say that true federalism is not known in the country to the requisite extent. This, undoubtedly, has been the thin end of the wedge. The Constituent Assembly, it seems, failed to note that India was not fully prepared for the federal systems.

Several provisions of the Constitution have been worded vaguely and ambiguously, and as it has been alleged, the Constitution has become a paradise for lawyers. It seems that litigation has become endless.

The Constituent Assembly, which was dominated by the Congress Party, in which Pandit Jawaharlal Nehru, Sardar Patel, Dr. Rajendra Prasad (the Permanent Chairman) and a few others could make themselves felt, must have presumed that the Congress was likely to remain in power for a long time. This presumption proved to be wrong, particularly after 100 Congress Ministers were unseated in the Fourth General Election (1967). However, later under St. Indira Gandhi leadership the Congress was strengthened and revitalised.

The federal pattern is in troubled waters. At the Centre, particularly after the break up of the Congress in August 1969, we saw for some time an undeclared coalition government at the Centre with Smt. Indira Gandhi of the Congress (R) as Prime Minister, Smt. Gandhi had to depend on the DMK and the Communist votes in the Lok Sabha for the stability of her Government from September 1969 to February 1971. This new development had a bearing on the Centre-State relations. Smt. Gandhi had been compelled to be soft towards the Tamil Nadu DMK Ministry, as the DMK support was needed in Parliament. The Prime Minister's attitude towards certain State Ministries was different from that towards certain other State Ministries.

As stated earlier, the situation changed to Mrs. Gandhi's advantage, when the routed her rivals in the March 1971 mid-term Lok Sabha poll and crippled the Congress (O). She could annex as many as 350 seats (6 more than two-thirds majority), and then silence the various opposition groups. She could easily pilot all bills in Parliament on which she had set her heart since August 1969.

Certain States, like Gujarat have alleged that the Centre is unfair to them, owing to political reasons, Mysore, now called

Karnataka, also felt sour about the attitude of the Centre. Thus in recent years, the misunderstanding between the Centre and the States has further complicated Centre-State relations.

One June 26, 1975, India which was already under an emergency owing to the threat of extent aggression, came under a double emergency, when the President, Mr. Fakhruddin Ali Ahmed, declared a state of Internal Emergency owing to a serious threat to the internal security of India.

Owing to the emergency excesses, the people voted out of power the Congress under Smt. Indira Gandhi's leadership and the Janata Party was able to rule from March 1977 for two and a half years. In 1980, owing to the failure of the janata, Smt. Gandhi came to power again. In January 1983 in the Assembly Elections, the Congress-I under Mr. Gundu Rao' leadership was thrown out of power in Karnataka and for the first time in Karnataka history Mr. Ramkrishan Hegde formed a Janata Ministry, Similarly, and at the same time, in Andhra Pradesh too the Congress-I was over thrown and Mr. N. T. Rama Rao formed for the first time the Telugu Deshan Ministry. Mr. Hegde called a meeting of all the non-Congress Chief Ministers to discuss the problems regarding Centre-State relations. They openly alleged that the Congress-I Government at the Centre was not fair towards the non-Congress Ministries in States like Karnataka, Andhra Pradesh, Tamil Nadu, Pondicherry and others. President Giani Zail Singh then appointed the Sarkaria Commission to review Centre-State relations.

I THE FUTURE OF THE FEDERAL SYSTEM

Strong Trend of Centralisation

In the USA

The actual difficulties experienced by federations like the USA, Switzerland and Australia make statesman and thinkers apply their minds seriously to the question of the position of the centre, J.P. Suda says on page 314 in *Elements of Political Science* (1952): "Writers hold conflicting views on the future of federalism. According to some. It is merely a transition stage bound to give way to the unitary principle in the long run." The principle of leaving the residuary powers to the units an experience bears witness, has weakened the position of the centre. This explains why in the USA the constitutional amendments were introduced.

In the light of the new difficulties experienced by the rulers in the USA, which perhaps the makers of the constitution did not anticipate, a broad interpretation of constitutional provisions in favour of the federal government was given. The Supreme Court which upheld the Doctrine of Implied Powers went far in strengthening the hands of the centre from time to time. According to this principle, the Congress in the USA, as Article 8 of the Constitution is interpreted, is authorized to enact legislation on subjects, which are implied or latent, though not specifically mentioned in the constitution.

Besides judicial decisions, the other factors, which faciliated centralisation were the centre-state, co-operation to deal with new problems and the participation of the national government in the financial affairs of units. J. A. Corry says: "By 1919, federal authority had been stretched to the point where it could employ two million civil servants on its legitimate peace-time concerns. The Supreme Court, aided by the arbitrament of arms in the Civil War, has confirmed the indissolubility of the Union and enormously strengthened the position of the federal government *vis-a-vis* the state". (*Democratic Government and Politics*, 1958: 558.)

In Canada

In Canada, the constitution-makers seeing the difficulties of the federal government in the USA decided to make the centre strong.

In India

In India, the constitution has a unitary basis. This again shows the trend of centralisation. The strong centre in India, in contrast to the relatively weak centres in other federations, can be explained by the peculiar conditions prevailing in India. The masses of people in India are not so advanced and well informed as the people in the USA.

In Australia and Switzerland

In Australia and Switzerland also there is an unmistaken trend towards centralisation.

The following factors explain the trend of centralisation:

1. *Complex Problems.* The problems of the twentieth century are more serious than those of the nineteenth century just as those of the ninetieth were more complex than those of the eighteenth. Leslie Lipson says on page 315 in *The Great Issues of Politics* that "order patterns of decentralization—whether in the form of local autonomy under a unitary system or of states' rights in a federal union—were doomed to dissolve in the corrosive acids of twentieth century politics, economics and technology. Virtually all the great driving forces in modern society combine in a centralist direction."
2. *Expansion of Social Services.* The concept of the welfare state calls upon all democratic governments including those having the federal pattern to render various kinds of social services. These are steadily expanding in recent years, and it becomes necessary to increase the powers of the centre. The expansion of social services is thus another factor in favour of centralisation. With the increase in population and the needs of the people, social services have to be rapidly multiplied.
3. *Wars.* The wars of the present century also favoured centralisation. Robert Rienow points out on page 205 in *Introduction to Government* (1960): "In an important sense the prosecution of war has been the greatest influence of all in centralising federal government. The outbreak of a war or the threat of war necessitates giving more powers to the centre in order to make adequate preparations on a large scale on a national basis. Questions pertaining to defence and war preparations cannot be left to the discretion of units in a state. The centre has to take the initiative, and mobilise resources to face the war situation. Two World Wars did much harm to the federal principle. J. A. Corry observes on page 586 in *Democratic Government and Polities* (1958); "If governmental management of the life of the people in peace time had stayed at the level reached in World War I, there is little doubt that federalism would be absolute. The federal governments ran the war and decided almost everything connected with it. The state governments remained in a condition of suspended

animation with no substantial sphere of independent initiative."

4. *National Emergency.* National emergencies like the one the USA had to face also favour the trend of centralisation. The problems created by a national calamity or emergency can be best tackled by the centre. For instance, when the most demoralising depression broke out in the USA about a decade after World War I ended, President F. D. Roosevelt introduced the *New Deal* to save the nation from disaster. The hands of the centre were strengthened by specific legislation to give effect to the *New Deal.* Had President Roosevelt left the situation as it was, the depression would have continued to spell more and more disaster on the USA. Seeing the realities, he change his attitude towards the centre-state relations and boldly introduced the *New Deal.* J. A. Corry says : "The New Deal brought a tremendous upsurge of federal government action in the United States. The federal government undertook large new activities or greatly expanded its former activities in relation to such matters a transport, public utilities, banking and credit, stock and commodity exchanges, labour-capital relations, agricultural production, housing, social security and conservation." (*Ibid.*, p. 572.)

Since then, the relations between the federal government and the states are quite different from those prevailing earlier. The times strengthened the centre, and made the states more and more dependent on it. For instance, the states receive grants from the federal government as federal-grants-in-aid on certain conditions which weaken their position in the face of the centre. It is idle to think in modern times, which have given rise to a bumper crop of knotty social and economic problems, that a weak centre with the units endlessly speaking of their full autonomy can be able to do full justice to the people scattered all over the federation.

In the USA, people were not slow to realise that the centre alone had the capacity to deal effectively with national problems. Robert Rienow says on page 206 in *Introduction to Government* (1960): "Unemployment, public works, security regulation—these are a major concern of central governments. No constitutional doctrine of federalism is able to withstand the clamour for governmental responsibility in the matter of guaranteeing jobs, production and smooth exchange of goods."

In India, the Chinese attack in 1962 and Pakistani attack in 1965 and 1971, enabled the Centre to make use of the Emergency Powers of the President. So also, the need to plan on a large scale with the help of the Planning Commission (which some regard as Super Cabinet at the Centre) greatly enhanced the powers of the Centre. The proclamation of Internal Emergency on June 26, 1975 for facing the threat of grave danger to the internal security of India even when the emergency of 1971 had not been ended made the Centre very strong.

Future not Bleak

The process of centralisation makes scholars think that the future of federalism is dark.

However, certain factors show that the future is not bleak. These are the following.

1. *Units not Subordinate*. The increase in the powers of the centre does not mean that units have become subservient to the centre. Constitutionally speaking, their position has not changed to one of subordination to the centre. K. C. Wheare points out that if the functions of the centre have increased in federations, functions of the units also have increased. If the centre is allowed to undertake works of national importance, it is because the units know that they are of national importance, and they will not be able to undertake them, if left alone without the aid of the centre.
2. *Centralisation Strengthens Federation*. The process of centralisation has added to the strength of federations, and has done away with disadvantages in the federal set-up coming in the way of national development. No sensible person will look suspiciously at the process of centralisation, if it is meaningful and is calculated to strengthen the bonds of national unity and improve the general conditions of the people. No federal state is prepared to sacrifice the interests of the nation in the name of regional independence

3. *Centralisation Meaningful*. There is danger to federalism only if the units in a federation are deliberately degraded to suit the whims and fancies of interested politicians at the centre. But, wherever there was centralisation in countries like the USA, it was not without justification. Wanton denigration of federated units has not taken place. In the USA, Switzerland and Australia, centralisation manifested itself to meet the urgent needs of the changing times.
4. *Federalism Spreading*. Federalism is speaking in the world. In recent years, countries which won their independence favoured federalism. India and the United Arab Republic can be given as examples.

World Federation

The functioning of federal government in the USA, Switzerland, Australia, Canada and the USSR holds out great hope for federalism in future. In these countries, perhaps a unitary system would have failed miserably.

Federalism is also the best remedy for curing the ills of the world. At a future date, when states decide to surrender sovereignty and to have a world government, they will have to choose a federal form and not a unitary one. R. G. Gettell says on page 136 in *Political Science* (1956): "Many writers have extolled the merits of the federal principle and have urged its further application in the formation of larger political units, even to the extent of a world federation," C. F. Strong says that "If the world is moving towards the organisation of a universal state out of the international anarchy which we have hitherto known, it is pretty certain that it is on federal lines that this will be achieved." (see *Modern Political Constitutions*—1958, p. 98.)

REFERENCES

Aiyar, S. P., and Usha Mehta (Ed.), *Essays on Indian Federalism*.

Beloff, M, *The* American Federal Government, 1959.

Corry, J. A., *Democratic Government and Politics*, 1958.

Finer, Herman *The Theory and Practice of Modern Government*, 1961.

Garner., J. W., *Political Science and Government*, 1955.

Gettell, R. G., *Political Science*, 1956.

Mogi, Sobei, *Problem of Federalism*, 1931.

Ogg and Zink, *Modern Foreign Government*, 1957.

Rienow, Robert, *Introduction to Government*, 1960.

Roy, N. C., The *Federal System of the USA*, 1940.

Santhanam, K., *Union-State Relations in India*.

Schulz, E. B., *Essentials of Government*, 1961.

Steware, Michael, *Modern Forms of Government*, 1959.

Suba, J. P., *Element of Political Science*, 1952.

Wheare, K. C., *Federal Government*, 1946.

Willoughby, F. W., *The Government of Modern States*, 1936.

9

The Executive

Its Functions

The Executive is the second main branch of government. The term is used in a broad sense to indicate 'the aggregate or totality of all the functionaries and agencies which are concerned with the execution of the will of the State as that will has been formulated and expressed in terms of law'.[1] In this sense, it includes not only those (like the President in the U.S.A. and the cabinet in Britain) who exercise supreme control but also the host of subordinate officials, like policemen and clerks, who simply carry out orders. It is more common in political science to restrict the use of the term Executive to those whose primary duty is rather that of 'seeing that laws are enforced' than that of 'doing the things which the laws call for'; the term the 'the Civil Service' is used to connote all other executive officials taken together.

Our survey of constitutions indicates that the functions of the Executive are not everywhere, or at all times, identical. They vary according to the type of Executive (being greater in respect of legislation in countries having a parliamentary Executive than in those having a non-parliamentary Executive), and according to the prevailing conceptions regarding the sphere of the State (being greater in totalitarian than in liberal States). An outline of the more important functions may, however, be attempted under three headings.

(i) Legislative

It has been noticed that while laws are everywhere passed by the Legislature, the Executive has some share, direct of indirect, in the process of legislation—recommending measures for its consideration, initiating bills, defending them in parliament, exercising a suspensive veto, etc. Besides, almost everywhere it has the power of delegated legislation, i.e. of issuing statutory orders an rules under the power vested in it by the Legislature. They power of summoning, proroguing and dissolving the Legislature (in countries where the constitution does not itself fix tenure and date of meeting) is also invariably vested in the Executive.

(ii) Administrative

Three kinds[2] of administrative duties may be distinguished. The first is the direction and supervision of the execution of laws. To enable the Executive to perform this duty efficiently, it is vested with the power of appointing and removing the higher officials, directing their work, and exercising disciplinary control over them. In some States, as in the U.S.A., the appointments may be made by the Chief Executive only with the consent of one chamber of the Legislature. The second is the military power; this includes the supreme command of the army, navy and air force, and, in some States, the power to declare war.[3]

"The command and application of the public force to execute the laws, to maintain peace, and to resist foreign invasion, are powers so obviously of an executive nature and require the exercise of qualities so peculiarly adapted to this department, that they have always been exclusively appropriated to it in every well-organized government on earth."[4]

And the third is the power to represent the Government in its relations with other States, conduct negotiations with them, and conclude treaties. In some States, treaties require for their validity the consent of the Legislature, or one of its chambers; in the U.S.A. all treaties require for their validity the consent of the Senate; in France (under the Third Republic) the consent of the Legislature was necessary for some treaties.

(iii) Judicial

In the main, this relates to the pardoning power vested in the Executive in almost every State (with or without limitations);[5] but it also includes in some countries, as in Britain, the quasi-judicial power of trying certain disputes between government officials and private citizens.

TYPES OF EXECUTIVE

Our study of constitutions, past and present, shows that there have been many different types of Executive. The executive power was vested in two kings in Sparta; but the kings were so far from being kings in the ordinary sense that they were not even chief magistrates. The real Executive was a Council, the College of Ephors[5] Rome in republican days vested the executive power in two consuls of equal power; but there were other magistrates also with 'though inferior in rank to the consuls, were still strictly co-ordinate with them, and were in no sense their agents or delegates'.[6] In the seventeenth-century European States the executive power was vested in one single hereditary monarch. In modern Britain, the real executive power is vested in a cabinet chosen from Parliament; in the U.S.A., in a President elected by an electoral college; in Switzerland, in a Federal Council of seven elected by the Legislature. In a short survey, like this, it is impossible to compare and contrast all types with one another; but two distinctions are pronounced in modern democratic States, and must be discussed.

Single and plural Executives

The primary difference between the single and plural Executive (illustrated respectively by the President of the U.S.A. and the Federal Council of Switzerland) is that in the former, the final control rests with one individual, whereas in the latter, it rests with a Council. The President of the U.S.A. has his ministers, but they are strictly *his* ministers, named by him and dependent on him; they are his advisers and agents, not his colleagues.[7] The position of the President of the Swiss Confederation, on the other hand, as has been noticed earlier, is wholly different. He is simply the chairman of the Federal Council and exercises the usual powers of a chairman. The other members of that Council are his colleagues, not merely his agents or advisers; executive acts are the acts of the Council as a body not of the President personally.[8]

The single Executive has one clear advantage. It secures the unity, singleness of purpose, energy and promptness of decision so necessary for the success of an Executive. This consideration is of particular importance at grave crises of national existence, when unity of control is absolutely essential. A collegial Executive, on the other hand, impairs unity of control by dividing responsibility. What a Board does, says J. S. Mill,[9] is the act of nobody for nobody can be made to answer for it.

A plural Executive has, however, its compensating advantages. It is a maxim of experience that in a multitude of counsellors there is wisdom.[10] A collegial Executive is safer thana single one. It renders more difficult the encroachment of the Executive on the liberties of the people in general. While it hinders the commonwealth from making the most of a great man, it prevents it from being dragged through the dirt by a small man.[11]

> 'The presidency of Washington and the presidency of Pierce are in Switzerland alike impossible.... America, with her personal chief, runs a risk which Switzerland avoids. As in all cases of risk, the more adventurous State sometimes reaps for itself advantages, and sometimes brings on itself evil, from both of which is less daring fellow is equally cut off. It may be that each system better suits the position of the nation which has adopted it.'[12]

Parliamentary and non-parliamentary Executive[13]

The second distinction is between an Executive (as in Britain) chosen from Parliament and holding office only so long as it commands the confidence of that Parliament, and another (as in the U.S.A.) chosen independently of the Legislature and holding office for a fixed term.

The parliamentary Executive has several advantages. (*i*) It ensures harmony and co-operation between the Executive and the Legislature, which makes for efficient legislation. The Executive's experience of the administrative process is useful in making the laws passed by the Legislature more realistic than they are otherwise likely to be. In Laski's expressive phrase, Congress in America legislates in a vacuum. The divorce of the Executive from the Legislature is 'the forcible disjunction of things naturally connected'; it is indeed injurious to both.

> 'The Executive is crippled by not getting the laws it needs, and the Legislature is spoiled by having to without responsibility: the Executive becomes unfit for its name, since it cannot execute what it decides on; the Legislature is demoralized by liberty, by taking decision of which others (and not itself) will suffer the effects.'[14]

(*ii*) It contributes to the efficiency of the administration by bringing the ministry into constant contact with the Opposition. The Opposition, eager 'to get in', keeps the ministry up to a high pitch of alertness through questions and vigorous criticism. (*iii*) It makes for responsibility to popular will. An Executive, liable to lose the confidence of Parliament as the result of the exercise of arbitrary power, is careful not to be autocratic. By its very nature, it is always induced to adopt a policy which has the support of public opinion. Even so 'autocratic' an Executive as the British cabinet always has its finger on the pulse of the House of Commons and of the larger public outside. (*iv*) It provides a simple method whereby persons fitted to be members of an Executive may make known their ability;[15] indeed, according to Laski there is no alternative method that in any degree approaches it.

But the parliamentary Executive has its defects. (*i*) Its tenure is uncertain, being liable to be upset at any moment by a breeze of popular disfavour, 'if the dominant party in the representative chamber is either small or wanting in coherence'. Cabinet government worked successfully in Britain because of the existence of two, and only tow, well-organized and powerful political parties, one of which was willing and able to take up the work of government when the other laid it down; when three parties so divided the House that no one party was able to command a majority (as happened between 1923 and 1929), it did not work well. In most other countries which have adopted the cabinet system of government, two strong parties have not developed, however. French experiences in this regard is typical. Ministries there were short-lived and uncertain of their period of office; the uncertainty rendered it difficult for them to adopt a farsighted and consistent policy. Under other conditions, where one party dominates the House, there is quite a different danger, which we have noticed in connexion with the British cabinet: there is a constant temptation to members to vote, not in what they may consider the best way, but in the way that will help to keep in or turn out the ministry, and this tends to make the cabinet autocratic. (*ii*) Ministers, are liable to be distracted from their executive duties by their parliamentary work. This is specially true in countries where the ministry has no stable majority; France under the Third Republic is a typical example. Further it happens that under such conditions the ministry is unwilling to propose measures, however salutary, that are likely to be unpopular, but is merely anxious to propose measures 'whose chief merit is their *vote-catching quality*'. *(iii) The choice of ministers in this system* is limited to members of the dominant party in Parliament; it is quite possible that they will not possess general administrative ability, still less the special knowledge required for particular departments.

By contrast, the great advantages of a presidential system of government are its stability and freedom from control by a fickle legislative majority. Thus the President of the U.S.A. is elected for a fixed term, and except in the case of some definite crime being judicially proved against him, he cannot be constitutionally removed before the end of that term. He is free to pursue a reasonably continuous and consistent policy; and, with nothing either to gain or fear from Congress, is free to think only of the welfare of the *people. Moreover, according to J. A. R. Marriott,* there is a real gain in efficiency of administration because ministers are not distracted by the necessity of constant attendance in the Legislature, and in efficiency of legislation because the minds of legislators are concentrated upon their special functions.[16]

These advantages, however, are gained at the cost of too great an isolation of the executive and legislative branches from each other, with all the attendant disadvantages noticed above and the possibility of deadlocks between two branches of government, which ought, if possible, to be avoided. In the U.S.A., if Congress and the President do not agree, neither party has any means of getting rid of the other. The President cannot dissolve Congress and he is in no way called on to resign has own office. A similar situation would be met in Britain either by the resignation of the ministry or by the dissolution of the House of Commons.

It may be, as Freeman suggests,[17] that each system is suited to the circumstances of the country where it prevails, for the great *lesson of political history* is that no kind of *government* worthy to be called government is universally good or bad in itself. Nevertheless, it is impossible to withhold admiration for the Swiss system which has the merits of both types of Executive and avoids the defects of both.

THE ORGANIZATION OF THE CIVIL SERVICE

We have earlier distinguished the Civil Service from the chief Executive, the duty of the former being to obey the orders of the latter. Briefly, it is 'a professional body of officials, permanent, paid and skilled'.[18] There was a time in history, as we have noticed with reference to Athens, when civil servants were not *permanent* officials, and were recruited for the most part from ordinary citizens, with no specialized training. That is a state of things which can hardly be revived, for the problems of modern government are very complex, requiring for their efficient solution a body of men who are trained for their job and who take to government service as a vocation for life.

The importance of the Civil Service has grown with the increased activity of the State. The modern State, we have noticed earlier, is not a police State, but a social service State, its functions have, therefore, increased enormously. As the scope of State activity widens, the Civil Service grows not only in numbers[19] but in power, for every extension of the area of State activity increases the points at which officials and citizens come into contact with each other. The greater the prohibitions and restrictions by Government on personal conduct, the greater, inevitably, the power of the Civil Service. The growth of delegated legislation and administrative justice, noticed earlier, must also be reckoned among the causes of the increasing importance of the Civil Service, for they increase the area of discretion vested in that service.

Three or four principles have gradually been established in the past hundred years regarding the organization of the Civil Service.

(i) The political Executive should have little control over the appointment of permanent officials because that might lead to party patronage, favoritism and insecurity of service. Men of ability and character will not be tempted to join the Service when no guarantee of continuous livelihood exists. Further, appointment by the political Executive may lead to corruption. The time and mind of ministers will be devoted to the rewarding of the followers of a party and to the interviewing of an endless number of candidates and those who come to plead on their behalf, rather than to the formulation of policies for the promotion of social good and their efficient administration. It is now recognized that to avoid these evils, members of the public Services must be appointed by persons other than those in the cabinet and under rules which reduce to a minimum the chances of personal favoritisms. A Public Service Commission, with members holding office during good behavior, is entrusted with the duty of recruiting men to the Service by open competition (supplemented by interviews in certain cases). The fundamental principles in the conduct of the Service thus constituted are permanence in office and the dissociation of tenure of office from the changes of government caused by the cabinet system. Once a candidate has been admitted to the Service, granted efficiency and good behaviour, he should be certain of keeping his place until the age of retirement. The Executive should have the right of dismissal, to be exercised only in cases of incompetence or neglect of duty, and never for political reasons or to make room for favorites.

(ii) Promotion must be on the basis of seniority tempered by factors of efficiency.

(iii) Members of the Civil Service must abstain from party politics, and loyally carry out the orders of their chief, whichever party be in power, in so far as they are within the limits of the law. They must, further, observe strict official secrecy.

(iv) The minister takes the responsibility for the action of his subordinates. It is a convention that no mention should be made in Parliament of a minister's permanent subordinates, either by way of praise or criticism; and no minister should take shelter behind the staff of his department.

In India, before the transfer of power to Indian hands in 1947, a further principle was recognized in the organization of the Civil Service, though luckily, only to a limited extent, viz. communal representation. Thus the Government of India had laid down the rule that 12½% of all vacancies to be filled by open competition should be reserved for the Scheduled Castes. This meant that if they obtained less than the prescribed percentage in open competition, this percentage would be secured to them by means of nomination. Similarly, in connexion with posts which were filled from the open market otherwise than by competition, recruitment was made approximately in proportion to the population of the various communities: Hindus excluding Scheduled Castes 60%, Scheduled Castes $16^{2}/_{3}$%, Muslims $13^{1}/_{3}$% and other communities 10%. Such discrimination in favour of minorities is not followed in European countries. The clause usually inserted in the constitutions of these countries is to the effect that differences of race, language or religion shall not prejudice any national in admission to public employment.

The *raison d'etre* of communal reservation in the Services was said to be the unequal cultural development of the communities in the State. It was based on the view that the efficiency of the public services was a function not merely of the qualifications of the entrants thereto but of the social harmony in the body politic they served. Such harmony, it was argued, could only be secured by the fair representation of the various communities in the services through reservation and the like. The principle, however, worked under two healthy safeguards; in order to secure a fair degree of (if not the maximum) efficiency, a minimum qualification was imposed; and communal representation was not taken into account in making promotions. If a senior found a junior promoted over him merely because he belonged to another community, there would be discontent within the Service. Such treatment would be going a long way on the road towards dividing the Service by communities; and 'a body which is divided against itself cannot have that loyalty and *esprit de corps* which are so vital in public service'.

The policy of the Government of India in regard to communal representation in the public Services was revised in 1950 in the light of the provisions of the constitution which lay down *inter alia* that with certain exceptions no discrimination should be made in the matter of appointments to the Services under the State on grounds of race, religion, caste, etc. The exceptions are that special provision shall be made for the Scheduled Castes and Scheduled Tribes in all Services and for Anglo-Indians in certain specified Services, as follows:

(i) *Scheduled Castes*. The existing reservation of 12½% of vacancies filled by direct recruitment in favour of the Scheduled Castes will continue in the case of recruitment to posts and Services made, on an all-India basis, by open competition. Where recruitment is made otherwise than by open competition the reservation for Scheduled Castes will be 16 2/3%

(ii) *Scheduled Tribes*. Both in recruitment by open competition and in recruitment made otherwise than by open competition there will be reservation in favour of members of the Scheduled Tribes of 5% of the vacancies filled by direct recruitment.

(iii) *Anglo-Indians*. The reservations which were in force in favour of Anglo-Indians in the Railway Services, the Posts and Telegraphs Department and the Customs Department on 14 August 1947 will be continued.[20]

The orders regarding reservation of vacancies in favour of the various communities will not apply to recruitment by promotion, which will continue to be made as heretofore irrespective of communal considerations and on the basis of seniority or merit as the case may be.

In all cases, certain minimum qualifications are prescribed and the reservations are subject to the overall condition that candidates of the requisite communities, possessing the prescribed qualifications and suitable in all respects for the appointment in question, are forthcoming in sufficient numbers for the vacancies reserved for them.

WHY THE POWER OF THE EXECUTIVE HAS GROWN

Before we pass on to the Judiciary, mention must be made of a remarkable trend in modern politics: the growth in the power of the Executive at the expense of the Legislature. This development it true not only of government in totalitarian States but also in democratic States. What are the reasons for this new development?

It might, indeed, be expected that the Legislature should generally be 'the great overruling power in every free community', for the will of the State must be expressed before it can be enforce, and that will is expressed by the Legislature. The Legislature has power over the purse, it has power to regulate matters the power over which has not been conferred on other departments; where a parliamentary Executive exists, the tenure of the Executive is controlled by the Legislature; and the importance of the legislative function has increased in proportion to the increase of collectivist legislation.

But in practice, the Executive tends to overshadow the Legislature for several reasons. (*i*) Modern executive business is concerned not only with the execution of laws, but also in many cases with the initiation of bills to be sanctioned by the Legislature. (*ii*) The increase of collectivist legislation, which increases the importance of the Legislature, *pari passu* increases also the importance of the Executive; for almost every law delegates to the Executive the power of enacting subsidiary legislation. (*iii*) In many States, the Executive has acquired quasi-judicial powers. (*iv*) War necessarily results in an increase in the power of the Executive; and the habit acquired in war-time tends to continue in peace-time as well. (*v*) Legislatures have everywhere been declining because of the inadequacy of the territorial basis of representation; the methods of election and the party system do not induce the best men to enter Parliament; the electorate, by demanding and acquiring powers of direct legislation, competes with the Legislature; other organizations like the Trade Union Congress and the press are similarly competing with the Legislature for power, and the Executive's control of the organs of public opinion, particularly the radio, necessarily operators to reduce the importance of the Legislature as a *fire* organ for the expression of public opinion. (*vi*) In totalitarian States, the concentration of power in the Executive is part of their very philosophy. (*vii*) Finally, the nature of modern government is such that leadership, continuous and acknowledged, concentrated and co-ordinating, adequately informed and equipped, is vitally necessary.

NOTES

1. Garner, *Political Science and Government*, p. 677.
2. Some writers would prefer to call the three duties here listed together as 'administrative' by three separate names, 'administrative', 'military' and 'diplomatic'
3. e. g. in Britain; in the U.S.A., Congress alone can declare war.

4. Kent, *Commentaries,* Vol. I, p. 283.
5. E. A. Freeman, *Historical Essays,* Essay XII.
6. Ibid.
7. Ibid.
8. Freeman, *op. cit.*
9. *Representative Government*, ch. XIV.
10. Ibid.
11. Freeman, *op. cit.*
12. Ibid.
13. The parliamentary Executive is also sometimes called the cabinet type of Executive: the non-parliamentary is called the fixed or presidential type. For example and characteristics of the parliamentary type, see chs. XVI, XVII, XIX: for the non-parliamentary, see ch. XVIII.
14. Bagehot, *The English Constitution,* ch. I.
15. Laski, *A Grammar of Politics,* pp. 299-300.
16. *The Mechanism of the Modern State,* Vol. II, pp. 113-114. Marriott, however, seems to discount the value of the increasing part that the American Executive plays in legislation. See above, ch. XVIII,.
17. op. cit.
18. Finer, *The Theory and Practice of Modern Government,* Vol. II, p. 1163.
19. From the statistics given by Herman Finer (*Theory and Practice of Modern Government*; 1949 ed., p. 760), the number of members in the Civil Service in Great Britain rose from 31,943 in 1861 to 717,000 in 1947.
20. Subject to certain specified conditions contained in Article 336 of the constitution.

REFERENCES

Bryce, J., *Modern Democracies,* Vol. II, ch. LXVII, Macmillan, 1921.

Finer, H., *The Theory and Practice of Modern Government,* Vol. II, Part VII, Methuen, 1932.

Freeman, E.A., *Historical Essays,* Essay XII, Macmillan, 1896.

Garner, F.W., *Political Science and Government*, ch. XXII, American Book Company, 1930.

Goodnow, F.J., *Principles of Constitutional Government*, ch, X, Harpers, 1916.

White, L.D., *The Civil Service in the Modern State*, University of Chicago .'ress, 1930.

White, L.D., *Introduction to the Study of Public Administration*, 2nd ed., Macmillan, 1939.

Willoughby, W.F., *Principles of Public Administration*, The Brookings Institution, 1939.

10

The Judiciary

ORGANIZATION OF THE JUDICIARY

'There is no better test of the excellence of a government than the efficiency of its judicial system',[1] for nothing more nearly touches the welfare and security of the citizen than his knowledge that he can rely on the certain, prompt, and impartial administration of justice. The judge, therefore, fulfils an onerous function in the community. His primary duty is to interpret law, to apply the existing law to individual cases, and, by so doing, to hold the scales even both between one private citizen and another, and between private citizens and members of the Government. Incidentally, however, in the process of interpretation, as we have seen, he cannot help making new law, this law-making function being relatively more important in federal States than in unitary States.

The role of the Judiciary being so important, it is obviously essential to choose men of honesty, impartiality, independence and legal knowledge to fill the places of judges. Three methods of appointing them are in vogue, as we have seen: nomination by the Executive,[2] election by the Legislature,[3] and election by the people.[4] There is no doubt that, of the three, the first is the best. A numerous Legislature can hardly be expected to estimate efficiently the legal knowledge required for judicial decisions, and, besides, is likely to be too much influenced by political considerations. For similar reasons, the popular election of judges is also open to objection. Only in three out of the thirty-eight American states where the system prevails has it given any satisfaction.[5]

Regarding the duration of their office, it is now recognized that the preservation of judicial independence requires that judges should hold office for life,[6] independent of the pleasure of the Executive, and that their salaries should not be diminished during their term of office. The extent to which these requirements are met and the methods by which they are met have been discussed elsewhere.

RELATION TO LEGISLATURE AND EXECUTIVE

Relation to the Legislature

What should be the relation of the Judiciary to the other departments of Government? So far as its relation to the Legislature is concerned, three or four principles may be formulated.

(i) The more the Judiciary is separated from party politics, the better. This means that the Legislature must not have the power to elect judges; and, further, it is desirable that no member of the Legislature should be eligible for a judicial office. (*ii*) The Legislature may be vested with the power of recommending the removal of judges either by the presentation of an address to the Executive as in Britian, or by impeachment as in the U.S.A. This power is necessary as an ultimate safeguard against a judge who abuses his power by receiving presents, for instance, None, not even a judge, can be entrusted with power without some guarantee against its abuse. (*iii*) The Judiciary in a unitary State (like France) need not have the power to question the validity of laws passed by the Legislature. (*iv*) In federal States, the power of the Judiciary to declare unconstitutional a law passed by the Legislatures is essential in order to maintain the supremacy of the constitution. Our survey shows that the Judiciary in India, the U.S.A. and Australia is vested with ample powers of this kind; but we find that in Canada and Switzerland the Judiciary has considerably reduced powers.

Relation to the Executive

In organizing the relation between the Judiciary and the Executive, the most important princip' clearly is that there must be a separation between the two. The separation is desirable because, as far as possible, no member of the Executive should have judicial functions (subject to the exceptions we have noted in connexion with administrative law in Britian); and because, while it may have the power of appointing judges, the Executive must not have the power of dismissing them. The reason for the second restriction has been explained above. The reason for the first is that such a combination involves damage to both liberty and efficiency. To liberty, because if the two are not separated, the Executive, as judge, has to sit in judgement over its own conduct, which is obviously injurious to freedom; to efficiency, because its members are not chosen for their capacity or training as judges.

But the Executive may be vested with two powers in relation to the judiciary. The first is the appointment of judges. The appointment of judges by the Executive also has defects; but alternative methods, such as popular election and election by the Legislature, are worse. The only ultimate guarantee that the best men are chosen as judges lies in a convention, supported by professional opinion, that judges must not be chosen for political or party reasons. The Executive's second power in connection with the Judiciary is the power of pardon.

In its turn, the Judiciary may be vested with the power to review the acts of the Executive. The government officer must be answerable in a court of law for his conduct as a government servant. This is an important safeguard of liberty. It has been noticed in the discussions of modern constitutions that, in general, States on the continent of Europe have established separate administrative courts for the trial of cases in which the Government or its servants are parties. The relative merits and defects of 'the rule of law' and 'administrative law' have also been examined in the same context.

EXECUTIVE AND JUDICIARY IN INDIA

We have pointed out earlier that in India a number of executive officials are transferred to the judicial department, and vice versa. For example, members of the revenue staff are chosen as sub-magistrates, and sub-magistrates rejoin the revenue staff as deputy collectors. Similarly a number of executive officials perform judicial functions; collectors, who are also district magistrates; revenue divisional officers, who are also subdivisional magistrates; and deputy *tahsildars*, who are also sub-magistrates. The district magistrate tries very few cases;[7] but the exercises administrative control over the sub-magistrates who try the bulk of the criminal cases in the district. These magistrates have to send to the district magistrate regular statements showing the nature of the cases they have tried, the alleged offences and the results of trials, as well as copies of their judgements. The admonitions of the district magistrate regarding delays or errors in the conduct of cases or the award of punishments are communicated to sub-magistrates subsequent to the disposal of the cases, with the intention of regulating their disposal of future cases. A district magistrate may also issue general circulars to all magistrates under his control for their instruction or guidance in dealing with cases.

The problem of the separation of executive and judicial powers thus centres in collectors, divisional officers, deputy tahsildars, and sub-magistrates.

That a man who is trying a criminal should try him in a purely judicial spirit and not be influenced by anxiety regarding promotion or prospects is admitted on all hands. This principle was indeed accepted by Sir Harvey Adamson (Home Member to the Government of India) in the Imperial Legislative Council in 1908.

> 'The exercise of executive control over the subordinate magistrate by whom the great bulk of criminal cases are tried is the point where the present system is defective. If the control is exercised by the officer who is responsible for the peace of the district there is the constant danger that the subordinate magistracy may be unconsciously guided by other than purely judicial considerations.'

It must be remembered too that the promotion and prospects of subordinate magistrates depend partly on the recommendation of the district magistrate as collector; it is therefore likely that they will subordinate their own views to what they assume to be his views.

There are disadvantages[8] too in members of the Indian Administrative Service being shifted from executive work to judicial work, because a district judge, for instance, trained in the executive field during his earlier years, may not possess those legal attainments or the judicial frame of mind necessary for an impartial administration of justice.

Progressive opinion in India, therefore, is in favour of effecting a separation of the Executive from the Judiciary. It demands that the control of the subordinate magistracy should be transferred to some authority independent of the district magistrate collector either to the district and sessions judge or to some officer appointed as his assistant for the purpose. Further, there should be separate officers to discharge the functions of divisional officers and deputy tahsildars, on the one hand, and of first-class and second-class magistrates on the other. Sub-Magistrates should be recruited from the bar and placed under the control of the High Court in the same way that district *munsiffs* are.

A section of opinion in India, however, still seems to fight shy of adopting these or similar proposals in the direction of separation.[9] Apart from the additional expenditure which any scheme of bifurcation necessarily involves, it is pointed out that the existing system secures administrative efficiency. At present magistrates subordinate to the district magistrate have the duty of taking preventive measures and quelling disturbances of the public peace; there is a side of magisterial work which must be regarded as preventive rather than punitive. The argument is that in India the head of the district has to deal with rebellions and local outbreaks, in which case he must be able to count on the support of the subordinate magistrates. For this purpose it is very desirable that he should be the chief magistrate of the district and that he should know his men. This advantage is now secured by the fact that sub-magistrates are chosen from revenue officials and are controlled by the collector who is also district magistrate. Further, any real scheme of separation will disintegrate the whole system of district administration, which has been built up as an organic whole, both the revenue and magisterial department being controlled by the district collector and magistrate. To transfer the magisterial powers of the collector to the district judge, or to another officer, will, it is feared, gravely lower his prestige and his value in the scheme of district administration, and lessen the opportunities available for the collector and the sub-divisional officers for keeping personal touch with the people in the district.

In conclusion, it is only necessary to remind the 'routine mind' of the dictum laid down by de Tocqueville that what we call necessary institutions are no more than institutions to which we are accustomed, and that the possibilities of experiment in the social constitution are far greater than most of us imagine.

NOTES

1. Bryce, *Modern Democracies*, Vol. II, p. 421.
2. In Britain, France the U.S.A., Canada, Australia, South Africa, Germany, Italy, and India.
3. In Switzerland and the U.S.S.R.
4. In some Swiss cantons and American states.
5. Ogg and Ray, *Introduction to American Government*, 8th ed., p.874.
6. This is sometimes expressed as 'holding office "during good behaviour"', i.e. so long as they are not guilty of any crime known to the law.
7. In Madras in 1926 he tried on the average one case and heard eight appeals.
8. It must be admitted that the system has its advantages also.
9. Several states including Madras and Uttar Pradesh have now adopted schemes for the separation of the Executive and Judiciary; in other states proposals to that effect are under consideration.

REFERENCES

Bryce, J., *Modern Democracies*, Vol. II, ch. LXVIII, Macmillan, 1921.

Goodnow, F.J., *Principles of Constitutional Government*, chs. XVII-XIX, Harpers, 1916.

Sidgwick, H., *The Elements of Politics*, ch. XXIV, Macmillan, 1908.

Willoughby, W.F., *Principles of Judicial Administration*, The Brookings Institution, 1939.

11

The Legislature

THE FUNCTION OF THE LEGISLATURE

Legislatures in modern States, we have seen, do not all perform identical functions. Everywhere they pass laws, determine the ways of raising and spending public revenue, and discuss matters of public importance. Almost everywhere they have some part in the process of amending the constitution. They control the Executive in States where, as in Britain and Canada, the Executive is a parliamentary one. Some Legislatures, as in Switzerland and the U.S.S.R., have elective functions. The upper Houses of several States (Britain, for instance) have judicial functions: the original and appellate. Some share in executive functions. The consent of the Senate is necessary in the U.S.A. for the appointment of officers and the making of treaties; in France, under the Third Republic, the Senate's consent was necessary for the dissolution of the lower House.[1] This variety can, of course, by explained only by the circumstances in which constitutions were framed and have developed in the respective countries. The judicial function of the House of Lords, for instance, is a historical survival, and is not of much significance, for, as we have seen. That function is in effect performed by the Lords of Appeal and the Lord Chancellor. The functions of the Senate of the United States of America in respect of appointments and treaties must be explained, partly at any rate, by the desire of the states on the establishment of the Federation to have some check on the new federal authority (to whom they were surrendering large powers); the Senate, being considered the guardian of state rights, was vested with these powers.

Practice apart, the question may be raised as to what is the proper function of a legislative body. We may discuss this under four heads: legislation, administration, finance, and the ventilation of grievances.

(i) Legislation

The first important function of a Legislature is, of course, to enact laws. The part that a legislative body (which is normally very large in size) should have, must, however, be correctly grasped. That great authority, J. S. Mill, has said: a numerous representative assembly is not fitted for the direct business of legislation, which is skilled work demanding study and experience. It is not competent to do work itself but it can cause it to be done, it is competent to determine to whom or to what sort of people this work shall be confided, and to give or withhold the national sanction when it has been done.

'Every provision of a law requires to be framed with the most accurate and long-sighted perception of its effect on all the other provisions; and the law when made should be capable of fitting into a consistent whole with the previously existing laws. It is impossible that these conditions should be in any degree fulfilled when laws are voted clause by clause.'[2]

The mere time necessarily occupied in getting through bills renders Parliament incapable of passing any except on broad principles. Mill himself suggested that the duty of making the laws should be entrusted to a small body of experts, a Commission of Legislation, not exceeding in number the members of a cabinet. No one would wish, he added, that this body should of itself have any power to *enact* laws; the Commission would only embody the element of intelligence in their construction; Parliament would represent that of will. Indeed, it should be a rule that no measure can become law until expressly sanctioned by Parliament. Technical knowledge needs to be tempered by the representatives' knowledge of social needs and the desires of the public. While Mill's specific suggestion has not anywhere been adopted, it is significant that the responsibility for the initiation of new legislation in most parliamentary democracies is vested in the Executive, which avails itself of the advice of experts and of advisory bodies representing special interests.

(ii) Administration

A popular assembly is still less fitted to administer or to dictate in detail to those who have the charge of administration. Here again its proper office is that of superintendence and check: to throw the light of publicity on the Government's acts; to censure them if found condemnable, and, if the men who compose the Government abuse their trust or fulfil it in a manner which conflicts with the deliberate sense of the nation, to expel them from office, and virtually appoint their successors.3

(iii) Finance

In matters of finance, it should be a rule that public money cannot be raised or spent without Parliament's sanction, but proposals for raising and spending money must come from the Executive. Further, the right of private members to propose new items of expenditure should be restricted, because this puts a premium upon particular interests instead of on the general interest, or upon the immediately apparent instead of the more essential.

(iv) The ventilation of grievances

Finally, a Legislature is a useful organ of public opinion, 'the nation's Committee of Grievances, and its Congress of Opinions', a place where every interest and shade of opinion can have its cause presented. This is a most important function in a democracy, which has been well described as a government controlled by public opinion.

BICAMERALISM

Most modern constitutions provide for a Legislature of two chambers, the lower and the upper. Among the exceptions are Greece, Turkey, two Balkan States (Yugoslavia and Bulgaria), some Canadian provinces,[4] some Swiss cantons,[5] and some Indian states.[6]

The more important arguments advanced in favour of a second chamber are the following:

(i) It is a safeguard against the despotism of a single chamber. Lecky and J. S. Mill are strong exponents of this view. Of all the forms of government that are possible among mankind, says the former, there is none which is likely to be worse than the government of a single omnipotent democratic chamber, it is at least as much susceptible as an individual despot to the temptations that grow out of the possession of uncontrolled power, and it is likely to act with much less sense of responsibility and much less real deliberation. Mill expressed himself equally strongly: the same reason, he said, which induced the Romans to have two consuls makes it desirable that there should be two chambers, so that neither of them may be exposed to the corrupting influence of undivided power, even for the space of a single year.

(ii) A second chamber serves as a check upon hasty and ill-considered legislation. An elected Legislative Assemble, it is argued, may be moved by strong passions and excitements; a second chamber, constituted differently and if possible with superior or supplementary intellectual qualifications, helps to restrain such tendencies and compels a careful, sober consideration of legislative projects. It is, as it were, an appeal from 'Philip drunk' to 'Philip sober'. It interposes a necessary delay between the introduction and the final passing of a measure, and subjects it to revision which may introduce improvements in form or substance.

(iii) It helps to provide adequate representation of the aristocratic element of the community. The lower, House, elected as it is on a wide suffrage, is bound to reflect the views of the *masses*; the upper House serves to balance this undue preponderance, and minimizes the danger of class legislation.

(iv) The constitution of a second chamber is the best way of providing adequate representation to certain 'interests' in a country, which need representation but which, for want of proper organization or other reasons, may not get such representation in the lower House Labour, Women, Landlords and Chambers of Commerce were thus given special representation under the Government of India Act, 1935.

(v) A second chamber makes it possible for people of political and administrative experience and ability (who for reasons of age, finance, or health are not likely to try to enter the lower House through the arduous process of electioneering) to be brought into public life and made available for the service of the State.

(vi) In federal States, the second chamber affords an opportunity for giving representation to the component units of the federation *as units*, the lower House being constituted on a population basis.

(vii) And, lastly, it is argued, particularly by J.A.R. Marriott, that the experience of history has been in favour of two chambers, No major State, whatever its form of government, whether federal or unitary, monarchical or republican, presidential or parliamentary, constitutionally flexible or rigid, has been willing to dispense with a second chamber. And even those States, like England, which tried the unicameral experiment during a period of social disorder, went back to the orthodox pattern after a time. It is not wise to disregard the lesson of history.

Bicameralism has not, however, had the unanimous support of political thinkers. At least from the time of the Abbe Sieyes, the dilemma has been posed that if a second chamber dissents from the first, it is mischievous; if it agrees with it, it is superfluous.[7] Further, the opponents of bicameralism suggest that it is unnecessary to have a second legislative chamber, with its attendant delay and expense, as a safeguard against the despotism of a majority in a single chamber. Other safeguards exist and are possible, e.g., the suspensive veto of the Executive, a second vote in the same chamber after an interval, and so on. In any case, as Mill rightly said,[8] the check 'which a second chamber can apply to as democracy otherwise unchecked' is not of much value, because few will then be disposed to listen to its opinion. Again, legislation, it is argued, is not so hasty or ill-considered as is often made out; almost any measure that is enacted becomes law as the *result of a long process of discussion and analysis*'; the committee system is especially useful in securing the necessary care in legislation. Finally, the difficulties in the construction of a second chamber in such a way that it will not compete with the first but will at the same time be constituted differently from it and will attract talent are too great to be overcome. Even the additional argument, applied to federal States, that a second chamber embodies the federal principle, is to be discounted, for experience shows that members of the second chamber often vote on party, rather than state, lines.

THE UPPER HOUSE

Disregarding the pros and cons and granting that it is decided to have a second chamber in a State, what are the considerations to be kept in view in constructing one—in respect of its composition, duration and powers?

The main principle is that it should be differently composed from the first so that legislative measures may receive consideration a second time by a body different in character from a primary representative Assembly, if possible with superior or supplementary intellectual qualifications; otherwise there will be duplication. This differentiation is usually brought about in the following ways.

(i) In the method of choice of members

The lower House is generally a directly elected body; the upper House is, in the main, a hereditary body, as in Britian, or a nominated body, as in Canada and Italy, or an indirectly elected one, as in France, or a partly nominated and partly (directly) elected body, as in India.[9] The objections to the hereditary principle are obvious: the qualities required for a legislator are not handed down from father to son; a hereditary body, is besides, an anachronism in a democratic age. Nomination has one merit: it enables men of character and ability who may not desire to contest elections to be made available for the service of the community (through nomination). A most serious objection to it is that the nomination is certain to be abused by being made on party lines; and, further, a nominated upper House, not being representative, may not command the confidence of the people. Indirect election gives some representative character to the body so elected, and presumably gives the choice of the legislators to people more competent than the primary voters; but it provides greater opportunity for corruption than direct election.

(ii) In the tenure of membership

In the United States of America, members of the lower House are elected for two years; but members of the upper House for six years; in France (under the Third Republic), the corresponding periods were four and nine years. Besides, as we have seen, the principle of partial renewal is applied to members of the upper House, one-third, for instance, retiring every two years in the United States of America.

(iii) In qualifications for membership

In the United States of American, for membership of the House of Representatives, the age qualification is 25; but for membership of the Senate, it is 30. Differentiation may also be made by prescribing a property or educational qualification, as was done for membership of the Indian Council of State.

The best method of constructing the upper House is, perhaps, the one recommended by Sidgwick in his *Elements of Politics,*[10] viz. a combination of nomination and indirect election. This gives it is differential character, makes it a partially representative body, and provides an opportunity for the nomination of the best men. A small body is preferable to a large one; two hundred ought to be the upper limit. The upper House so constituted may be given a fairly long tenure, say six years; it could also be renewed partially, say one-third every two years. Its powers should be on the lines recommended by the Bryce Conference Committee, which we have already cited, the essential idea being that the upper House should not obstruct the will of the lower House, but should be helpful in revising the laws passed by the lower. Further, it must have power to interpose such delay in the passing of a bill into law as may be needed to enable the opinion of the nation to be adequately expressed upon it.

THE LOWER HOUSE

That the lower House, should be elected by the people hardly needs special mention. The organization of the electorate and the methods of election and of voting (in both theory and pracuce) have been discussed elsewhere. The size of the House is also a matter for careful consideration. The principles are clear enough: it should not be too large to make effective deliberation possible: it should not be too small to make the formation of reasonably small constituencies easy, for if the constituencies become very large, members cannot maintain effective contact with their electors. In fixing the actual number, the area of the State and the population must, of course, be taken into consideration; five hundred would be a reasonable minimum. Regarding the tenure of he House, the principle is that it must be sufficiently long to enable members to familiarize themselves with procedure and to settle down to useful work; a very long period may result in members losing touch with the electorate. Perhaps a period of not less than four years nor more than five is the best, subject to the qualification that the House may be dissolved earlier by the Executive when the electorate has to be consulted on an issue which was not placed before it at the general election. The functions of a body so constituted must be more or less the functions which we have discussed in of this chapter. It must make the final decision in matters of legislation and finance, the initi..tive being with the Executive, and the revision, subject to the final sanction of the lower House, being left to the upper House. It should besides, be the organ of public opinion on all matters of public importance. Above all, it must watch and control the Government, compelling it to justify all its acts before the Legislature and before the public; and 'if the men who compose the Government abuse their trust or fulfil it in a manner which conflicts with the deliberate sense of the nation', it must have power to expel them from office, and either expressly or virtually appoint their successors. This last function it can, of course, only perform efficiently where the Executive is a parliamentary one; where a non-parliamentary Executive prevails, its function in this regard must necessarily be secondary and indirect.

NOTES

1. The consent was necessary according to the law of the constitution, though it had, by convention, fallen into disuse for a considerable time.
2. Mill, *Representative Government*, ch. V.
3. Ibid.
4. All except Quebec and Nova Scotia.
5. With the exception of six cantons, each has a unicameral legislature. See Brooks, *The Government and Politics of Switzerland*, p. 313.
6. Madhya Pradesh, Orissa and East Punjab.

7. For a modern version of the dilemma, see Laski, *A Grammar of Politics*, p. 331. The first part of the dilemma assumes, it may be added, that the will of the people is reflected in the lower House; and that an upper House, which is nominated or hereditary, as no authority to oppose it.
8. *Representative Government*, ch. XIII.
9. In the U.S.A., the U.S.S.R., Australia, and Switzerland (almost wholly) the upper House is also directly elected, but differentiations are made in other ways.
10. pp. 476-7. H. B. Lees-Smith in his *Second Chambers in Theory and Practice*, pp. 216ff., recommends the Norwegian system, in which the second chamber is a small body elected by the first, and roughly proportionate to the composition of the latter. Laski also commends the scheme in *A Grammar of Polities*, pp. 332-3.

REFERENCES

Laski, H.J., *A Grammar of Politics*, ch. VIII, Allen & Unwin, 1930.

Lees-Smiteh, H.B., *Second Chambers in Theory and Practice*, Allen & Unwin, 1923

Marriott, J.A.R., *Second Chambers*, Oxford, 2nd ed., 1927

J. S. Mill, *Representative Government*, chs. IX-XIII, 'World's Classics' No. 170, Oxford

Willoughby, W.F., *Principles of Legislative Organization and Administration*. The Brookings Institution, 1934.

12

The Electorate

SUFFRAGE

Representative government as distinguished from direct democracy is based on the principle that popular *sovereignty* can exist without popular *government*. The primary means by which the people exercise their sovereignty is the vote. Those who are qualified by the law of the State to elect members of the Legislature form the electorate.

As ou survey has shown, there is no uniformity in modern States regarding the constitution of the electorate. The broad distinction is between States in which the right to vote is given to all adult citizens,[1] and those in which the right to vote is restricted to adults, or only men, who possess specified qualifications in respect of race, property or eduction. Britain, the U.S.A., Canada, Australia, Weimar Germany, India and the U.S.S.R. are instances of the former; South Africa and Switzerland, of the latter. Everywhere, too, those who cannot or those who are obviously unfit to use the vote (such as persons of unsound mind and criminals) are disfranchised. A residence requirement, of three to six months' stay in a constituency, is also invariably insisted upon.

The point naturally arises as to the principle on which a State may decide in favour of adult or restricted suffrage; or having decided against adult suffrage, its grounds for deciding on a particular kind of restriction such as property, education, race, or sex. It was widely held by theorists in the nineteenth century that every individual had the inalienable and sacred right' to participate in the formation of the law and that no one could be deprived of this 'upon any pretext or in any government'. The Declaration of the Rights of Man roundly asserted:

> 'The law is an expression of the will of the community; *all* citizens have the right to concur, either personally or by their representatives, in its formation.'

Adult suffrage may indeed the supported by several strong arguments, (*i*) It is a personal injustice to withhold from any one, unless for the prevention of greater evils, the ordinary privilege of having his voice reckoned in the disposal of affairs in which he has the same interest as other people.[2] 'If he is compelled to pay, if he may be compelled to fight, if he is required implicitly to obey, he should legally be entitled to be told what for; to have his consent asked, and his opinion counted at its worth.' (*ii*) Political equality is a basic principle of democracy; any form of restricted franchise necessarily infringes the principle of equality between individuals in some degree. (*iii*) If the right to vote is denied to some, their interests may be overlooked by the Legislature. As J. S. Mill pointed out:

> 'Rulers and ruling classes are under a necessity of considering the interests and wishes of those who have the suffrage; but of those who are excluded, it is in their option whether they will do so or not, and however honestly disposed, they are in general too fully occupied with things which they *must* attend to, to have much room in their thoughts for anything which they can with impunity disregard.'[3]

These arguments have not, however, been allowed to pass unchallenged. It has been urged[4] that (*i*) where there is *prima facie* proof that those who have been excluded will not suffer by exclusion, their interests being adequately cared for by the representatives of those included, their disfranchisement is justified. The political interests of wives, daughters, and sisters, for instance, are safe in the hands of husbands, fathers, and brothers, on account of the intimate relations of affection that bind the members of the family. (*ii*) The exclusion of a class is justifiable when that class is likely to make a dangerously bad use of the vote. The ignorant masses, according to many competent writers,[5] come under this category. Enfranchising them might, thought Macaulay, lead to one 'vast spoliation'; 'a few half-naked fishermen would divide with the owls and foxes the ruins of the greatest of European cities.'[6] It might, thought Sir Henry Maine, work against scientific progress.

> 'Universal suffrage, which today excludes free trade from the United States, would certainly have prohibited the spinning jenny and the power loom. It would certainly have prohibited the threshing machine. It would have prevented the adoption of the Gregorian calendar, and it would have restored the Stuarts.'[7]

Sir James Stephen went so far as to remark that universal suffrage tended to invert what he regarded as 'the true and natural relation between wisdom and folly'[8] The main deduction made from these counter-arguments is that suffrage should be based in part upon education and property, so that only those who are able to read and write, and those who have some stake in the country, should be allowed to elect representatives to the Legislature.

These considerations suggest the thought, that while adult suffrage is certainly the ideal, the constitution of the electorate at any particular time is a matter is be adjusted in accordance with the particular conditions of each State. Take, for instance, the enfranchisement of women. As Willoughby suggests,[3] this should be influenced largely by the attitude taken by women themselves, the legal and social status of the women in the community concerned, and the extent and character of their education and general training. Again, the extension of the franchise, which might be feasible and desirable in a settled community long accustomed to the exercise of the powers of self-government, might be impracticable and undesirable in the case of a community beginning to learn the art of self-government. The extent of literacy is a factor to be taken into consideration. If universal suffrage is introduced in a community, the vast majority of whom are illiterate, multitudes may simple cast their votes as directed by other individuals or organizations. Under such conditions, Mill's wise saying that universal teaching must be precede universal enfranchisement must be heeded. The administrative difficulty of managing a vast electorate, of ensuring an adequate supply of reliable and impartial returning officers and polling officers, is sometimes a major consideration, as it was in India when the electorate was extend under the constitution of 1935.

MODES OF ELECTION AND OF VOTING

Should election be direct or indirect?[10] Of the (elected) legislative bodies we have studied, only the French Council of the Republic and the Senate of South Africa are indirectly elected bodies. All others are directly elected. The system also obtains, at least in name, in respect of the election of the Presidents of the United States of America and India.

The argument for indirect election is, in theory, a strong one. The electors who are finally to choose the members of the Legislature may be expected to be more competent at their job than the citizens who elect them. Being comparatively few, they should be less moved than the demos by the gusts of popular passion; and, therefore, their choice should be more careful and enlightened, and be made with a greater feeling of responsibility, than election by the masses themselves. This should tend to improve the quality of the Legislature.

But experience with the indirect system of election has not confirmed this deduction from abstract reasoning. The successful working of the system demands an honesty of purpose and independence, in both the primary voters and the intermediate electors, which rarely obtain. If the latter are chosen under pledges, as invariably they are, the whole meaning of indirect election is lost. Indirect election also has positive disadvantages. As the number of persons in whom the final selection is vested is comparatively small, it affords additional facilities for intrigue and for every form of corruption compatible with the station in life of the electors'. The possibility of corruption is increased by the fact that, holding no permanent office or position in the public eye, the electors 'would risk nothing by a corrupt vote except what they would care little for, not to be appointed electors again'. Secondly, indirect election is decidedly inferior to direct election as a means of cultivating public spirit; interest in public affairs is considerably less when a middleman is interposed between the voter and his representative.

Secret v. Public voting

Vote by ballot (or some form of secret voting) is now the universal practice. But this fact must not lead one to think that public voting was at no time prevalent or that it has no advantages.

It was in use till recently in Denmark,[11] Prussia,[12] and the U.S.S.R.[13] The case for public voting is in theory unassailable: voting is a public responsibility, and, therefore, its exercise should also be public. If the suffrage is a trust, asked Mill,[14] if the public are entitled to a person's vote, are they not entitled to know his vote? Under the system of secret voting, the voter is free from the sense of shame or public responsibility; he may, therefore, be tempted to abuse his trust, to further his own or a class interest.

If, in spite of such a clear case, public voting has disappeared in modern States, it is because its working revealed a serious practical defect: the possibility of the coercion of the voter. If a citizen has to vote in public, he may be compelled to vote for particular persons, whose pressure he may not be able to withstand. The experience of Prussia till 1920 may be cited in proof.[15] The Government took advantage of the opportunity which public voting afforded to exert pressure upon the electors to vote for Government candidates; and landholders and employers did likewise in respect of those who were more or less subject to their control. The result was that large numbers of voters, rather than be exposed to intimidation of this kind or to loss of their positions through having their votes known to the public, abstained from voting.

Clearly, in circumstances like these, where a *free* vote cannot be given secret voting is preferable to public voting. But, where a community is sufficiently enlightened and its members are sufficiently courageous to withstand improper pressure, public voting is certainly desirable.

THE DUTY OF A REPRESENTATIVE

There are two views concerning the essential nature of an elected representative. According to one, he is simply an agent or delegate, an ambassador, who has to vote in the Legislature according to the instructions, the mandate, of his constituents. According to the other, he is a senator, who is chosen fo his superior wisdom and integrity, and who is, therefore, free to use his best judgement upon the issues he is called upon to decide. The former may be called the theory of instructed representation;[16] that latter, of uninstructed representation.

The theory of instructed representation errs in several respects.

(*i*) It is impossible in practice for any member to state his total views partly because there is not the time to do so, partly because new issues are bound to arise. 'And upon those new issue, he cannot, item by item, consult their considered judgement.' Nor is it possible for the constituency, on their initiative, to instruct their member in all matters that come up before the Legislature. (*ii*) It makes deliberation in Parliament ineffective, for, by assumption, the number has arrived at his final decision before Parliamentary deliberation begins. Indeed, as Burke rightly saw,[17] it would result in an absurd state of affairs in which the determination precedes discussion, in which one set of men deliberates and another decides, and where those who form the conclusion are far away from those who hear the arguments. (*iii*) It is immoral, for it demands the sacrifice of the judgement and conviction of the representative in favour of those of others. (*iv*) It may affect the quality of the Legislature. Men of superior intellect and integrity will hardly seek election to a place in which they are not free to think for themselves, and vote according to their conscience. The community is therefore the loser. (*v*) It emphasizes local interests and local opinion to the possible prejudice of common interests and of the 'the general good resulting from the general reason of the whole'.

On the other hand, we should not jump to the opposite conclusion and say that the representative is a master who is always at liberty to disregard the fundamental convictions of his constituency. The right view to take is somewhat as follows: A representative is elected by a constituency to confer with representatives who come from other parts of the country as to what is best for the nation as a whole. He must be reasonably consistent in his views. Plainly, as Laski suggests, he is not entitled to get elected as a free trader and to vote at once for a protective tariff. The electors are, therefore, 'entitled to a full knowledge of the political opinions and sentiments of the candidate; and not only entitled, but often bound, to reject one who differs from themselves on the few articles which are the foundation of their political belief.[18] The representative must also be reasonably industrious. Burke has said that it ought to be the happiness and glory of a representative to live in the strictest union, the closest correspondence and the most unreserved communication with his constituents. Their wishes ought to have great weight with him; their opinions, high respect; their business, unremitted attention; otherwise, indeed, the simply does not perform his duty. From his central position in the constituency, he has a unique opportunity to instruct his constituents and to broaden their horizon. And, finally, the representative should be allowed freedom of judgement, i.e. freedom to vote according to *his* judgement, even when it differs from that of his constituents. The whole matter is authoritatively summed up in Burke's eloquent address to the electors of Bristol.

'To deliver a opinion is the right of all men; that of constituents is a weighty and respectable opinion, which a representative ought always to rejoice to hear; and which he ought always most seriously to consider. But *authoritative* instructions, mandates issued, which the member is bound blindly and implicitly to obey, to vote, and to argue for, though contrary to the clearest conviction of his judgement and conscience—these are things utterly unknown to the laws of this land, and which arise from a fundamental mistake of the whole order and tenor of our constitution.

Parliament is not a *congress* of ambassadors from different and hostile interests; which interests each must maintain, as an agent and advocate, against other agents and advocates; but Parliament is a *deliberative* assembly of *one* nation, with *one* interest, that of the whole; where, not local purposes, not local prejudices, ought to guide, but the general good resulting from the general reason of the whole. You choose a member indeed, but when you have chosen him, he is not member of Bristol, but he is a member of *Parliament*.

SINGLE - V. MULTI-MEMBER CONSTITUENCIES

It is the practice in all countries to divide the whole territory into convenient electoral districts (single-member or multi-member) primarily for the purpose of enabling the member to keep in touch with his constituency. Practically every State in our survey, except Germany, Italy and to some extent India, has adopted the single-member plan; Weimar Germany had a multi-member system; Mussolini's Italy, a corporative structure which, as has been explained, is somewhat peculiar, and India has both single-member and multi-member constituencies

The single-member constituency (sometimes called the district system) satisfies one important requisite of a good electoral system: that areas which return members to the Legislature must be small enough to enable candidates to be known in a genuine way, and also to enable the finally elected member to keep in close touch with his constituents. It is simple and economical, especially for the candidates; therefore it is more democratic because the poor candidates; is not at such a disadvantage as he would be in a larger constituency. It is more likely to encourage local talent than the larger multi-member constituency, because men of moderate means and position will feel more confidence where the constituency is small and their local influence counts. Further, it is clearly an advantage that more and more leaders of the community should be induced to take an active interest in the political process. Above all, the working of electoral systems throughout the world points to the fact that the single member system tends to provide a more stable majority in a Legislature than the multi-member system, and thereby helps to form a strong Executive. The multi-member system, generally coupled with provisions for minority representation, encourages the multiplication of groups[1] in a Legislature, making it difficult for any group to command a majority, and, therefore, to work a parliamentary Executive.

The single-member system, however, is not without its defects. (*i*) Election from small districts greatly facilitates the power of the Government to control the elections, for the smaller the district the more easily can it influence a sufficient number of voters to obtain the return of Government candidates. This was the experience of France under the single-member system, and constituted one of the principal reasons which induced her, in 1919, to abandon it for a time. (*ii*) It leads to the choice of men who regard themselves as representatives of local interests rather than as representatives of the interests of the country as a whole. The experience of both France and Italy with the single-member system of choosing deputies substantiates this.[19] As Gambetta once said, it made the Chamber of Deputies a broken mirror in which France could not recognize her own image'. (*iii*) It increases powerfully the temptation of legislative majorities to 'gerrymader' the State, that is, to construct the electoral districts in such a way as to give the majority party more representatives than its voting strength entitles it to. (*iv*) In certain conditions, it results in the return of the candidate disliked by the bulk of the constituency, thus tending to distort the representative system. This might occur when more than two candidates contest the one seat, as the following hypothetical instance shows. Suppose at an election 1,000 votes are cast, divided amongst four candidates as follows: A 280; B 260; C 240; D 220. A is returned. But it is quite possible that A is disliked by the majority of the voters. The inadequacy of the system increases with the number of candidates. And if a number of members were returned in this way, the majority in the Legislature might well be elected by a minority of voters. Thus, in 1924, the Conservative Party in Britain secured 412 seats out of a total of 615, though they had the support of only 48% of the voters. (*v*) Finally, it is possible under this system that minorities may not be adequately represented in the Legislature. The inadequacy varies according to the distribution of the minorities in the country. Theoretically it is possible for a minority group to be a minority in every constituency, and therefore, to go without any representation at all. But this rarely obtains. It is significant that Gladstone, while introducing the Redistribution Bill of 1885, defended the single-member system on the ground that it provides for minority representation.

'The recommendations of this system I think are these—that it is very economical, it is very simple, and it goes a very long way towards that which many gentlemen have much at heart—namely, what is roughly termed representation of minorities. It may be termed the representation of minorities; it may be termed the representation of separate interests and pursuits; but give it what name you like, there is no doubt that by means of one-member districts, you will obtain a very large diversity of representation.'[20]

Nevertheless there is the possibility that the minorities may not be represented adequately, i.e. in proportion to their voting strength. Thus in the British election of 1924, referred to above, the Liberal Party secured less than 8% of the seats though their voting strength was as high as 20% and the Labor Party, 25%, though their voting strength was about 34% of the whole.[21]

THE REPRESENTATION OF MINORITIES

Minorities are of various kinds: political, national, racial, linguistic, and communal. It is an accepted proposition in Politics that the minority in a democratic State have the right to *decide* on the passing of a law; it is equally accepted that in the *deliberation* which precedes decision, the voice of the minorities should be heard through representatives who enjoy their confidence. For law must be built on the widest acquiescence if it is to command effective obedience; and the best way to ensure such wide acquiescence is to provide opportunities for the adequate expression of minority opinion, and for the majority to accept the reasonable wishes of minorities. Where large groups of men feel that their wishes are not taken into consideration in the framing of the laws which they are compelled to obey, the way is open for discontent and rebellion.

Among the methods which have been adopted for the adequate representation of minorities, the most important are described under the five following headings.

(i) Proportional representation

The principle underlying this system is that, in a real democracy, every section of opinion should be represented in the Legislature in proportion to its strength in the country. 'A majority of the electors would always have a majority of the representatives; but a minority of the electors would always have a minority of the representatives.' Proportional representation may be achieved by two methods: by the single transferable vote or by the list system.

The essentials of the 'single transferable vote' are the multi-member constituency, the quota, the possession by the voter of only *one* vote, the marking of preferences, and the transfer of votes. The system demands multi-member constituencies; indeed this type of constituency is essential to any form of minority representation. Further, to be elected, a candidate, instead of getting an absolute majority of votes or a particular, meets only the quota i.e. the total number of votes divided by the number of seats.[22] Again, it is essential to the system that, though the constituency returns more than one member, the voter has only *one* vote. He may, however, indicate his preferences for other candidates besides his first choice. Thus if there are eight candidates and only three seats to be filled, the voter may place beside three of the names the numbers I, 2, 3. His vote is credited to his first choice unless it is found *either* that his first choice does not need it as he has reached his quota, *or* because he has secured so few votes that it cannot possibly help him to be elected. In such a case, the elector's vote is credited to his later choices. When the voting papers are counted, the first choices of the voters are first reckoned. If all the seats are not filled, owing to the fact that a sufficient number of candidates do not get the quota, the other seats are filled by reckoning the second preferences indicated in the surplus votes of the successful candidates. If a sufficient number still do not get the quota, the candidate with there lowest number of votes is eliminated, and his votes are added to others according to the preferences expressed therein, and so on, until the required number of candidates is returned.

It will be observed that every minority which is strong enough to get the quota by itself, or through the aid of other groups as expressed, say, in the second and third preferences, is assured of representation; it will not be sure of it, if a majority of votes or plurality is insisted upon as the criterion of success in election.

This system prevails in Great Britain for the election of members for the National Assembly of the Church of England; for Education Authorities in Scotland; in Northern Ireland for both Houses of Parliament; in Eire for elections to the lower House; in South Africa for Senatorial elections and in certain municipalities; in Canada for some municipal elections and in India for the election of the President of the Union.[23]

The list system also demands a multi-member constituency. Every party prepares a list of candidates for each constituency. The voter votes for the list he likes (not the candidate); and the seats are divided among the parties in proportion to the number of votes each list has secured. This method was once in vogue in Austria, Belgium, Czechoslovakia, Finland, Germany, Latvia, Lithuania, Poland and Yugoslavia.[24]

The merit of proportional representation is obvious; it ensures the representation of every group in the Legislature in proportion to its strength, so necessary to give it a sense of security in the State. Parliament will truly be a mirror of the nation, as it must be in a democracy 'which professes equality as its very root and foundation'. The single transferable vote also develops civic interest, for the system of preferences implies that the voter must give some time to consider the issues involved.

But it may justly be contended that proportional representation, 'however useful for a debating society, is useless as a means of establishing an instrument of government'. For it has been the 'experience of most countries which have worked it that it leads to the return of a large number of small parties. A system which makes it possible for all parties, however small,[25] to obtain separate representation necessarily encourages such disintegration. This, in turn, leads to the instability of the Executive by necessitating fragile coalition governments, which fall when any section of opinion is outraged. Further, legislation under such conditions is likely to lose all coherence and creative force, because it will be the result of enforced compromise to me the wishes of several groups. The system encourages 'minority thinking,' the voters and the leaders all being encouraged to think in terms of, and to fight for, sectional interests. A legislature elected on this basis represents a number of isolated interests; it hardly helps to form the general will of the nation. The tie between the elector and the member is bound to be less direct and personal on account of the enlargement of the area of the constituency. In the list system, the freedom of choice of the voter is severely curtailed as he cannot express his preference for an individual without voting for the whole party list; and *pari passu* the party organization gains in power. The single transferable vote may be puzzling to voters, and besides, being so complicated in the process of counting, may place them at the mercy of the counting authority. For these reasons, the bulk of competent opinion is against proportional representation.[26] To establish the system... is to organize disorder and emasculate the legislative power; it is to render cabinets unstable, destroy their homogeneity, and make parliamentary government impossible.

(ii) The single non-transferable, vote

The distinctive element of this scheme is that each elector may exercise only one vote, no matter how many representatives are to be elected. In a constituency having 500 voters and five representatives, each voter will be given only one vote. There will therefore be 500 votes and no more. If any candidate obtains 100 votes, he will be sure of election. Thus the system ensures representation for minorities of any considerable size.

(iii) The limited vote

The limited vote is so called because each voter is allowed to vote only for a limited number of candidates, i.e. a number less than that of the seats to be filled. For instance in a constituency returning five members, each elector may be allowed only four votes, or less; no party can then monopolize the representation of the constituency. This system has been tried in Portugal and in some of the states of the U.S.A.

(iv) The cumulative vote

Under this system the voter is given as many votes as there are seats to be filled by the constituency; but he may spread them over several candidates or concentrate them on one. The power of accumulation enables a numerically weak party to secure some representation by the concentration of its voting power on its own candidate. This has been tried for elections to school boards in England and for electing local officers in some states of the U.S.A.

(v) Communal representation

Communal representation may be secured either by (*a*) separate electorates where the voters of each community vote separately for candidates of their own community, e.g. Hindus vote for Hindu candidates, Muslims for Muslim candidates and so on; or by (b) the reservation of seats in a joint electorate, in which case the voters may vote for candidates of communities other than their own, but the member of the community (for whom seats have been reserved) securing the highest votes among the candidates of his community will be declared elected in preference to members of other communities who might have secured a larger number of votes. Sets are reserved in this way for the Scheduled Castes within the 'general' seats in Madras. Communal representation was introduced in India for the first time in 1909, at the request of the Muslim community.

The argument urged in favour of communal representation is, primarily, that when people are so divided by race, religion, and caste as to be unable to consider the interests of any but their own community, and when one community, does not trust another, communal representation is not merely inevitable but is actually best because it appeals to those instincts which are strongest. Indeed, according to this view, it is an inevitable and even a healthy stage in the development of a non-political people. It is realistic because it takes note of actual conditions, and avoids wishful thinking. Secondly, there is the argument of *status quo*: a safeguard exists and should not be taken away without the consent of the communities concerned; its abolition without their consent would be considered a breach of faith, a cancellation of assurances on which they have been relying for their security.

But, with equal force, it may be urged,[28] communal representation is fraught with the most disastrous consequences for the healthy political development of a nation. (*a*) As the authors of the Montagu-Chelmsford Report realized, the crucial test to which a proposal of the kind should be subjected is whether it will or will not help to carry India towards responsible government; and they had no hesitation in stating that communal representation would not help in achieving that object. For responsible government rests on an effective sense of common interests. 'The history of self-government among the nations who developed it, any spread in through the world, is decisively against the admission by the State of any divided allegiance against the State's arranging its members in any way which encourages them to think of themselves primarily as citizens of any smaller unit than itself.' (*b*) Again, communal representation perpetuates existing class divisions. It teachers men to think as partisans and not as citizens, and 'it is difficult to see how the change from this system to national representation is ever to occur'. That the authors of the joint report were correct in this judgement is proved by events since their time; the division of India into two States is but the logical corollary of the introduction of separate electorates. (*c*) The communal system stereotypes existing relations.

'A minority which is given special representation owing to its weak and backward state is positively encouraged to settle down into a feeling of satisfied security; it is under no inducement to educate and qualify itself to make good the ground which it has lost compared with the stronger majority. On the other hand the latter will be tempted to feel that they have done all they need do for their weaker fellow-countrymen, and that they are free to use their power for their own purposes. The give and take which is the essence of political life is lacking. There is no inducement on the one side to forbear, or to the other to exert itself.'[29]

Unqualified joint electorates are, therefore, the ideal. For a transitional period, i.e. until the minorities learn to have confidence in the reasonableness of the majority, the reservation of seats in a joint electorate may be tried with advantage as a step in promoting that confidence. The argument sometimes urged against this, that the candidate elected under this system is bound to be less communal in so far as he has to seek the votes of all communities, should in reality be considered its strong recommendation.

Separate electorates were tried in India from 1921 to 1947, and .he experiment offers conclusive evidence against them as a method of ensuring minority representation. In the 1950 constitution, India has wisely discarded them in favour of joint electorates while retaining reservation of seats for the Scheduled Castes.

POLITICAL PARTIES

Their merits

The representative system is the modern State is closely connected with the political party. A political party is a more or less organized group of citizens who act together as a political unit, have distinctive aims and opinions on the leading political questions of controversy in the State, and who, by acting together as a political unit, seek to obtain control of the Government. It is based on two fundamentals of human nature: men differ in their opinions, and are gregarious; they try to achieve by combination what they cannot achieve individually. Religious and communal loyalties, and the attachment to a dynasty or leader, also help parties to develop. Party enthusiasm is maintained by such elements of human nature as sympathy, imitation, competition, and pugnacity.

Parties fulfil certain necessary functions, so necessary, indeed, that many competent thinkers consider them essential to the working of representative government. They enable men and women who think alike on public questions to unite in support of a common body of principles and policies and to work together to see that those principles and policies are adopted by the Government of the day. In the mass and without organization, the people can neither formulate principles nor agree on policy. Parties make articulate the inarticulate desires of the masses. Out of the innumerable problems which call for solution in a State, they select those which are the more urgent, study them, think out solutions and present them to the people. They act, in Lowell's phrase, as the brokers of ideas. They preserve a sense of continuity in public policy. They organize and educate the electorate, and help to carry on elections. They dramatise polities and keep the nation politically alive. They sometimes help to discover ability, although only as part compensation for the repression of other abilities. Under a two-party system, moreover, they help to maintain a keen and responsible Opposition which puts the Government on their mettle, and induces in them the strength and confidence necessary to enable them to plan long-term policies.

Their defects

The party system has serious defects, however. It lowers the moral tone and the intellectual standards of society. Adhesion to the party creed becomes the supreme political virtue. Moreover, to keep up the vigour and zeal on one's own side, one has to pretend that there is agreement on the political principles of one's party. The party leader has to make the worse seem the better reason; he can seldom afford to speak the whole truth, except perhaps to his intimate circle. The party system thus encourages hollowness and insincerity. Intellectual honesty is at a discount, for an appeal to the honour of the party is considered sufficient to silence possible opposition. Political conformity is applauded and political difference derided. The system thus puts a premium on cowardice in public life and obstructs the free course of opinion. Tact, agreeableness, flattery, 'the gift of the gab' and other such adventitious social qualities receive undue importance; truth, justice and reason recede into the background.

While the individual is thus silenced by the moral oppression of numbers, all those who exploit the public interest may manipulate the party as they please. The party becomes a tool for the use of private interests under cover of serving the public weal; elections to the Legislature, which it conducts, while ostensibly national, really turn on selfish interests. That is why it is said of the House of Representatives in the U.S.A. that it represents every interest except the public interest ! Corruption becomes a fine art and incidentally drives the finer sort of men away from polities. All this criticism means that the party is in effect a *faction*; it aims at securing personal and sectional benefits rather than at carrying out a programme of public policy. Alexander Pope's definition of party as 'the madness of the many for the gain of the few' is seen to be more realistic than its broader and more well-known formulation by Burke[30] in terms of national interest.

A non-party democracy

Doubtless it was some such realization as this that led Rousseau to declare that any community in which parties existed was incapable of a true common will. A non-party democracy is therefore hailed by thinkers (both in the West and in the East) as the only remedy which will make representation more real and public life more honest. It has the support of America's first and greatest President. In his farewell address, Washington warned the Americans against the party spirit. The alternating domination of one faction over another, sharpened by the spirit of revenge natural to party dissension which in different ages and countries has perpetuated the most horrid enormities, is itself a frightful despotism.

'The disorders and miseries gradually incline the minds of men to seek security and repose in the absolute power of an individual; and sooner or later the chief of some prevailing faction, more able or more fortunate than his competitors, turns this despotism to the purpose of his own elevation on the ruins of public liberty. A fire not to be quenched, it demands a uniform vigilance to prevent its burning into a flame, lest, instead of warming, it should consume.'

Attractive as a non-party democracy would appear to be, we suggest it is practicable, even if it were desirable. If we were writing on a clean slate, it might perhaps be possible by means of a constitutional provision to prohibit party organization and party funds; but we have to deal with States where parties have come to stay. There is the initial difficulty: who is to bell the cat? If a Government in power (itself a party government) prohibits parties, will it apply the rule to the party from which it is chosen? If it does not, the road to one-party dictatorship is clear—a possibility with which one has to reckon in this imperfect world.

Further, the desirability of abolishing parties is open to question; for, in spite of their defects, they perform, as we have seen, certain essential functions. In a non-party democracy, the only means for the education of the electorate are the speeches of independent candidates, discussions in the Legislature, and agitation in the press. But without the association and discipline provided by the parties, these are likely to lack a sense of unity, responsibility, and continuity. Politics will lose its 'colour' and interest. No Government in power will be able to reckon in advance the support which it can normally command, and therefore by bold enough to cope adequately with its problems. These are serious defects which a government system can have, and would have to be met before the non-party system could be adopted.

It is better, then, frankly to recognize the existence of parties and to regulate them. More stringent laws to root out corruption and fraud in making up the party roll and in the conduct of business at party meetings and for the prevention of bribery and undue influence at elections may go some way to improve matters. The more active participation of upright and public spirited citizens in party polities is essential. The more they keep out of them the more do they help to increase the evils which they hate. Further, the rigidity of parties in the Legislature has to be lessened by the provision of greater opportunities for the 'free' vote of members. Finally, we must rely on the existence of a mobile body of public opinion, 'owing no permanent allegiance to any party, and therefore ably, by its instinctive reaction against extravagant movements on one side or the other, to keep the vessel on an even keel'.

THE TWO-PARTY V. MULTIPLE-PARTY SYSTEM

Granted parties are tolerated, the question arises as to which system is preferable, the two-party or the multiple-party?

The multiple-party, or group-system as it is sometimes known, has some advantages. It reflects perhaps more accurately than the two-party system the way in which the popular mind is actually divided. And further, where parties are numerous there is likely to be less of the uncritical sentiment of loyalty to party, less probability that their members will regard will questions habitually and systematically from a party point of view.

But, nevertheless, if a choice were possible, the two-party system is preferable to the multiple-party. (*i*) It gives the necessary strength and stability which enable the Government to attempt great measures. Long-term planning of policy can be successfully attempted only by a Government which is certain of a reasonably long period in office; that certainty can be provided, if at all, only under a dual party system. (*ii*) The multiple-party system not only enfeebles the Executive, but gives a disproportionate power to self-seeking minorities; it turns important branches of legislation into class bribery and thus lowers the tone of public life. (*iii*) The dual party system leads further to a more regular, systematic, and sober criticism of the Government than is likely under the group-system. The object of the Opposition being 'to get in', it is the business of its leaders to scrutinize the measures of the ministry carefully in order to expose all their weak points. At the same time there are strong inducements for them to abstain from attacking measures which are wisely chosen, because they expect to come to power and the blow may recoil on themselves. (*iv*) The superiority of a two-party system over a multiplicity of groups is to be found, above all, in the fact that it provides the only method by which the people at the electoral period can directly choose their government.

'It enables that government to drive its policy to the statute-book. It makes known and intelligible the results of its failure. It brings an alternative-government into immediate being. The group-system always means that no government can be formed until after the people has chosen the legislative assembly.'[31]

THE REFERENDUM AND THE INITIATIVE

So far the organization of the electorate has been considered; a word may be added about its powers. Its most important power, of course, is that of periodically electing its representatives to the Legislature. Can it be entrusted with any other functions in respect of legislation, administration, or judicial work?

In our survey of modern constitutions, two other ways in which the voters in some States—Australia, Switzerland (both in the Federal Government and in the Cantons), Germany, and the U.S.S.R.—share more directly in legislation have been noticed, viz. through the referendum and the initiative.[32] The referendum, it has been seen, is made use of in both its forms, the compulsory and the optional; it is applied to constitutional as well as to ordinary laws. The initiative is applied in some States to constitutional laws only, elsewhere to ordinary laws as well. What are the merits and defects of these methods of direct (popular) legislation?

Strictly from the point of view of democratic theory, the referendum and the initiative have some definite merits. They embody the principle of popular sovereignty better than the Legislature can; and, therefore, when a law has received the approval of the people themselves, it is likely to command more willing obedience than when it has only received the approval of the Legislature. The referendum ensures that laws opposed to the popular will are not passed; the initiative ensures that the people are not denied the laws they desire because of the unwillingness of the legislature, controlled as it sometimes is by vested interests, to pass them. Indeed, the demand for the grant of these rights is often made because of a belief among the people that the Legislature has failed more or less to translate the people's wishes into laws. The referendum is particularly useful as a check on legislative bodies, where, as in Switzerland, the Executive has no veto on the bills passed by them. Direct legislation, by means of the referendum and the initiative, is also of high value as a means of political education. In campaigns for the choice of legislators, personalities necessarily play come part; but in initiative referendum campaigns there is the maximum opportunity to hear and decide solely on the basis of the facts and principles involved. The Swiss people have repeatedly shown ability to learn and to change their opinions upon questions submitted to them.[33]

While the referendum thus primarily serves as a check on the Legislature and as an agency of political education, it serves other purposes also. It is an excellent barometer of the political atmosphere, and a Legislature ought to welcome the opportunities it affords for discovering the real wishes of the people which it seeks to represent. It also helps to resolve deadlocks between the two chambers of the Legislature (as under the Australian constitution and under the Weimar constitution of Germany), or between the Legislature and the Executive (as under the constitutions of Czechoslovakia, Lithuania and the Free City of Danzig).[34] Thirdly, the referendum places before the voter a particular issue for consideration, making it easier for him to give his considered judgment, especially as contrasted with a general election campaign, in which he has, through his one vote, to elect his representative to the Legislature and simultaneously give his verdict on an omnibus party programme raising several issues.

A study of the working of the referendum and the initiative in those States where they have been in operation causes two reflections, however. First the theoretical advantages referred to above have not been realized in all States, at any rate to the same extent. Second, direct legislation also has certain positive limitations which considerably lessen its value as a governmental institution. Regarding the first, it is sufficient to cite the authority of Bryce; after a survey of modern democracies he comes to the general conclusion that while the Swiss are well qualified by intelligence and knowledge of public affairs and their conservative nature to profit by the referendum and the initiative, it is more difficult to speak in the same terms of other States. That it has done little good, and perhaps done positive harm, would appear to be the prevalent opinion in America.[35] The proportion of people who vote at referenda is less than at ordinary elections; further, where the referendum is optimal it is little resorted to. These facts suggest the thought that people are more willing to choose between men than between laws; at any rate, the educative value of the referendum in practice is not as great as was expected. Where the initiative exists, the methods employed to get the signatures of the people are not always fair, also, the bills and amendments are not skilfully drawn up.

The referendum has five positive limitations. (*i*) It tends to weaken, if not to paralyse, the sense of responsibility under which the Legislature does its work; for the feeling might develop that the ultimate responsibility for any given measure rests not upon its members, but upon the voters, and this in turn is likely to react on the quality of membership of the Legislature. It is true that fear of the popular veto may tend to make some legislators timid rather than reckless;[36] but timidity, it may be argued, is equally undesirable in so far as it leads to conservatism or even reaction. (*ii*) Experience shows that the proportion who actually vote at referenda is invariably less than fifty per cent of the qualified voters, for people develop 'electoral fatigue'. Thus the decision arrived at its invariably that of a minority, which is contrary to democratic principles. The argument that since it is open to all to vote, failure to do so must be taken to mean approval, ignores the reasons why many people do not, in practice, turn up to vote. If, to cure this defect, voting is made compulsory, it is found that, in sheer disgust, voters drop blank papers in the ballot box! (*iii*) The number of specific questions capable of decision by mass voting is very small. What is significant in legislation is not the acceptance or rejection of a simple principle, say of protection or free trade, but its translation into terms of a statute with all its details, exceptions and delimitations. 'The difficulty, in fact, which direct government involves is the final difficulty, that it is by its nature far too crude an instrument to find room for the nice distinctions in the art of government.'[37] On many subjects, an opinion can be formed only after long and careful examination of the points at issue; the busy and ignorant voter hardly seems the person qualified or likely to make that examination. Indeed the referendum is an appeal from responsibility to irresponsibility, from knowledge to ignorance. This defect is much greater in respect of the initiative, for unless under that system an examination of the initiative bills by the Legislature is made compulsory, it brings before the people bills that have not run the gauntlet of parliamentary criticism. (*iv*) Where the Executive is of the parliamentary type as an Britain, the referendum is likely to embarrass and confuse the Government.

'Unless there should occur a complete break with English political tradition, it is hardly conceivable that a ministry could with self-respect, or indeed with advantage to the country, remain in office after the rejection by the electorate of a government bill of first-rate importance. Could Mr Baldwin have retained office in 1924 if a scheme of Tariff Reform, declared by him to be essential to a solution of the problem of unemployment, had been rejected on referendum?'[38]

Incidentally, this explains why the referendum has not been introduced in the English system of government (*v*) Direct legislation causes delay, and complicates the process of legislation.

Some of these defects may be overcome or lessened by the adoption of certain devices. When a bill is to be submitted to the people, the voter may be supplied in advance not only with the text of the bill, but a concise statement of its purpose and a summary of its contents. The initiative may be required to be drafted by an official (or recognized) draftsman, and it may have to be signed in the presence of a public authority, And before the opinion of the people is sought, the Legislature may in every case be given an opportunity to discuss it, and if necessary, to submit to the voters along with it a statement embodying its own views or even a counter-proposal. The small size of the electorate, the absence of wide divergences of economic and social interests and of party influences, the presence of literacy and of an independent opinion are conditions which facilitate successful popular legislation. Nevertheless, it is advisable to restrict its use, as far as possible, to simple and intelligible issues, concerning the fundamentals of the constitution, on which a direct expression of opinion by the electorate may be helpful and desirable.

THE PLEBISCITE AND THE RECALL

Two other political devices call for mention in this context as being connected with the powers of the electorate on legislation and other matters of political importance. They are the plebiscite and the recall.

The plebiscite, like the referendum, is a vote of the people on a matter referred to them; but unlike it, it is a vote on some important public question (rather than on a law). The political destiny of a State or part of a State or of a national minority are points on which plebiscites are taken. For example, a plebiscite was taken in 1935 in respect of the Saar in order to decide whether it should be returned to Germany. In 1942 Canada took a plebiscite on the issue of conscription for overseas service.

The recall means the 'calling back' of elected legislators, executive officers or judges before the expiration of the period for which they were elected, followed by the election of others to fill the places left vacant. This device is prevalent in many American states. In the state of Oregon, for instance it is provided that when a prescribed percentage of electors in any electoral area have signed a petition demanding a vote on the dismissal of an elected official, a popular vote shall be held on the matter (unless the official immediately resigns), and if the vote by a majority goes against the official, he shall be dismissed and a new election shall be held for the choice of his successor for the unexpired residue of his term.[39] This procedure has been adopted by other American states and has been frequently successful,[40] though very rarely in the case of members of the Legislature. Judges may be recalled by popular vote in six states; even judicial decisions may be reserved by popular vote in the state of Colorado.

Outside the American states, there used to be provision for executive recall in Germany and Latvia. In Germany, the Reichstag could, by a two-thirds majority vote, bring before the electorate a proposal to recall the President. The Latvian President could be recalled by a specified majority of the Legislature. The constitutions of twelve German states contained provision for the recall of the Legislature or of the Executive, on a petition initiated by the electorate. In eight Swiss cantons, the people may, by a specified majority, demand the dissolution and reelection of the cantonal Legislature before the expiration of its term.[41]

There can be no two opinions on the under desirability of the recall. If is wrong and mischievous. It asks too much of the average voter. If it is applied to the legislator there is a real danger of turning him into a mere mouthpiece of the voters mandate, contrary to the sound principles laid down by Burke. If it is applied to the executive official, it tends to make him timid and corrupt. If it is applied to the judge (or to his decisions) it destroys the independence which is so necessary for the proper administration of justice.

NOTES

1. The age at which a person is considered to be an adult for purposes of voting varies from State. In Russia it is eighteen; in Germany, twenty; in India, Great Britain and the U.S.A., twenty-one; in Norway, twenty-three; in Denmark and Japan, twenty-five.
2. Mill, *Representative Government*, ch. VIII
3. ibid.

4. See Sidgwick, *The Elements of Politics*, p. 379.
5. e.g. Macaulay, W. E. H. Lecky, H. S. Maine, and Sir James Stephen.
6. Quoted by Fisher in *The Republican Tradition in Europe*, p. 274.
7. *Popular Government*, p. 36.
8. Liberty, *Equality, Fraternity*, pp. 258-9.
9. *The Government of Modern States*, p. 273.
10. See Mill on this subject in *Representative Government*, ch. IX.
11. Till 1901
12. Till 1920
13. Till 1936.
14. Representative Government, ch. X.
15. Garner, *Political Science and Government*, p. 585.
16. Sometimes also called the telephone theory of representation.
17. Speech to the electors of Bristol, on 3 November 1774. *The Works of Edmund Burke*, Vol. II,' The World's Classics', pp. 159-66.
18. Mill, *Representative Government*, ch. XII
19. Garner, in *The American Political Science Review*, Vol VII, pp. 610 ff.
20. Quoted in the *Report of the Royal Commission appointed to inquire into Electoral System*, 1910, p. 2.
21. Conservative Party 7,451,132 votes 412 seats
    Liberal Party 3,008,474 votes 46 seats
    Labour party 5,484,760 votes 151 seats
22. This is only one (and perhaps the simplest) of the many ways of reckoning the quotes. Another is

$$\frac{\text{Total No. of votes}}{\text{No. of seats} + 1} + 1$$

23. Strong, *Modern Political Constitutions*, p. 178.
24. A. J. Zurcher, *The Experiment with Democracy in Central Europe*, ch. V.
25. Provided, of course, they are able to secure to quota.
26. H. Sidgwick, H. Finer, and H. J. Laski, among others, are against it. The late Ramsay Muir, however, was in favour of it.
27. Also called the Japanese system because it was in use for some years in Japan.
28. On this whole subject see the *Report on Indian Constitutional Reforms*, 1918, paras, 227-31.

29. ibid.
30. 'Party is a body of men united, for promoting by their joint endeavours the national interest, upon some particular principle in which they are all agreed',—*Thoughts on the Cause of the Present Discontents.*
31. Laski, *A Grammar of Politics,* p. 314.
32. In chs, XIX, XX, XXI. These are also in use in Eire and in the states of America. The constitutions of several of the new States created after the Great War (1914-18)—Latvia, Estonia, Lithuania, Austria and Czechoslovakia—also provided for some form of popular legislative activity. See Zurcher, *op. cit.,* p. 93
33. Brooks, *The Government and Policies of Switzerland,* p. 163.
34. Zurcher, *op. cit.,* p. 98.
35. H. Finer, *The Theory and Practice of Modern Government,* Vol. II, p. 931.
36. Brooks, *op. cit.,* p. 162.
37. Laski, *op. cit.,* p. 322.
38. Marriott, *The Mechanism of the Modern State,* Vol. I, p. 462.
39. Bryce, *Modern Democracies,* Vol. II, p. 162.
40. Strong, *op. cit.,* p. 291.
41. Here the recall is usually applicable to the legislative body as a whole and in a few instances to the members of either House from a single electoral district. See Brooks, *op. cit.,* p. 322.

REFERENCES

Finer, H., *The Theory and Practice of Modern Government,* Vol, I. Part IV, Methuen, 1932.

Garner, J.W., *Political Science and Government,* ch. XIX, American Book Company, 1932

Hoag, C.G. and G. H. Hallett, *Proportional Representation,* Macmillan, 1926.

Mill, J.S., *Representative Government,* 'World's Classics' No. 170 Oxford

Ostrogorski, M., (Tr. F. Clarke), *Democracy and the Organization of Political Parties,* 2 vols., Macmillan, 1902.

Report on Indian Constitutional Reforms, ch. VIII, Government Printing Office, Calcutta, 1918.

Report of the Royal Commission appointed to inquire into Electoral System, 1910, H. M. Stationery Office, 1929

Sidgwick, H., *The Elements of Politics,* ch. XX, Macmillan, 1908.

Willoughby, W.F., *Principles of Legislative Organization and Administration,* The Brookings Institution, 1934.

13

The Classification of States

INTRODUCTORY

In our analysis of the subject-matter of Politics we indicated that from a study of government in the past and in the present, we should be in a position to formulate, by an inductive process, principles regarding the organization of government, its structure and working. To this we now turn.

There is, however, one preliminary inquiry to make. There are, as our survey has shown, different types of States. A discussion of principles relating to organization of government, to be realistic, must needs take into account the similarities and differences between States; these are best studied by a classification of States.[1]

EARLY CLASSIFICATIONS

Aristotle was among the earliest thinkers to attempt a comprehensive classification. The basis of his classification is at once quantitative and qualitative. He takes into account the *number* of those in whom sovereign power is vested, and the *end* to which the conduct of government is directed. The supreme power in a State must necessarily be in the hands of one person, or of a few, or of many. The one, or the few, or the many, may government the community for the common good or for their own selfish or class interests. The first type of constitution is a *normal* one; the second, a *perverted* one. Taking these two principles together, Aristotle arrived at the conclusion that six kinds of State are possible; monarchy and its perversion, tyranny; aristocracy and its perversion, oligarchy; polity and its perversion, democracy.

Two observations are necessary to help us to understand

Aristotle's account correctly. First, he used the term 'polity' to describe the unselfish rule of the masses; 'democracy' was for him a perversion. To us, the former is a somewhat unfamiliar term, and the latter does not necessarily indicate the arbitrary or selfish rule of the demos. Aristotle's dislike to 'democracy' must be explained by the degeneration of Greek democracies in his day. Second, in his definition of oligarchy and of democracy Aristotle was not entirely logical. He defined oligarchy as the rule of the rich in the interests of the rich, be they few or many; and democracy, as the rule of the poor, be they many or few, in the interests of the poor.[2] On his own first principles, a constitution in which the rich ruling in the interests of the rich are in a majority should have been called a democracy; and one in which the poor ruling in the interests of the poor are in a minority, an oligarchy. Aristotle was aware of this illogicality, but after a thorough discussion,[3] he decided that the question of numbers was accidental; that of wealth, essential. To keep to the facts of life is more important than to attempt a meaningless logical precision; Aristotle knew that normally 'there wee many poor and few rich.'

A few of the later classifications—by Polybius, Hobbes, Locke, Montesquieu, and Rousseau—will also be briefly referred to. In all of them the influence of Aristotle may be traced.

Like Aristotle, Polybius adopted an ethical standard when marking off one State from another. 'The rule of one may be held to be a kingship only when his rule "is accepted voluntarily and is directed by an appeal to reason rather than to fear and force". Otherwise it is a *despotism*. Nor can every oligarchy be properly described as an aristocracy, but only where "the power is wielded by the justiest and wisest men select on their merits". Similarly the rule of the many may easily become nothing but *mob-rule*; the honourable designation of a democracy must be reserved for a government where "reverence to the gods, succor of parents, respect to elders, obedience to laws are traditional and habitual".[4]

Hobbes is content with a threefold classification, basing it entirely on the location of sovereign power in the one, the few, or the many, and paying no heed to the ethical *differentiae* noted by Aristotle and Polybius.

'The difference of Commonwealths consisteth in the difference of the Sovereign, or the Person representative of all and every one of the Multitude... When the Representative is one man, then is the Commonwealth a Monarchy: when an Assembly of All that will come together, then it is a Democracy, or Popular Commonwealth: when an Assembly of a Part only then it is called in Aristocracy. Other kind of Commonwealth there can be none: for either One, or More, or All, must have the Sovereign Power (which I have shewn to be indivisible entire.'[5]

Hobbes was aware of other names of government such as Tyranny, Oligarchy and Anarchy, but he refused to consider them as other *forms* of government. Those who were discontented under Monarchy called it Tyranny; those who were displeased with Aristocracy called it Oligarchy; and those who nursed grievances against Democracy called it Anarchy.

Locke substantially follows Hobbes in his classification, with some differences of detail. Thus he says, 'according as the power of making laws is placed, such is the form of the Commonwealth.[6] If the majority, in whom the whole power of the community is placed at the dawn of civil society, retain the legislative power in their own hands and execute those laws by officers of their own appointing, the form of the government is a perfect democracy; if they put the power of making laws into the hands of a few select men and their heirs or successors, then it is an oligarchy; if into the hands of one man, then it is a monarchy, hereditary or elective.

Montesquieu (1699-1785), the French poetical philosopher, held that States are of three types, the republican, the monarchic and the despotic. If all or part of the people have the sovereign power, the State is a republic, a democratic or an aristocratic one. A monarchy is the rule of a single person according to law; a despotism, the rule of a single person arbitrarily. Montesquieu indicates the various principles animating the various forms of government, the sustaining and driving power behind them. Thus the virtue of the citizens is the principle of a republic. In a democracy, this virtue takes the shape of love of country and desire for equality. That the members of a ruling class will be moderate towards the people, maintain equality among themselves, an enforce the laws against persons of rank—this is the virtue of an aristocracy. The mainspring of monarchy is honor:

the confidence or conceit of the individual and of the governing classes concerning their own special importance, a confidence which spurs men to accomplish things quite as much as virtue itself. Despotism requires neither virtue nor honour, but fear which suppresses both courage and ambition among subjects.

Rousseau, like Hobbes, is content with a numerical *differentia*: governments are monarchies, aristocracies or democracies.

Their inapplicability to modern conditions

Whatever was the value of these classifications at the time when they were formulated, it should be clear to the student of modern constitutions that they are quite inapplicable to existing poetical conditions. They do not help one to understand the resemblances and differences between States, which is the object of a classification. To illustrate: Under the classification adopted by Aristotle, almost every State in the preceding survey should be termed a democracy (or a polity); we know, however, that there are marked differences between them. Britain is a unitary State the U.S.A., a federal one. The U.S.A. is a federal State with a non-parliamentary Executive; Australia is a federal State but with a parliamentary Executive. Switzerland is also federal but with an Executive which is at once both parliamentary and non-parliamentary. The inapplicability of older classification is primarily due to the developments in political constitutionalism in recent times. The authors whom we have cited were classifying States with which they were familiar. But we have to frame a classification which is more in accordance with modern conditions.

A CLASSIFICATION OF MODERN STATES

The classification outlined below is based upon the suggestions made by Bryce, Marriott, Strong and Lindsay. While it applies to most modern States, it does not claim to be applicable to all.

The terms used in the classification have been defined in Part I and in Part II, Book II. Three explanation may be added.

(*i*) The classification is framed on two major bases. 'I. The conception regarding the sphere of the State', Whether liberal or totalitarian. This *differentia* has assumed such importance in modern times that it deserves emphasis in any scheme of classification. The life of the people in liberal States has a quality all its own, different not only in degree but in kind from that of the people in totalitarian States. As has been indicated elsewhere, totalitarian States themselves fall into two types, the communist and the fascist, the former abolishing, and the latter retaining, private capital. 'II. The nature of the political organization.' Under this heading three *differentiae* are noteworthy, viz. the nature of the State (unitary or federal); the nature of the constitution (flexible or rigid); and the structure of the Government (the electorate, the Legislature, the Executive and the Judiciary).

		Basis of Division	A	B
I	1	The conception regarding the sphere of the State	Liberal	Totalitarian (*a*) communist (*b*) fascist
II		The nature of the pclitical organization		
	2	The nature of the State	Unitary	Federal
	3	The nature of the Constitution	Flexible	Rigid
	4	The nature of the electorate	(*i*) Adult suffrage (*ii*) Single-memgber[8] constituency	(*i*) Restricted surrage[7] constituency[8]
	5	The nature of the Legislature	Bicameral (*a*) elective or partially elective second chamber (*b*) non-elective second chamber	Unicameral[0]
	6	The nature of the Executive	Parliamentary	Non-parliamentary
	7	the nature of the judiciary	The rule of law law	Administrative law

(*ii*) It cannot be assumed that a State which comes under A in respect of I comes under A also in respect of 2, 3, 4, 5,

6 and 7. Thus the U.S.A. is a Liberal State (1), but is not a unitary State (2); her constitution is not a flexible one (3); and her Executives is not a parliamentary one (6).

(*iii*) As we adopt in effect seven bases of classification, it is necessary to deal with each State seven times in order to place it properly. Thus:

Britain

Liberal, unitary State, flexible constitution, adult suffrage and single-member constituency, bicameral Legislature with a non-elective second chamber, parliamentary Executive, and the rule of law.

The French Republic

Liberal, unitary State, rigid constitution, adult suffrage and multi-member constituency, bicameral Legislature with an elective second chamber, parliamentary Executive, and administrative law. And so on.

The rest of the book follows the order of the principles of classification laid down in the Table under 'II.' The nature of political organization.' A chapter on 'The Separation of Powers' has, however, been added before a consideration of the electorate, the Legislature, the Executive, and the Judiciary.

NOTES

1. Some writers like Gilchrist (*Principles of Political, Science*, p. 231) prefer the term 'the classification of the forms of government' on the ground that the 'form of States' is really the form of government. Willoughby (*The Nature of the State*, ch. XIII) goes so far as to say that there can be no such thing as a classification of States: 'In essence they are all alike—each and all being distinguished by the same sovereign attributes.' With Leacock (*Elements of Political Science*, p. 109), we may say that this objection does not seem very strong: 'The differences in structure of government constitute the basis of classification, but we may on that basis either speak of the various "forms of government" or "forms of the State".' When we consider the fact that States differ not only in their forms of government, but in their professed *end* (e.g. totalitarian States v. democratic States) and in their very nature (e.g. unitary v. federal), the term 'the classification of States', seems even preferable; it has, besides, the support of

writers like Hobbes and Locke, and in recent times, Bluntschli and Marriott.

2. *Polities,* bk. IV, ch. IV.
3. Ibid.
4. Polybius, cited by Marriott in *The Mechanism of the Modern State,* Vol I, p. 26.
5. Hobbes, *Leviathan,* pp. 96-7.
6. *Of civil Government,* bk, II, ch. X.
7. Restricted suffrage indicates the restriction of the right to vote to men, as in Switzerland; or to men and women in possession of prescribed educational or property qualifications as under the Government of India Act of 1935.
8. Consisting of two chambers.
9. Consisting of one chamber.

REFERENCES

Aristotle, *Policies,* Bk. IV, 'Everyman's Library', Dent

Bryce, J., *Studies in History and 'jurisprudence,* Vol. I, Essay III, Oxford, 1901.

Hobbes, T., *Leviathan,* ch. XIX, 'Everyman's Library', Dent J. Locke, Of Civil Government, ch. X, in Social Contract, 'World's Classics' No. 511, Oxford

Marriott, J. A. R., *The Mechanism of the Modern State,* Vol. I, ch, II, Oxford, 1927

Rousseau, J. J., *The Social Contract,* Bk. III, chs. III to VIII, in *Social Contract,* 'World's Classics' No. 511, Oxford

Strong, G. F., *Modern Political Constitutions,* ch. III, Sidgwick & Jackson, 1930.

14

Unitary and Federal States

UNITARY AND FEDERAL STATES

A unitary State may be defined as one organized under a single central government; and unitarianism, as the habitual exercise of supreme legislative authority by one central power. Britain, France and Italy are unitary States: South Africa and India have some characteristics of the unitary State, but they have also some of the characteristics of the federal State.

A federal State is one in which there is a central authority that represents the whole, and acts on behalf of the whole in external affairs and in such internal affairs as are held to be of common interest; and in which there are also provincial or state authorities with powers of legislation and administration within the sphere allotted to them by the constitution.[1] It is, in the words of hamilton, 'an association of States that forms a new one'; or, as Dicey put it, it is a political contrivance intended to reconcile national unity with the maintenance of the state rights. The U.S.A., Canada, Australis, Switzerland and the U.S.S.R. are federal States.

The distinctive feature of federation is the formal division of governmental powers by a constitution between the constituent units (states, provinces, or cantons) and the larger State which they compose. The units have power to pass laws on the subjects allotted to them and to administer and interpret them; and the Federal Authority has similar power on the subjects allotted to it. Both the units and the Federal Authority may exercise their legislative, administrative and judicial powers and within the limits set by the constitution. The supremacy of the constitution is, therefore, a second important feature of federation. The constitution of the U.S.A., for instance, explicitly declares: 'This constitution and the laws of the U.S.A. which shall be made in pursuance thereof . . . shall be supreme law of the land, and the judges in every state shall be bound thereby, anything in the constitution or laws of any state to the contrary notwithstanding.' This supremacy implies that the laws passed by any authority in the State, if contrary to the constitution, may be declared *ultra vires*; some authority, such as a Supreme Court to interpret the constitution and decide conflicts of jurisdiction between the Centre and the units is therefore essential. If also means that neither the Federal Authority, nor any unit thereof, has the power to change the constitution as it likes; for then one of the two, and not the constitution, becomes supreme. In other words, a federal State has necessarily a rigid constitution. Normally, the machinery to amend the constitution is one in which both the Federal Authority and the units have a definite place. The U.S.A, Australia and Switzerland are instances of this. These then are the essential features of federation: the division of powers, the supremacy of the constitutions, the existence of a court to interpret the constitution, and the rigidity of the constitution.

By contrast, in a unitary State there is no constitutional division of powers between the Centre and local territorial divisions; at any rate it is one which the Centre is not powerless to alter. The distinguishing mark of a unitary State is that all local governing authorities within the State (provinces, counties, districts) are created, their powers defined, their form of organization determined by the Central Government. That Central Government may be limited by a superior constitution in a number of ways without affecting the unitary character of the State; but if the constitution gives power to the local bodies independent of, and not modifiable by, the Central Government, the political system partakes of the essential nature of federation. Therefore, it is by the nature of the relationship of the Centre to the local bodies that one determines whether a State is federal or unitary. Briefly, in the former, both the central and local authorities derive their power from a common source; in the latter the Central Government has authority legally to determine the powers, indeed the very existence, of the local authorities. It follows that in the unitary State, the constitution need not *necessarily* be supreme, for the Centre may have the power to modify it, as an Britain; there is no need to have an authority to decide conflicts of jurisdiction between the Centre and the local authorities; and the constitution need not *necessarily* by rigid.

FEDERATION AND CONFEDERATION

A federation must be distinguished from a confederation. The League of Nations was an example of the latter. The American Confederation, whose articles were drawn up by the Continental Congress in 1777, and which lasted from 1781 to 1789, is another. Here each one of its thirteen State-members was a sovereign body-politic. The only form of common control was exercised through the Congress, 'a body of delegates which had no power to compel the States to its will, and no power to command or to tax the individual citizens of the thirteen States'. Congress was primarily to look after foreign relations, declare and conduct war, build and equip a navy, and issue requisitions upon the States for soldiers and for funds. The working of the system for eight years proved its inadequacy, for while Congress could pass resolutions 'it had no authority to make law, in the sense of regulations backed up with a power of enforcement'. The confederation gave place to a federation. The German Confederation, as it existed from 1815 to 1866, is a third example. This was a union of 39 States, including kingdoms, free cities, and principalities. The primary aim of the union was the external and internal security of the States. The common authority was the Central Assembly called the Diet, consisting of delegates of the Governments of the States. But no central Executive was established, each State acting as the executor of the resolution of the union. In 1866 it had to be dissolved to give place (later, in 1871) to the Federation of the German Empire.

A confederation, like a federation, is a union of States with a common recognized authority in certain matters affecting the whole, and especially in respect of external relations. But it differs from a federation in that it is a league of sovereign States (*Staatenbund* is the expressive German term, *Staaten* being plural); whereas federation creates a new State (*Bundesstaat, Staat* being singular). In the former, sovereignty rests with the component States; in the latter, the component States give up their sovereignty in favor of the new State, sovereignty in the new State being exercised by the amending body of its constitution. If follows that while the units of a confederation have the legal right of secession, the units of a federation have not.[2] The distinction between the two forms of union is therefore fundamental, founded upon the source of ultimate authority, sovereignty.

Another difference between the two is that the common authority of a confederation deals only with the Government of the constituent units, and not, as in a federation, directly with their individual citizens. The citizen in a confederation therefore has to obey only one Government, that of his own State; the orders of the common authority are binding on him only in so far as they are imposed on him by the Government of his own State. The citizen in a federal State, on the other hand, has to obey two Governments, that of his state and that of the Federal Authority.

From these two differences may be deduced a third: the confederation, being a looser union than the federation, is generally less stable.

CONDITIONS OF FEDERALISM

The normal method of establishing a federation has been the coming together of a number of States, formerly separate and sovereign, to establish a common government for better security. This was how the United States, Switzerland, and Australia came into existence. Sometimes it has been the other way round. In Canada, for instance, an originally unitary State was converted into a federal one by a constitution marking out the spheres of the provinces, and making each of them part of a federal State. This is a process of devolution or decentralization, designed to secure a more efficient government.

The conditions which favour the establishment and continuance of a federation are as follows.

(i) The desire for union

Obviously unless some political units desire to unite and establish a common government for their common interests, there is no basis for federation. This desire normally arises when a number of small independent States, locally adjacent, come to feel that if they do not unite, their independence will be threatened by the more powerful States. It will not arise where the separate States are so powerful as to be able to rely, for protection against foreign encroachment, on their individual strength. 'If they are', said J.S. Mill, 'they will be apt to think that they do not gain, by union with others, the equivalent of what they sacrifice in their own liberty of action; and consequently, whenever the policy of the (con) federation, in things reserved to its cognizance, is different from that which any one of its members would separately pursue, the internal and sectional branch will, through absence of sufficient anxiety to preserve the union, be in danger of going so far as to dissolve it.'[3] The felt need for strength in external relations is invariably coupled with the desire of the separate States, by conjoint action, to develop foreign trade, remove internal trade barriers and prevent internecine warfare. The thirteen American States, which joined to form the U.S.A., were eager not only to stabilize their hard-won independence of England, but also to adopt a uniform commercial policy, and generally to make the maximum use of the opportunities afforded by union to advance their general prosperity. The six colonies which federated to form the Commonwealth of Australia in 1900 'would not have done so except under the dread of danger from imperializing Powers in the Pacific, a danger not apparent until the closing years of the last century'.[4] At the same time 'there was a general feeling that an authority with wider powers than any existing before the federation was necessary for industrial and social development, and that a supreme judicial authority ought to be established to avoid the expense and delay involved in carrying cases to the Privy Council in London'.[5] These two instances also remind us that the sentiment of union is induced by community of blood, language and culture, and the similarity of political institutions. These create and keep up common sympathy along the peoples concerned and conduce to an identity of political interest without which a federation cannot come into being, or if forcibly created, cannot last long.

(ii) The desire for local independence

While there must be a desire for union, this desire should not be so great as to result in the demand for the establishment of a unitary State. A desire among the component states for the preservation of their independence in all but essentially common matters is a precondition for this form of political organization. Federalism is a natural constitution only for a body of States which desire union and do not desire unity.[6]

(iii) Geographical contiguity

The physical contiguity of countries which are to form a federation 'is certainly a favorable, and possibly a necessary, condition for the success of federal government'. It they are widely separated, the desire for union cannot easily emerge, as the advantages to be obtained do not appear real enough to make the necessary sacrifice worth while. The proposal for a federation of the countries which form part of the British Commonwealth, which found some support in the last century, fell through partly because these countries were physically wide apart.

(iv) The absence of marked inequalities among the component units

If there is any State so much more powerful than the rest as to be capable of vying in strength with many of them combined 'it will insist on being master of the joint deliberations: if there be two, they will be irresistible when they agree; and whenever they differ everything will be decided by a struggle for ascendancy between the rivals'.[7] The classic instance of this is the German Empire, established in 1871; the predominance of Prussia vitiated the federal principle.

(v) Political education and legalism

The permanence of a federation demands a capacity on the part of the people to appreciate the meaning of a double allegiance, and the ability to prevent the centrifugal principle of political action from overcoming the centripetal. It also means a developed sense of legalism, or in other words 'a general willingness to yield to the authority of the law courts' which decide indeed what the constitution at any moment is.

PROBLEMS OF FEDERAL GOVERNMENT

The federal State, differing as it does from the unitary in essential features, has to face a number of problems which the latter has not. The most important of these are:

(i) A satisfactory division of powers

The problem which all federal States have to solve is how to secure an efficient Central Government, while allowing scope for the diversities, and free play to the authorities, of the units. It is, to adopt Bryce's metaphor, to keep the centrifugal and centripetal forces in equilibrium, so that neither the planet states shall fly off into space, of the sun of the Central Government draw them into its consuming fires. The general principle on which the division of powers should rest is fairly obvious. 'Whatever concerns the nation as a whole should be placed under the control of the national Government. All matters which are not primarily of common interest should remain in the hands of the several states.'[8] Such subjects as foreign affairs, defence, the control of the armed forces, foreign trade, maritime shipping and currency, are clearly of common interest and are everywhere federal; municipal institutions, hospitals, local public works, property and civil rights, and the administration of justice within the state, are clearly of a local nature and are everywhere allotted to the units. On a number of subjects, however, the common interest, or the purely local interest, is not quite so clear, and, therefore, the details of the division vary under different federal conditions.

There is a variation not only in the particular subjects which fall within the sphere of the Center and of the units, but also in the way in which the division is effected. Broadly speaking, our survey suggests, there are three such methods.

(a) In the U.S.A., Australis, Switzerland, Weimar Germany, and the U.S.S.R., the powers of the Centre are enumerated in the constitutions; the residue is left to the units. The enumeration itself is not of a uniform type; in the U.S.A., there is one list of exclusively federal subjects allotted to the Centre, with some prohibitions both on the Centre and on the units; in Australia, Switzerland, and Weimar Germany, the Centre has power to pass laws on an exclusively federal list as well as on a concurrent list, Central laws in respect of concurrent subjects prevailing over those of the units; in the U.S.S.R., there is only an exclusively federal list. The device of concurrent powers is specially noteworthy as it provides a plan by which the Centre can step in some matters when the Government of a unit is lazy or unprogressive and when the need for uniformity demands its interference, while leaving the initiative in the first instance to the units.

(b) In Canada, the powers of the provinces are enumerated;

the residue is left to the Centre, though, as has been indicated in the section on Canada, this is qualified in some ways by the powers granted to the provinces in respect of matters of a 'merely local or private nature'.

(c) In the federal scheme for India, as outlined under the Act of 1935, the powers of the Centre and of the provinces were more or less exhaustively enumerated in three lists, the exclusively federal, the concurrent and the exclusively provincial; further, the residuary power as such was neither with the Centre nor with the provinces, but was to be allotted (as and when each specific case arose) to the Centre or to the provinces by the Governor-General in his discretion.

A word may be added about the 'enumerated' and the 'residuary' powers. The object of enumerating the powers of any authority is to limit it. Where, then, a federal constitution enumerates the powers of the Centre, as in the U.S.A., the object clearly is to limit its powers as against the units, and enable the latter to retain all the rest; conversely, where it enumerates the powers of the units, as in Canada, the object is to limit their powers as against the Centre. In general, therefore, it is true to say that the greater the 'reserve of powers' with the units, the more markedly federal is the State whose constitution permits such reserve to them.[9]

But three things must be emphasized. (*a*) The 'more markedly federal' nature depends not on the mere fact that the residue is allotted to the units, but on the content of that residue; it would be absurd, for instance, to consider Weimar Germany markedly federal *because* the residue was left with the states. (*b*) The idea of the residuary powers has little significance, as in the federal scheme for India referred to above, where care was taken to enumerate every conceivable power, so that very little was left as the 'reserve of powers'. (*c*) Under modern economic and social conditions, where an increasing number of problems can be met only by an authority representing the general interest, it seems the wisest policy (if it were possible) to enumerate the powers of the units and leave a large reserve of powers to the Centre.

The governmental powers must not only be satisfactorily distributed between the Centre and the units, but provision must be made to prevent either from encroaching upon a sphere allotted to the other, Here, again, federations differ in respect of the safeguards provided against this possibility, and their efficacy. The most common safeguard is the establishment of an independent court to interpret the constitution and decide conflicts of jurisdiction between the Centre and the units. The American and the Australian courts are the best instances of this; in Switzerland and in the U.S.S.R. the Supreme Court has no power to declare the federal law unconstitutional and, to that extent, the judicial 'safeguard is ineffective as a means of protecting the rights of the units. A second safeguard is the power given to the people, as in Switzerland, by the referendum and the initiative to decide finally on constitutional laws, the opinion of a majority of the people being, as it ought to be, final. Thirdly, the constitution is made rigid, i.e., not alterable, by the ordinary law-making body of the Centre or of the states. Invariably, too, some part is given to both the Centre and the units in the process of amending the constitution, the U.S.S.R. being an exception in that it ignores the units; again invariably, the part assigned to the units is greater that allotted to the Centre. The central Legislature is given the power to *propose* amendments in the U.S.A., Australia, and Switzerland; the final *ratification* by a majority of the units is made essential (in the U.S.A. by three-fourths of the states). Further, some fundamental rights of the units (as, for instance, the right to equal membership in the Senate in the U.S.A., and territorial limits in Australia) are made unalterable except with the consent of the states affected.

(ii) Protection of the smaller units against dominance by the larger

As the units in no federation are identical in size and population, it is possible that the larger units may have a predominant influence in legislation on account of their larger representation in the lower House of the central legislature (everywhere constituted on the basis on population). Two provisions are generally adopted to prevent this evil. (*a*) In the second chamber of the central Legislature, every unit is given equal representation (in the U.S.A., Australia, Switzerland, and the U.S.S.R.), or a provision is made, as in Weimar Germany, restricting the number of members that may be sent to the second chamber by *any* unit to less than one half of its total strength. Further, in the first four States mentioned, the second chamber is given powers equal, or very nearly equal, to those of the first. The constitution of the U.S.A. goes further and gives the Senate two important powers denied to the House of Representatives, those of consenting or refusing its assent to appointments and treaties made by the President. (*b*) It is stated (in Australia and Switzerland) that no amendments to the constitution may become valid until they have been ratified not only by a majority of the whole people, but also by a majority of the federal units. In the U.S.A. the consent of three-fourths of the states is necessary.

(iii) Organization of the relation between the Centre and the units

Ideally, in a federal State, the Centre and the units ought to be mutually independent in the spheres allotted to each by the constitution—in legislation, in administration, and in finance. This mutual independence is indeed the distinguishing principle of federalism and it can be truly said that the greater the independence of the units from the Centre in their defined spheres, the more truly is the political system federal in character. In actual practice, this ideal condition rarely obtains. Various points of contact are established between the two, partly by law and partly be usage.

In our survey of federal States, several methods of federal control over the units sanctioned by the constitution have been noticed: the federal guarantee to every state in the U.S.A. of a republican form of government and of protection against invasion and, on the application of the state authorities, against domestic violence; the power of the Governor-General in Canada to veto provincial laws and to appoint the Governors of the provinces; the control of the Governor-General in the abortive Indian federation over the Governors whenever the latter acted in their individual judgement or in their discretion; and the administration of many federal laws through the administrative machinery of the units in Switzerland and Weimar Germany, which, to this extent, is placed in a position subordinate which, to the Federal Governments. The last is particularly noteworthy. Experience shows that such administrative decentralization has at least two advantages: it makes the administration of federal laws more popular (being in the hands of local men) than it otherwise would be; and, secondly, by avoiding unnecessary duplication of the administrative machinery, it secures economy.

Of the instruments of federal control over the units established by usage, the most noteworthy is the system of grants-in-aid given by the Federal Government in the U.S.A. to the states in recent years. These grants are made for the development of agricultural and vocational eduction, for the construction of roads, for maternity and infancy aid and so on, and in 1946 entailed congressional appropriations of nearly $743,000,000. The states are not bound to accept them, but once they accept them, they subject themselves in some degree to federal control over the activities for which the money is voted.

(iv) Organization of the relation among the units

Each state is more or less independent not only of the Centre but of other states as well. Such provisions as are included in federal constitutions to regulate their relationship are calculated to secure harmony among them in respect of certain essential matters, and to prevent any two or more of them from conspiring against the interests of the whole. Thus every state is enjoined to give full faith and credit to the public acts, records and judicial proceedings of every other state; the citizens of every unit are declared to be entitled to the privileges and immunities of citizens of every other; it is required (with exceptions in certain constitutions, e.g., India) that all articles grown, produced or manufactured by any one of the units shall be admitted free into every other; all separate alliances and treaties of a political character between the units are forbidden; and so on.[10]

(v) A satisfactory method of amendment

The peculiar problems of federal States is regard to the amending body are that (a) neither the Centre nor the units by themselves should be given the power to alter the constitution, as such power is likely to affect one of the essential features of federalism, viz, the supremacy of the constitution; and (*b*) it is desirable that in the body which is authorized to change the constitution, both the Centre and the units are given some place, and further the smaller states must be protected against dominance by the larger. How these problems are faced by the different federations has already been indicated in (*i*) and (*ii*) above.

(vi) *Secession*. It is possible that one or more of the units may, as the southern states of the U.S.A. did in 1861, claim the right of secession from the whole. The sensationalists in the U.S.A. argued that the general government emanated from the people of the several states, forming distinct political communities and acting in their separate and sovereign capacity, and not from all the people forming one aggregate political community. 'The constitution of the United States is, in fact compact to which *each State is a party* . . ., the several states or parties have a right to judge of its infractions; and in case of a deliberate, palpable, and dangerous exercise of power not delegated, have the right also, in the last resort, to interpose for arresting the progress of the evil, and for maintaining within their respective limits, the authorities, rights and liberties appertaining to them.' Those who opposed the right of secession argued the *people of the country as a whole* were the real parties to the union, and not the states, and cited in evidence the preamble to the constitution:

> 'We, the people of the United States, in order to form a more perfect union, establish justice ensure domestic tranquillity, provide for the common defence, promote the general welfare, and secure the blessings of liberty to ourselves and our posterity, do ordain and establish this constitution for the United States of America.'

Arguments apart, the issue in the U.S.A. was decided, by force of arms, against session. It is interesting to note that the constitution of the U.S.S.R. is unique in recognizing the legal right of secession. Where such a right is not recognized by the constitution, it seems clear, as a matter of constitutional theory, that the units do not have it. The only legal method for a unit to regain its sovereignty would appear to be an amendment of the constitution permitting the unit to go out of the Union. Sovereignty in a federal State 'lies in the body, wherever and whatever it may be, which has power to amend the constitution. Legally speaking, this sovereign body can entirely abolish the federation and restore each member of it its original independenc'.[11] It is difficult, however, to see how a federal State an prevent a determined unit from seceding except by force of arms; no constitutional provisions seem adequate to meet such a situation.

MERITS AND DEFECTS

The unitary State has, as compared with the federal State, two distinct advantages.

(i) 'The whole problem of the organization of a government is enormously simplified when the decision is made to establish a unitary government.'[12] The constitution-making body does not have to concern itself, as it must in a federation, with the manner in which the territory shall be divided into political divisions nor the manner in which governmental powers shall be divided between two authorities. The territorial distribution of power (between the Centre and local bodies) is a matter of internal organization to be decided by the Central Government. The prolonged discussions at the Round Table Conferences in London, which set about drawing up' a federal constitution for India, afford ample illustration of the difficulties in a federal constitution. Further the distribution of powers made by the constitution of a federal State is modified only by a special procedure, for federal constitutions must necessarily be rigid. And it is found, notably in the U.S.A. and in Australia, that because of the difficulty of getting the amending body into operation, the changes in the constitution do not keep pace with the changes in the social and economic life of the State. For example, child labour could be abolished easily in England; its abolition was found difficult in the U.S.A. In the unitary State also, the identical difficulty may arise when its amending body is of the same cumbrous type; but at any rate the difficulty is not further complicated by a constitutional division of powers with its attendant traditions of state loyalty and the support of vested interests. Federalism, therefore, incidentally tends to produce conservatism. "The difficulty of altering the constitution produces conservative sentiment, the national conservatism doubles the difficulty of altering the constitution.'[13]

(ii) A unitary State is, other things being equal, stronger than a federal one. Here, all the powers of government are concentrated in the hands of one single set of authorities.

> All the force of government can, therefore, 'be brought to bear directly upon the problems of administration to be solved. There can be no conflict of authority, no conflict or confusion regarding responsibility for work to be performed, no overlapping of jurisdictions, no duplication of work, plant, or organization which cannot be immediately adjusted.'[14] By contrast, in a federal State there are two sets of authorities, each limited by the powers given to the other. That is why, as Dicey said, the comparative weakness of federalism is no accident, it is inherent in it.

'The distribution of all the powers of the State among coordinate authorities necessarily leads to the result that no one authority can wield the same amount of power as under a unitarian constitution is possessed by the sovereign. A scheme again of checks and balances in which the strength of the common government is, so to speak, pitted against that of the state governments leads, on the face of it, to a certain waste of energy. A federation therefore will always be at a disadvantage in a contest with unitarian States of equal resources.'[15]

When a question of external policy arises which interests only one part of the union, the existence of states feeling themselves specially affected is apt to have a strong and probably an unfortunate influence. Another source of weakness in a federation is the divided allegiance of the citizens. This may give rise to the dissolution of the State by the rebellion or secession of states, and to division into groups and factions by the formation of separate combinations of the component states.

The great advantage of the federal State is the principle of compromise between unity and diversity which it embodies. It provides the means of uniting a number of small states into one nation under one national government, without extinguishing their separate Legislatures and Administrations.[16] The argument of the preceding paragraph, that the federal government is weak as compared with a unitary one, presupposes that a choice is open between them. But the history of federations shows that often the choice is only between complete independence of the units, with the consequent weakness of all, and federalism with greater strength for every one. As Dicey truly says, 'a federal system sometimes makes it possible for different communities to be united as one State when they otherwise could not be united at all. The bond of federal union may be weak, but it may be the strongest bound which circumstances allow'. In such circumstances, federalism helps a number of small states to obtain greater strength through union while ensuring their individuality in essentially local matters. It recognizes the fact that closer union is necessary for some purposes, while separate existence is necessary to provide for diversity. It thereby prevents the rise (by force) of a despotic Central Government absorbing other powers and menacing the private liberties of the citizen; and, by creating many local Legislatures with wide powers, relieves the national Legislature of a part of that large mass of functions which may otherwise prove too heavy for it.

There is another series of advantages which a federal State provides; but they apply equally to unitary States which allow a large measure of decentralization. These are the advantages pertaining to local self-government on a large scale. Self-government stimulates the interest of people in the affairs of their neighbourhood, sustains local political life, educates the citizen in his daily round of civic duty, teachers him that perpetual vigilance and the sacrifice of his own time and labour are the price that must be paid for individual liberty and collective prosperity. Further it conduces to the good administration of local affairs by giving the inhabitants of each locality due means of overseeing the conduct of their daily administration.[17]

NOTES

1. H. Samuel in *The Nineteenth Century*, No. 428, p. 676.
2. The U.S.S.R. is an exception. See, however, above, ch. XXI,.
3. *Representative Government*, ch. XVII.
4. Strong, *Modern Political Constitutions*, pp. 111-12.
5. Ibid.
6. Dicey, *Introduction to the Study of the Law of the Constitution*.
7. Mill, *op. cit.*, ch. XVII.
8. Dicey, *op. cit.*, p. 143.
9. Strong, *op. cit.*, p. 101.

10. Article 118 of the constitution of Australia; Articles I and IV of the constitution of the U.S.A.; Articles 7 and 60 of the constitution of Switzerland; and Article 121 of the constitution of Canada. The relevant Articles in the constitution of India are 301, 302 and 303. Article 301 lays down the general rule that trade, commerce and intercourse throughout the territory of India shall be free; exceptions to this rule are stated in Articles 302 and 303: thus power is conferred on Parliament by Article 302 to impose restrictions on trade, commerce and intercourse between one state and another in the interest of the public; Article 303 stipulates that such power should not be abused by the Parliament of the State Legislature by preferring one State to another, or by making discrimination between one State and another.
11. Leacock, *Elements of Political Science*, p. 228.
12. Willoughby, *The Government of Modern States*, p. 174.
13. Dicey, *op. cit.*, pp. 173-4.
14. Willoughby, *op. cit.*, p. 177.
15. Dicey, op cit., pp. 171-2; and p. 605.
16. See Bryce, *The American Commonwealth*, ch. XXX, for a good disc sion of the merits of federation.
17. Bryee, op.cit.

REFERENCES

Bryce, J., *The American Commonwealth*, Macmillan, 1910

Dicey, A.V., *Introduction to the Study of the Law of the Constitution*, ch. III and Appendix IV, 9th ed., Macmillan, 1939

Hamilton, A., J. Jay, and J. Madison, *The Federalist*, 'Everyman's Library', Dent

Karve, D. G., *Federations*, Oxford, 1932

Mill, JS., *Representative Government*, ch. XVII, 'World's Classics' No. 170, Oxford

Newton, A.P., *Federal and Unified Constitutions*, Longmans, 1923

Venkatrangaiya, M., *Federalism in Government*, Andhra University, Waltair, 1935

Willoughby, W.F., *The Government of Modern States*, chs, XII and XIII, Appleton Century, 1936

Wheare, K.C., *Federal Government*, Oxford, 1946.

15

Rigid and Flexible Constitutions

WRITTEN AND UNWRITTEN CONSTITUTIONS

States, we have said earlier, may be classified according to the nature of their constitutions, whether they are flexible or rigid. The question may be raised whether constitutions may also be classified according as to whether they are written or unwritten.

A written constitution may be described as one in which the fundamental principles concerning the organization of a government, the powers of its various agencies and the rights of the subjects, are written down in one document (or a few documents as in the French constitution of 1875). Thus the constitution of the United States of America (1789) outlines the composition of the Legislature, the Executive, and the Judiciary and their powers, and the fundamental rights of citizens; and besides, mentions a method for its amendment.

An unwritten constitution, by contrast, is one in which the fundamental principles of the organization and powers of a government are not codified in one document, but where many of them are followed as a matter of usage. The constitution of Britain is a good example.

'The English have left the different parts of their constitution just where the wave of history had deposited them; they have not attempted to bring them together, to classify or complete them, or to make a consistent and coherent whole'[1]

Of the eleven modern constitutions we have surveyed, the British constitution alone is unwritten.

It is interesting to note that, as a matter of history, written constitutions have been, relatively speaking, of recent growth. The first considerable attempts at written constitutions in modern times were made in the American colonies[2] when they became independent of Great Britain. New Hampshire, South Carolina, Virginia, Pennsylvania and Maryland among others, each adopted a written constitution in 1776; Georgia and New York flowered suit in 1777, and Massachusetts in 1780. The U.S.A. adopted its constitution in 1789. On the continent of Europe, France set the example, After the *ancien regime* was destroyed by the Revolution of 1789, she adopted a written constitution in 1791; since then France has tried twelve other written constitutions and the thirteenth is now being worked. One after another, the European States followed the French example[3] and adopted written constitutions; indeed, not only in Europe but in Asia, America, and Australia the written constitution became the rule. Further, no State which has once tried the written constitution has ever returned to the unwritten type.

The documentary constitution differs from the unwritten one not only because it is a document. It supplies a standard of reference to which the acts of the Government of the day may always be compared. And, since its framers contemplate it as the fundamental law of the nation, which ought not to be lightly changed, they invariably[4] make it rigid, i.e. unalterable by the ordinary law-making process; unwritten constitutions can hardly be rigid.

While the written constitution can thus in a general way be distinguished from the unwritten one, it is hardly adequate to classify constitutions on the ground of their written or unwritten nature; for the written or unwritten nature *as such* has not much political significance. Further, such a classification is on the whole misleading. First, it wrongly suggests the idea that the written constitutions have no unwritten elements, and vice versa. Our survey, particularly of the governments of the United States of America and Britain, makes it clear that constitutions in general contain both elements, the written and the unwritten. Second, it wrongly suggests, at any rate to the layman, that the Acts of the Legislature in every State with a written constitution are void if repugnant to that constitution. Indeed, in a famous judgement,[5] Chief Justice Marshall himself expressed this view:

'Certainly all those who have framed written constitutions contemplate them as forming the fundamental paramount law of the nation, and consequently the theory of *every* such government must be that an act of the Legislature, repugnant to the constitution, is void.'

As a matter of fact, this is not true. In France, under the Third Republic, the Judiciary did not claim the power to declare the Acts of the Legislature unconstitutional, primarily because the Judiciary did not owe its existence to the constitution but was itself created by an Act of the Legislature, and that Legislature could take effective steps to prevent the Judiciary from exercising any such power. The new constitution of France, as indicated already, sets up a constitutional committee which has in effect the power to decide on the constitutionality of laws. In Switzerland, the constitution itself, as we have seen, specially lays down that the Federal Tribunal shall administer the laws passed by the Federal Assembly. A somewhat similar provisions is found in the constitution of the U.S.S.R. The Italian constitution of 1848 made no provision for its amendment; the absence of any such provision has been interpreted to mean that the Legislature can make amendments to the constitution; and no question of repugnancy arises.

RIGID AND FLEXIBLE CONSTITUTIONS

A more adequate basis on which constitutions may be classified is the method for their amendment. If that method is the same as that for the passing of ordinary laws, the constitutions is 'flexibly'; if it is a different one, the constitution is 'rigid'. Britain and Italy[6] have flexible constitutions; all the other States in our survey have rigid constitutions.

Rigid constitutions, however, vary considerably both in the methods they provide for constitutional amendment and in the extent of difficulty they experience in adjusting themselves to changing times. Our survey suggests that rigid constitutions are, broadly, or four types.

(i) Those in which the Legislature may make constitutional amendments, but subject to certain restrictions not prescribed for passing ordinary laws. The constitutions of the French Republic, South Africa, and the U.S.S.R. fall under this head. The restrictions themselves are not the same everywhere. A joint session of the chambers of the Legislature with an absolute majority for the passing of constitutional amendments magnets, as in France; a joint session with a two-thirds majority for the passing of *some* constitutional amendments, as in South Africa;' and a two-thires majority in each of the two chambers of the Legislature, as in the U.S.S.R., are illustrations.

(ii) Those in which the final decision is with the people. Australia and Switzerland, as we have seen, make the consent of a majority of the voters necessary for constitutional amendment. In both, the initiative in proposing amendments to the constitution it taken by the Legislature; in Switzerland, in addition, 50,000 voters may also take the initiative. The Weimar constitution also provided for the referendum and the initiative for the passing of such amendment.

(iii) Those in which the final decision is with a prescribed majority of the component units of the federation. Thus Australia and Switzerland make the consent of a majority of the units essential in addition to the consent of a majority of the voters. The United States of America requires a three-fourths majority of the states. In Australia and the United States of America another restriction is added: in respect of amendments to certain essential matters, such as the changing of the territorial limits of the states in Australia, the consent of the affected state is required. The motive for prescribing restrictions of this kind (to protect the smaller units of a federation from being dominated by the larger) has been noted elsewhere. It is, however, noteworthy that *all* federations do not prescribe these conditions; the U.S.S.R. and Canada are exceptions.

(iv) Those which leave the final decision in the hands of an outside authority. Canada, for instance, leaves the decision to the king in Parliament in Britain.

Merits and defects

The flexible constitution has, clearly, one advantage. In a

period of great social changes, new ideas can make their way without being compelled to pass through the complicated machinery for amendment framed in an earlier period. Thus child labour in factories could be abolished easily in England; the proposal for its abolition, made by Congress in the U.S.A. in 1924, has not yet been ratified by the required of states. As Bryce remarks,[7] flexible constitutions 'can be stretched or bent so as to meet emergencies without breaking their framework; and when the emergency has passed, they slip back into their old form, like a tree whose outer branches have been pulled on one side to let a vehicle pass'.

That is why it has been said of the English constitution that it bends but does not break.

But the defect of a flexible constitution is that it may be in a state of perpetual flux, and may be the plaything of politicians. Because of the ease with which fundamental changes may be made, valuable rules and institutions may be abolished in a transient gust of unpopularity, and thus lose irreparably the stability given by antiquity and unbroken custom.[8] As Sidgwick recognized, this danger varies according to the manner of composition of the Legislature; but certainly it is important enough in the modern democratic State, in which the Legislature is popularly elected for short periods varying from two to five years. In any case, in a properly organized society, it is desirable to impose some restrictions on the power of the Legislature to interfere with such fundamental rights of the citizen as freedom of speech and of religion.

The advantage of a rigid constitution is that it recognizes that there are some fundamentals, be they the rights of citizens or the rules relating to the composition and powers of the agencies of government, which ought not to be lightly changed, and it ensures that adequate consideration will be given to them when it is sought to change them.

On the other hand, the rigid constitution has at least two serious defects. It is not easily adaptable, and it may break under changing conditions or emergencies. This danger is greater in a federal than in a unitary State, on account of the complication cause by the division of powers. It also varies according to the difficulty of the particular amending process; for instance, it is greater in the United States of America than in the U.S.S.R. Secondly, under a rigid constitution, the Judiciary may have too much power to decide upon the constitutionality of laws. It is better not to give judges such power, for the constitution will always reflect the spirit of the time at which it was made, and the judges will, in interpreting the constitution, be better acquainted with that spirit than with the new.[9] If, on the other hand, they try to interpret differently, to adjust the constitution to the changing times, they may be drawn into party conflict, and the confidence in their impartiality thereby be impaired.

> 'And from the same cause, there arises a further danger that the Legislature of the Executive may be tempted to misuse its control over the appointment and dismissal of judges in order to obtain a tribunal subservient to its wishes; while yet the withdrawal of all control of this kind would leave the judges in too independent a position.'[10]

To avoid both these defects, the following method suggested by H. J. Laski[11] seems the best for constitutional amendment: in unitary States, let a two-thirds majority in Parliament be secured for the passing of constitutional laws; in federal States, let a constitutional law be passed by the federal Legislature by a two-thirds majority in two successive sessions, and if a majority of the states protest against any such change, let it again secure a two-thirds majority in order to become law.

NOTES

1. M.E. Boutmy. *Studies in Constitutional Law*, p, 7, cited by Marriott in *The Mechanism of the Modern State*, Vol. I, p. 153.
2. Britain tried two experiments in this direction, 'the agreement of the People' (1649) and 'the Instrument of Government' (1963) but neither became a permanent part of her constitution.
3. e.g. Spain in 1808, 1812 and 1876; Bavaria in 1818; Italy in 1848; Prussia in 1850; Germany in 1919; and so on.
4. There are written constitutions which are flexible, e.g. Italy, New
5. Marr [illegible]
6. Other States with flexible constitutions are New Zealand and Finland.
7. *Studies in History and Jurisprudence*, Vol, I. p. 168.

8 Sidgwick, *The Elements of Politics*, pp. 561-2.
9. Laski, *A Grammar of Politics*, p. 304.
10. Sidgwick, *The Elements of Politics*, p. 564.
11. Laski, op cit., pp. 305-8.

REFERENCES

Bryce, J., *Studies in History and Jurisprudence*, Vol. I, Essay III, Oxford, 1901.

Finer, H., *The Theory and practice of Modern Government*, Vol. I, ch. VII, Methuen, 1932

Sidgwick, H., *The Elements of Politics*, ch. XXVII, Macmillan, 1908

Strong, C.F., *Modern Political Constitutions*, chs. VI-VII, Sidgwick & Jackson, 1930.

16

The Separation of Powers

THE THEORY OF SEPARATION OF POWERS

Governmental power expresses itself in three forms: legislation, administration and judicial decision. It is of prime importance to the theory of the organization of government to determine whether, and to what extent, these powers should be combined in the same persons or body of persons, or should be entrusted to three separate agencies, co-ordinate and mutually independent.

Early in the modern period Bodin,[1] the French writer, pointed out in *The Republic* (1576) that some separation was essential. The Prince, he thought, ought not to administer justice in person, but should leave such matters to independent judges.

> 'To be at once legislator and judge is to mingle together justice and the prerogative of mercy, adherence to the law and arbitrary departure from it: if justice is not well administered, the litigating parties are not free enough, they are crushed by the authority of the sovereign.'[2]

The theory of separation of power was, however, clearly formulated for the first time by Montesquieu in *The Spirit of Laws* (1748):

> 'When the legislative and executive powers are united in the same person, or in the same body of magistrates, there can be no liberty; because apprehensions may arise, lest the same monarch or senate should enact tyrannical laws, to executive them in a tyrannical manner.'

Again, there is no liberty, if the judiciary power be not separated from the legislative and executive. Were it joined with the legislative, the life and liberty of the subject would be exposed to arbitrary control; for the judge would be then the legislator. Were it joined to the executive power, the judge might behave with violence and oppression.

There would be an end of everything, were the same man or the same body, whether of the nobles or of the people, to exercise those three powers, that of enacting laws, that of executing the public resolutions, and of trying the causes of individuals.'[3]

Seventeen years later Blackstone, an English jurist, gave expression to similar views:

> 'In all tyrannical governments the supreme magistracy, or the right both of *making* and of *enforcing* the laws, is vested in one and the same man, or one and the same body of men; and wherever these two powers are united together, there can be no public liberty. The magistrate may enact tyrannical laws, and execute them in a tyrannical manner, since he is possessed in quality of dispenser of justice with all the power which he as legislator thinks proper to give himself. . . . Were it [the judicial power] joined with the legislative, the life, liberty, and property of the subject would be in the hands of arbitrary judges, whose decisions would be ten regulated only by their own opinions, and not by any fundamental principles of law; which, though legislators may depart from, yet judges are bound to observe. Were it joined with the executive, this union might soon be an overbalance for the legislative.'[4]

And, finally, we may cite an American classic, *The Federalist* (1788), for another authoritative exposition of the theory:

> 'The accumulation of all powers, legislative, executive, and judiciary, in the same hands, whether on one, a few, or many, and whether hereditary, self-appointed, or elective, may justly be pronounced the very definition of tyranny.'[5]

There has been some controversy[6] among students of political science whether Montesquieu, the author of the theory (and others who followed him), contemplated an absolute or only a limited separation of the three powers. There is no doubt that the sound opinion, as *The Federalist* pointed out,[7] is that he did *not* mean that the three departments ought to have no *partial agency* in, or no *control* over, the acts of each other. His meaning, as his own words import, and still more conclusively as illustrated by the example in his eye (viz. the British constitution), can amount to no more than this, that 'where the *whole* power of one department is exercised by the same hands which possess the *whole* power of another department, the fundamental principles of a free constitution are subverted.'

Rightly interpreted, therefore, the theory of separation of powers merely means that a different body of persons is to administers each of the three departments of government; and that no one of them is to have a *controlling* power over either of the others. Such separation is necessary for the purpose of preserving the liberty of the individual and for avoiding tyranny.

ITS APPLICATION TO MODERN GOVERNMENTS

Before we consider to what extent the legislative, the executive, and the judicial powers in modern governments are combined and separated, it is useful to have some idea of what complete separation involves. It means a Legislature elected directly by the people for a fixed term; an Executive elected directly by the people, or indirectly by an electoral college as in the United States of America, for a fixed term and independent of the Legislature in discharging its function; and judges similarly elected, and independent of both the Legislature and the Executive in respect of their term of office and their salary. The Legislature will not have the power of choosing, controlling, or dismissing the Executive or the Judiciary; the Executive will not have the power of dissolving the Legislature or vetoing laws or of appointing and dismissing judges; the judges will not ave. the power of declaring laws unconstitutional or of trying executive officers.

If we look into the constitutions of several States, we find that there is not a single instance in which the three departments or powers have been kept absolutely separate and distinct. Instead, we find some union and some separation. This may be illustrated from Britain, the United States of America, and the French Republic.

Britain

In Britain the Executive forms an integral part of the Legislature, the cabinet being considered as 'the first legislative chamber'. The cabinet is chosen from the Legislature. Ministers take part in its proceedings, initiate laws, and have power to issue statutory orders. The cabinet has power to advise the dissolving of the House of Commons before its normal term of five years is over, and to recommend the creation of peers in the House of Lords. On the other hand, the legislature has power, by refusal of supply and other methods, to terminate the term of the cabinet.

The Executive appoints the judges; and, further, it has been vested in recent times with power to try certain cases. On the other hand, according to the principle of the rule of law, the judges have power to sit in judgement on the conduct of government officials.

The Legislature has power to present an address to the Crown for the removal of judges. The second chamber is also the final court of appeal for the United Kingdom of Great Britain and Northern Ireland.

But there is *some* separation of powers as well in the British constitution:

> 'A close study of the English Government in its practical working shows, that, *organically,* the principle of the separation of powers has been carried out with a rigidity that is found in few or no other governments.'[8]

The exercise of legislative power is vested in the Legislature, which is a department of government distinct from the Executive.[9] The executive power is vested in the Crown, and Parliament never attempts to deprive it of any of its executive powers, nor takes to itself the function of administration.[10]

In like manner, the Judiciary has been established as a distinct and independent branch of the government. Judges hold office during good behavior, and are not liable to be dismissed by the Executive. Their salaries are independent of annual budgetary provision, being a permanent charge on the Consolidated Fund.

The United States of America

The framers of the constitutions of the states in the United States of America consciously adopted the principle of the separation of powers. The Massachusetts constitution of 1780 explicitly declared:[11]

> 'In the government of this commonwealth, the Legislative department shall never exercise the executive and judicial powers or either or them; the executive shall never exercise the legislative and judicial powers or either of them; the judicial shall never exercise the legislative and executive powers or either of them to the end it may be a government of laws and not of men.'

The popular election of executive officials and of judges so widely prevalent in the states is an attempt at a rigid application of the theory. So too the constitution of the United States of America is an essay in the theory of separation. The separation is evident in the relations between the Legislature and the Executive. Congress and the President are (the former directly and the latter indirectly) elected by the people for fixed terms; the President and the heads of departments do not sit in Congress, or initiative laws; and Congress cannot be dissolved by the President before it has run its term. The separation is also evident in the relation between the Executive and the Judiciary: the term of the judges is made independent of the Executive.

Yet, even here, there are many points of contact between the Legislature, the Executive, and the Judiciary. The President sends messages to Congress; he has a suspensive veto over the laws passed by it; and heads of departments appear before the committees of Congress. The Senate's consent is necessary for the appointment made by the President, and the treaties negotiated by him. The House of Representatives may impeach the President before the Senate. The President appoints the judges, and has the power of pardon except in cases of impeachment. Judges may sit in judgement over the conduct of government officials, and they have the power to declare laws passed by Congress unconstitutional.

The French Republic

In the government of the French Republic, also, we find some union of powers and some separation. The election of the President by the Legislature, the President's suspensive veto, the cabinet system, the power of the National Assembly to indict the President and the ministers before the High Court of Justice, and there President's power of pardon illustrate the former; the existence, as elsewhere, of three distinct organs of Government to perform the work of legislation, administration and judicial decision, and the system of administrative jurisprudence, illustrate the latter.

IS SEPARATION DESIRABLE AND PRACTICABLE?

Sufficient has been said to indicate that a complete separation of the Legislature, the Executive and the Judiciary is not found in any modern constitution. All constitutions recognize the fact that government is an organic whole. Therefore, the separation of powers necessary for the maintenance of liberty has to be reconciled with the need for their co-operation with, and dependence on, each other. They realize that some union of powers promotes harmony in government and some separation makes for liberty, while both are essential for efficiency. The question naturally arises as to what extent separation is desirable and practicable.

A detailed study of the proper organization of the relationship of the Legislature to the Executive, the Legislature to the Judiciary, and the Executive to the Judiciary—which allows for partial union as well as partial separation—is attempted in the chapters that follow: here it is sufficient to draw attention to two general principles. First, the principle of vesting the exercise of the three powers of government—the legislative, the executive, and judicial—in three distinct organs, which Willoughby has called an *organic* separation of powers as distinct from a *personal* separation, is fundamental to the efficient working of government. More than one department may be under the *direction* of the same persons as regards their superior officers, as the legislative and the executive departments in Britain are directed by the cabinet; what is essential is that each department should in the main confine itself to the work which properly belongs to it. This is merely the political application of the economic principle of division on labour; it makes for specialization and efficiency. It is obvious, for instance, that the Legislature as a body is unfit to undertake the work of judges, because it is subject to the influences of party polities, 'because its organization as well as its temper is out of accord with the judicial spirit, and because its members are not chosen for their capacity or training'. And, second, no one department should have *absolute* control over the other two, for that is inimical to liberty. If, for instance, the Executive has absolute control over the Judiciary, justice cannot be impartial, and the freedom of the individual is bound to suffer. Within the limits set by these two general principles, there must be points of contact and interaction between the three departments, so that there may be the maximum harmony and co-operation between them in the essential tasks of government.

NOTES

1. 1530-96.
2. Cited by Bluntschli in *The Theory of the State,* p. 517.
3. *The spirit of Laws,* bk. XI, ch. VI.
4. 1765, *Commentaries on the Laws of England,* Vol, I. pp. 146 and 269.
5. *The Federalist,* Essay XLVII.
6. See, e.g. G. H. Sabine, *A History of Political Theory,* p. 559-
7. loc. cit.
8. Willoughby, op. cit., p. 238; italics ours.
9. Though members of the cabinet are chosen from Parliament, the Executive is only a part of the Legislature and not the whole of it.
10. In the U.S.A. treaties and appointments require confirmation by the Senate for their validity; no such rule obtains in Britain.
11. Article XXX.

REFERENCES

Hamilton, A., J. Jay and J. Madison, *The Federalist,* 'Everyman's Library', Dent.

Montesquieu, *The Spirit of Laws.*

Willoughby, W. F., *The Government of Modern States,* Appleton Century, 1936.

Bibliography

Adams, H., *The Degradation of Democratic Dogma.*

Aiyar and Srinivasan (ED.), *Studies in Indian Democracy,* 1965.

Aiyar, S.P., and Usha Mehta (Ed.), *Essays on Indian Federalism.*

Allen, C.K., *Democracy and the Individual.*

Almond, G.A.and Powell, G.B., *Comparative Politics, A Developmental Approach,* 1972, Amerind Publishing Co.Pvt.Ltd., New Delhi.

Aristotle, *Policies,* Bk. IV, 'Everyman's Library', Dent

Asirvatham, Eddy, *Political Theory,* 1968, Upper India Publishing House, Lucknow.

Asirvatham, Eddy, *Political Theory,* 1968, Upper India Publishing House, Lucknow,

Ball, Alan R., *Modern Politics and Government,* 1971, Macmillan.

Barker, Ernest (Tr.and ed.), *The Politics of Aristotle,* 1946, Oxford.

Beloff, M, *The* American Federal Government, 1959.

Benn and Peters, *Social Principles and the Democratic State, 1951.*

Blondel Jean, *Comparative Government,* 1969, Amerind Publishing Co.Pvt.Ltd., New Delhi.

Blunt, E., *The I.C.S.*

Bryce, J., *Modern Democracies,* Vol.II, ch.LXVII, Macmillan, 1921.

Bryce, J., *Studies in History and 'jurisprudence,* Vol. I, Essay III, Oxford, 1901.

Bryce, J., *The American Commonwealth,* Macmillan, 1910

Burns, C.D., *Democracy,* 1935.

Burns, C.D., *The Challenge to Democracy.*

Burns, E.M., *Ideas in Conflict,* 1960.

Butler, D.E., *The study of Political Behaviour,* 1958, Hutchinson of London.

Cobban, Alfred, *Dictatorship.*

Coker, F.W., *Recent Political Thought,* 1947, The World Press, Calcutta.

Corry, J.A., *Democratic Government and Politics,* 1958.

Cum ıngs, M.C., and Wise, David, *Democracy Under Pressure.*

Dahl, Robert A., *Modern Political Analysis,* 1963, Prentice Hall, New Jersy.

Dahl, Robert A., *Pluralist Democracy in the United States,* 1967, Scientific Books Agency, Calcutta.

Dahl, Robert, A., *Modern Political Analysis,* 1963, Prentice Hall, New Jersey.

Dicey, A.V., *Introduction to the Study of the Law of the Constitution,* ch. III and Appendix IV, 9th ed., Macmillan, 1939

Dicey, A.V., *The Law of the Constitution.*

Dyke, Vernon, Van, *Political Science, A Political Analysis,* 1960, Standard University Press, California.

Easton, David, *The Political System,* 1959, Alfred Knopf, New York.

Eckstein and Apter (Ed.), *Comparative Politics,* 1963, The Free Press, Glencoe, London.

Eckstein and Apter, *Comparative Politics,* 1963, Free Press of Glencoe, London.

Faguet, E., *The Cult of Incompetence.*

Feith, H., *The Decline of Constitutional Democracy in Indonesia,* 1962.

Field, G.L, *..omparative Political Development,* 1967.

Finer, H., *The British Civil Service.*

Finer, H., *The Theory and Practice of Modern Government,* 1960, Asia Publishing House, Bombay.

Ford, G.S., *Dictatorship in the Modern World.*

Freeman, E.A., *Comparative Politics,* 1873.

Freeman, E.A., *Historical Essays,* Essay XII, Macmillan, 1896.

Fried, R.C., *Comparative Political Institutions,* 1966.

Friendrich, C.I. and Brezezinski, Z.K., *Totalitarian Dictatorship and Autocracy,* 1969, Harvard University Press.

Garner, F.W., *Political Science and Government,* ch.XXII, American Book Company, 1930.

Garner, J.W., *Political Science and Government,* 1955, The World Press, Calcutta.

Get□tell, R.G., *Introduction to Political Science.*

Gettel, R.G., *Political Science,* 1956.

Gilchrist, R.N., *Principles of Political Science.*

Goodnow, F.J., *Principles of Constitutional Government,* Harpers, 1916.

Hamilton, A., J. Jay, and J. Madison, *The Federalist*, 'Everyman's Library', Dent

Hearnshaw, F.J.C., *Democracy at the Crossways.*

Heckscher, Gunnar, *The Study of Comparative Government and Politics.*

Hoag, C.G. and G. H. Hallett, *Proportional Representation*, Macmillan, 1926.

Hobbes, T., *Leviathan*, ch. XIX, 'Everyman's Library', Dent J. Locke, Of Civil Government, ch. X, in Social Contract, 'World's Classics' No. 511, Oxford

Hoover, C.B., *Doctorship and Democracies.*

Iyengar, S.S., *Problems of Indian Democracy.*

Johari, J.C., *Comparative Politics*, 1972.

Karve, D. G., *Federations*, Oxford, 1932

Kavanagh, Dennis, *Political Culture*, 1972, Macmillan.

Labin, Suzanne, *The Secret of Democracy*, 1958, Comet Books, Collins, London.

Laski, H.J., *A Grammar of Politics*, ch. VIII, Allen & Unwin, 1930.

Lasswell, Harold D., *The Policy Orientation of Political Science*, 1971, Lakshmi Narain Agarwal, Agra 3.

Leacock, Stephen, *Elements of Political Science*, 1938.

Lees-Smiteh, H.B., *Second Chambers in Theory and Practice*, Allen & Unwin, 1923.

Lindsay A.D., *The Modern Democratic State.*

Lindsay, A.D., *Essentials of Democracy.*

MacIver, *The Web of government*, 1959.

MacPherson, C.B., *The Real World of Democracy.*

Macridis, R.C.and Brown, E., *Comparative Politics : Notes and Readings*, 1968.

Maine, H., *Popular Government.*

Marriott, J.A.R., *Second Chambers*, Oxford, 2nd ed., 1927.

Marriott, J.A.R., *The Mechanism of the Modern State*, Oxford, 1927.

Maxey, C.C., *Political Philosophies*, 1959.

Mayo, H.B., *An Introduction to Democratic Theory*, 1960.

McIlwain, *The Growth of Political Thought in the West*, 1932, London.

Mill, J.S., *Representative Government*, 'World's Classics' No. 170 Oxford

Mogi, Sobei, *Problem of Federalism*, 1931.

Montesquieu, *The Spirit of Laws.*

Neumann, F., *The Democratic and the Authoritarian State,* 1957.

Newton, A.P., *Federal and Unified Constitutions,* Longmans, 1923

Ogg and Zink, *Modern Foreign Government,* 1957.

Ogg, F.A., *English Government and Politics.*

Ostrogorski, M., (Tr. F. Clarke), *Democracy and the Organization of Political Parties,* 2 vols., Macmillan, 1902.

Palmer, N.D., *The Indian Political System,* 1961.

Panikkar, K.M., *The Afro-Asian States and Their Problems,* 1946.

Park and Tinker, *Leadership and Political Institutions in India,* 1951.

Parkinson, N.C., *The Evolution of Political Thought.*

Pinney, B.L.*Comparative Politics and Politics,* 1966.

Prasad, Beni, *The Democratic Process.*

Pye and Verba (Ed.), *Political Culture and Political Development,* 1969, Princeton University, New Jersy.

Pye, Lucian, *Politics, Personality and Nation Building,* 1962, New Haven.

Ramaiyer, *Politics.*

Report of the Royal Commission appointed to inquire into Electoral System, 1910, H. M. Stationery Office, 1929

Report on Indian Constitutional Reforms, ch. VIII, Government Printing Office, Calcutta, 1918.

Rienow, Robert, *Introduction to Government,* 1960.

Rockefeller Panel Report on American Democracy, *The Power of the Democratic Idea,* 1967, Popular Prakashan, Bombay.

Roucek, J.S.and others, *Introduction to Political Science,* 1954.

Rousseau, J. J., *The Social Contract,* Bk. III, chs. III to VIII, in *Social Contract,* 'World's Classics' No. 511, Oxford

Roy, N.C., The *Federal System of the USA,* 1940.

Sabine, S.H., *A History of Political Theory*-1957, George Harrap & Co., London.

Sait, E.M., *Democracy,* 1929.

Santhanam, K., *Union-State Relations in India.*

Sartori, Giovanni, *Democratic Theory,* 1962.

Schulz, E.B., *Essentials of Government,* 1961.

Sidgwick, H., *The Elements of Politics,* Macmillan, 1908.

Simon, Y.R., *Philosophy of Democratic Government*, 1951.

Soltau, R.H., *Introduction to Politics*, 1959, Longmans, Green & Co.

Steware, Michael, *Modern Forms of Government*, 1959.

Strong, C.F., *Modern Political Constitutions*, Sidgwick & Jackson, 1930.

Suba, J.P., *Element of Political Science*, 1952.

UNESCO, *Contemporary Political Science, 1950.*

Venkatrangaiya, M., *Federalism in Government*, Andhra University, Waltair, 1935

Waldo, Dwight, *Political Science in the United States of America*, UNESCO.

Weldon, T.D., *The Vocabulary of Politics*, 1953, Penguin Books, London.

Wells, H.G., *Democracy under Revision*.

Wheare, K.C., *Federal Government*, Oxford, 1946.

White, L.D., *Introduction to the Study of Public Administration*, 2nd ed., Macmillan, 1939.

White, L.D., *The Civil Service in the Modern State*, University of Chicago Press, 1930.

Willoughby, W. F., *The Government of Modern States*, Appleton Century, 1936.

Willoughby, W.F., *Principles of Legislative Organization and Administration*, The Brookings Institution, 1934.

Willoughby, W.F., *The Nature of the State*.

Index